Dictionary of Classical Mythology

BROCKHAMPTON PRESS
LONDON

This edition published 1995 by Brockhampton Press, a member of the Hodder Headline PLC Group.

ISBN 1 86019 088 X

Printed and bound in Slovenia.

A

Abaris the Scythian in Greek mythology, a priest of Apollo to whom the god gave a golden arrow on which to ride through the air. This dart ('the dart of Abaris') rendered him invisible; it also cured diseases and gave oracles. Abaris is said to have given it to the philosopher Pythagoras.

Abas in Greek mythology, the twelfth king of Argos, son of Lynceus (1) and Hypermnestra, grandson of Danaus and father of Acrisius and Proetus, and, in some accounts, of Idmon. He was given his grandfather's shield, which was sacred to Hera and the sight of which was capable of subduing people.

Abdera an ancient Greek city on the Thracian coast, east of the river Nestus, the birthplace of the philosophers Democritus, Anaxarcoras and Protagoras. Despite this, its inhabitants became proverbial for dullness and stupidity. According to Greek mythology, it was founded by Heracles in honour of his friend Abderus.

Abderus in Greek mythology, a friend of Heracles, devoured by the horses of Diomedes, king of Thrace. Diomedes gave him his horses to hold, and they devoured him.

Absyrtus *or* **Apsyrtus** in Greek mythology, a son of Aeëtes, king of Colchis and brother of Medea. When Medea fled with Jason she took Absyrtus with her, and when she was nearly overtaken by her father she murdered her brother, cut his body in pieces and strewed them on the road so that her father would be detained by gathering the limbs of his child.

Acacetus one who does nothing badly. It was a name given to Hermes because of his eloquence.

Acamas *see* **Demophon**.

Acarnania the most westerly portion of northern Greece, bounded on the north by the Ambracian Gulf, on the northeast by Amphilochia, on the west and southwest by the Ionian Sea and on the east by AETOLIA. One of the original independent states of ancient Greece, its inhabitants, the Acarnanians, were considered to be behind the other Greeks in civilization, living by robbery and piracy.

Acastus in Greek mythology, a son of PELIAS, king of IOLCUS. He was one of the ARGONAUTS and also took part in the CALYDONIAN BOAR hunt. His wife, Astydamia, fell in love with PELEUS.

Acestes according to Virgil's *Aeneid*, in a trial of skill Acestes the Sicilian discharged his arrow with such force that it took fire ('the arrow of Acestes').

Achaea *see* **Achaia**.

Achaeans *or* **Achaians** one of the four races into which the ancient Greeks were divided. In early times they inhabited a part of northern Greece and of the PELOPONNESUS. They are represented by Homer as a brave and warlike people, and so distinguished were they that he usually calls the Greeks in general Achaeans. Afterwards they settled in the district of the Peloponnesus, called ACHAIA (2) after them and forming a narrow belt of coast on the south side of the Gulf of CORINTH.

Achaeus in Greek mythology, son of XUTHUS and CREUSA, and consequently the brother of ION and grandson of HELLEN. He returned to THESSALY and recovered the dominions of which his father had been deprived.

Achaia *or* **Achaea** (1) a district in the south of THESSALY in which PHTHIA and HELLAS were situated. It appears to have been the original home of the ACHAEANS, who were hence called Phthiotan Achaeans to distinguish them from the Achaeans in PELOPONNESUS. It was from this part of Thessaly that ACHILLES came, and Homer says that the subjects of this hero were called MYRMIDONS, HELLENES and ACHAEANS.

Achaia *or* **Achaea** (2) a district in PELOPONNESUS where the ACHAEANS settled.

Achates in Greek mythology, a companion of AENEAS in his wanderings subsequent to his flight from TROY. He is always distinguished in Virgil's *Aeneid* by the epithet *fidus*, 'faithful', and has become typical of a faithful friend and companion.

Achelous the largest river in Greece, which rises in Mount Pindus and flows mainly north-south to the Ionian Sea. In Greek mythology, it was regarded as the ruler and representative of all fresh water in HELLAS and was worshipped as a mighty god throughout Greece. The river-god is celebrated on account of his combat with HERACLES for the possession of DEÏANEIRA. Achelous first attacked Heracles in the form of a serpent, and on being worsted assumed the shape of a bull. Heracles wrenched off one of his horns, which forthwith became a cornucopia, or horn of plenty. This legend alludes apparently to some efforts made at an early period to check the ravages of the inundations of the river and by thus damming it creating a land of plenty.

Achemon *or* **Achmon** and his brother Basalas in Greek mythology, two CERCOPES who were forever quarrelling. One day they saw HERACLES asleep under a tree and insulted him, but Heracles tied them by their feet to his club and walked off with them, heads downwards, like a brace of hares. Everyone laughed at the sight, and it became a proverbial cry among the Greeks, when two men were seen quarrelling 'Look out for Melampygos!' (i.e. Heracles).

Acheron the ancient name of several rivers in Greece and Italy, all of which were connected by legend with the lower world. The principal was a river of Thesprotia in EPIRUS (the 'River of Sorrows), which passes through Lake Acherusia and flows into the Ionian Sea. Homer speaks of Acheron as a river of the lower world, and late Greek writers also use the name to designate the lower world.

Acherontian Books the most celebrated books of augury in the world. They are the books which the Etruscans received from TAGES.

Acherusia a cavern on the borders of PONTUS, in Greek mythology said to lead down to the infernal regions. It was through this cavern that HERACLES dragged CERBERUS to earth.

Achilles a Greek legendary hero, the chief character in Homer's *Iliad.* His father was PELEUS, ruler of PHTHIA in THESSALY, his mother the sea-goddess THETIS. When only six years of age he was able to overcome lions and bears. His guardian, CHIRON the Centaur, having declared that TROY could not be taken without his aid, his mother, fearing for his safety, disguised him as a girl, and introduced him among the daughters of LYCOMEDES of Scyros. Her desire for his safety made her also try to make him invulnerable when a child by anointing him with ambrosia, and again by dipping him in the River STYX, from which he came out proof against all wounds except in the heel by which she had held him. When his hiding place was discovered by ODYSSEUS, Achilles promised his assistance to the Greeks against Troy. Accompanied by his close friend, PATROCLUS, he joined the expedition with a body of followers (MYRMIDONS) in fifty ships, and occupied nine years in raids upon the towns neighbouring Troy, after which the siege proper commenced. On being deprived of his prize, the maiden BRISEÏS, by AGAMEMNON, Achilles refused to take any further part in the war, and disaster attended the Greeks. Patroclus persuaded Achilles to allow him to lead the Myrmidons into battle dressed in his armour, and when Patroclus was slain by HECTOR, Achilles vowed revenge on the Trojans, and forgot his anger against the Greeks. He attacked the Trojans and drove them back behind their walls, slaying them in great numbers. He chased Hector, who fled before him three times round the walls of Troy, slew him, and dragged his body at his chariot wheels, but afterwards gave it up to King PRIAM, who had come in person to beg for it. He then performed the funeral rites of Patroclus, with which the *Iliad* closes. He was killed in a battle at the Scaean Gate of Troy by an arrow from the bow of PARIS, which struck his vulnerable heel. In discussions on the origin of Homeric poems the term *Achilleid* is often applied to those books of the

Iliad in which Achilles is prominent, and which some suppose to have formed the original nucleus of the poem.

Acis in Greek mythology, a beautiful shepherd of Sicily, loved by GALATEA and crushed to death by his rival, the Cyclops POLYPHEMUS. His blood, flowing from beneath the rock which crushed him, was changed by Galatea into a river bearing his name, and renowned for the coldness of its water.

Achmon see **Achemon**.

Acrisius in Greek mythology, son of ABAS and twin brother of PROETUS, with whom he is said to have quarrelled even in the womb, and father of DANAË. After the death of Abas, he expelled Proetus from his inheritance, but Proetus, supported by IOBATES, returned and Acrisius was compelled to give him TIRYNS while he kept ARGOS.

acropolis the citadel or chief place of an ancient Greek city, usually on an eminence commanding the town. The Acropolis of ATHENS contained some of the finest buildings in the world, such as the Parthenon, Erechtheum, etc.

Actaeon in Greek mythology, son of Autonoë, a great hunter who was turned into a stag by ARTEMIS for looking on her when she was bathing and torn to pieces by his own dogs.

Actor *see* **Eurytion**.

Admetus in Greek mythology, king of PHERAE in THESSALY, and husband of ALCESTIS, who gave signal proof of her love by consenting to die in order to prolong her husband's life.

Adonis originally a deity of the Phoenicians but borrowed into Greek mythology. He was represented as being a great favourite of APHRODITE, who accompanied him when engaged in hunting, of which he was very fond. He received a mortal wound from the tusk of a wild boar, and when the goddess hurried to his assistance she found him lifeless, whereupon she caused his blood to give rise to the anemone flower. The worship of Adonis, which began in Phoenicia was afterwards widely spread round the Mediterranean. He is the reproductive principle, nature's decay in winter and its revival in spring.

Adonis a small river rising in Lebanon and flowing to the Mediterranean. When in flood it is tinged with a red colour, and so is connected with the legend of ADONIS.

Adrasteia *see* **Ida**; **Titans**.

Adrastus in Greek mythology, a king of ARGOS, whose daughter married POLYNICES of THEBES, who had been exiled from his native city by his brother ETEOCLES. Adrastus led the expedition of the SEVEN AGAINST THEBES to restore his son-in-law to his right, and, as had been foretold by AMPHIARAUS, was the only who survived. Ten years later he led the six sons of the heroes who had fallen to a new attack on Thebes, the war of the EPIGONI. This attack was successful, but a son of Adrastus fell, and the father died of grief.

Aea a name given by very early writers to COLCHIS as residence of AEËTES.

Aeacus in Greek mythology, son of ZEUS and AEGINA, born on the island of AEGINA, of which he became the ruler. His sons TELAMON and PELEUS abandoned the island, Telamon going to SALAMIS and Peleus to PHTHIA. After his death Zeus made him a judge of the shades in HADES with MINOS and RHADAMANTHUS.

Aechmodius *see* **Echetus**.

Aeëtes in Greek mythology, a son of HELIOS, brother of CIRCE, PASIPHAË and PERSES (3). He was married to EIDYIA, by whom he had two daughters, MEDEA and Chalciope, and one son, ABSYRTUS. He was king of COLCHIS at the time when PHRIXUS brought there the GOLDEN FLEECE. At one time he was expelled from his kingdom by his brother Perses, but was restored by his daughter Medea.

Aegaeon *see* **Briareus**.

Aegean Sea that part of the Mediterranean which washes the eastern shores of Greece and the western coast of Asia Minor.

Aegeus in Greek mythology, son of PANDION (2), king of ATHENS and Pylia. Pandion had been expelled from his kingdom by the Metionids, but Aegeus with his brothers PALLAS (3), NISUS and LYCUS (3) restored him, and Aegeus being the eldest succeeded.

Neither of his first two wifes bore him children. He ascribed this misfortune to the anger of APHRODITE and to conciliate her introduced her worship at Athens. Afterwards he begot THESEUS by AETHRA (1) at Troezen. When Theseus had grown to manhood he went to Athens and defeated the fifty sons of his uncle Pallas, who had deposed Aegeus and also wished to exclude Theseus from the succession. Aegeus was restored, but died soon after. When Theseus went to Crete to deliver Athens from the tribute it had to pay to MINOS, he promised his father that on his resturn he would hoist white sails as a signal of his safety. On his approach to the coat of ATTICA he forgot his promise, and his father, who was watching on a rock on the coast, on seeing the black sails thought that his son had perished and threw himself into the sea, which according to some traditions received from this event the name of the AEGAEAN SEA. MEDEA, who was believed to have spent some time at Athens on her return from CORINTH to COLCHIS, is said to have become mother of a son, Medos, by Aegeus.

Aegialeia an ancient town of SICYON, its name derived either from AEGIALEUS (2) or from a brother of PHORONEUS and first king of Sicyon, to whom the foundation of the town was ascribed.

Aegialeus (1) in Greek mythology, a son of ADRASTUS and Amphithea or Demoanassa. He was the only one of the EPIGONI who was killed.

Aegialeus (2) in Greek mythology, a son of INACHUS and the Oceanid MELIA, from whom the part of PELOPONNESUS afterwards called ACHAIA (2) derived its name of AEGIALEIA.

Aegina in Greek mythology, the daughter of the river-god, ASOPUS. ZEUS carried her to the island of Oenone or Oenopia, where she bore him a son, AEACUS. The island took her name.

Aegina a mountainous Greek island in the Gulf of Aegina, south of Athens, triangular in form. It was one of the most celebrated islands in Greece. In Greek mythology it was called Oenone or Oenopia and received the name of Aegina from AEGINA, who there bore ZEUS a son, AEACUS. At this time Aegina was uninhabited, and Zeus changed the ants of the island into people, the MYRMIDONS, over whom Aeacus ruled.

Aegipan *see* **Delphyne**.

aegis in Greek mythology, the shield of ZEUS, according to Homer, but according to later writers and artists a metal cuirass or breastplate, in which was set the head of the Gorgon MEDUSA, and with which ATHENA is often represented as being protected. In a figurative sense the word is used to denote some shielding or protecting power.

Aegisthus in Greek mythology, a son of THYESTES and cousin of AGAMEMNON, king of MYCENAE. He became the lover of the queen, CLYTEMNESTRA, with whom he killed Agamemnon. He helped Clytemnestra rule Mycenae for seven years, and was slain with her by ORESTES, the son of Agamemnon.

Aegyptus in Greek mythology, a son of BELUS (1) and twin brother of DANAUS. Belus assigned to Danaus the sovereignty of Libya and to Aegyptus he gave Arabia. Aegyptus also subdued the country of Melampodes, which he called Aegypt after his own name. All his fifty sons except LYNCEUS (1) were killed by their brides, the daughters of DANAUS. *See* DANAÏDES.

Aello *see* **Harpies**.

Aeneas the hero of Virgil's *Aeneid*, a Trojan, who, according to Homer, was, next to HECTOR, the bravest of the warriors of TROY. When Troy was taken and set on fire, Aeneas, according to Virgil, with his father, son, and wife CREUSA (2), fled, but the latter was lost in the confusion of the fight. Having collected a fleet, Aeneas sailed for Italy, but after numerous adventures he was driven by a tempest to the coast of Africa, where Queen DIDO of CARTHAGE received him kindly and would have married him. ZEUS, however, sent HERMES to Aeneas and commanded him to sail to Italy. While the deserted Dido ended her life on the funeral pile, Aeneas set sail with his companions, and after further adventures by land and sea reached the country of King LATINUS, in Italy. The king's daughter LAVINIA was destined by an oracle to wed a stranger, this stranger being Aeneas, but had been promised by her mother to TURNUS, king of the RUTULI. The result was a war, which was ended by Aeneas slaying Turnus and marrying Lavinia. *See also* ROME.

Aeneïd *see* **Virgil**.

Aeolian Islands a group of volcanic islands in the Tyrrhenian Sea. One of the islands, Strongyle is an active volcano and in Roman mythology was considered the home of VULCAN.

Aeolians one of the four races into which the ancient Greeks were divided, orginally inhabiting the district of Aeolis, in THESSALY, from which they spread over other parts of Greece. In Greek mythology they are represented as descendants of AEOLUS, the son of HELLEN. In early times they were the most numerous and powerful of the HELLENES, chiefly inhabiting northern Greece and the western side of PELOPONNESUS, although latterly a portion of them went to LESBOS and TENEDOS and the northwest shores of Asia Minor, where they possessed a number of cities.

Aeolus (1) in Greek mythology, the god of the winds, which he kept confined in a cave in the AEOLIAN ISLANDS, releasing them when he wished or when he was commanded by the superior gods.

Aeolus (2) in Greek mythology, a son of HELLEN, to whom Hellen is said to have left his kingdom in THESSALY and from whom the AEOLIANS were descended.

Aerope *see* **Atreus**; **Nauplius** (3).

Aeropus *see* **Echemus**.

Aeschylus the first of the three great tragic poets of Greece, the others being SOPHOCLES and EURIPIDES. He was born at Eleusis, in Attica, 525 BC, died in Sicily 456. Only seven of his tragedies are extant: *The Persians, Seven against Thebes, Suppliants, Prometheus, Agamemnon, Choephori*, and *Eumenides*, the last three forming a trilogy on the story of ORESTES.

Aesculapius *or* **Asclepius** in Greek mythology, the god of medicine. He was afterwards adopted by the Romans. He is usually said to have been a son of Apollo and Coronis (1). He was worshipped in particular at Epidaurus, in the Peloponnesus, where a temple with a grove was dedicated to him. The sick who visited his temple had to spend one or more nights in the sanctuary, after which the remedies to be used were revealed in a dream. Those who were cured offered a sacrifice to Aesculapius, commonly a cock. He is often represented with a large beard, holding a knotty staff, around which is entwined a serpent, the serpent being specially his symbol.

Aeson in Greek mythology, son of Cretheus and heir to the throne of Iolcus, and father of Jason. Usurped by his half-brother, Pelias, he sent Jason to Chiron the Centaur for protection.

Aeson *or* **Aesonis** a town of Magnesia in Thessaly, the name of which is derived from Aeson, the father of Jason.

Aethalia the ancient name of the island of Elba.

Aether in Greek mythology, the personification of the clear upper air breathed by the Olympians, son of Erebus and his sister Nyx.

Aethices a barbarous Epirot clan, who lived by robbery, placed by Strabo on the Thessalian side of Pindus. They are mentioned by Homer, who relates that the centaurs, expelled by Peirithous from Mount Pelion, took refuge among the Aethices.

Aethra (1) in Greek mythology, a daughter of King Pittheus of Troezen. Bellerophon sued for her hand but was banished from Corinth before the nuptials took place. She later became the mother of Theseus by Aegeus. She went to Attica from where she was carried off to Lacedaemon (2) by Castor and Pollux and became a slave of Helen, with whom she was taken to Troy. At the taking of Troy she came to the camp of the Greeks where she was recognized by her grandsons, and Demophon, one of them, asked Agamemnon to free her. Agamemnon accordingly sent a messenger to Helen to request her to give up Aethra. This was granted, and Aethra became free again.

Aethra (2) in Greek mythology, a daughter of Oceanus by whom Atlas fathered the twelve Hyades and a son, Hyas.

Aetna, Mount *see* **Etna, Mount**.

Aetolia a western division of northern Greece, separated on the west by the River ACHELOUS from ACARNANIA and washed by the Corinthian Gulf on the south. It was one of the original independent states of Greece. In Greek mythology MELEAGER slew the CALYDONIAN BOAR here.

Aetolus in Greek mythology, a hero who invaded the country of DORUS (2) and his brothers, killed them and founded AETOLIA.

Agamemnon in Greek mythology, son of ATREUS, king of MYCENAE and ARGOS, brother of MENELAUS, and commander of the allied Greeks at the siege of TROY. Returning home after the fall of Troy, he was treacherously assassinated by his wife, CLYTEMNESTRA, and her lover, AEGISTHUS, Agamemnon's cousin. He was the father of ORESTES, IPHIGENIA, and ELECTRA.

Aganippe (1) in Greek mythology, daughter of the river-god Parmesses, or Termessos, and nymph of a fountain on Mount Helicon, sacred to the MUSES, which had the property of inspiring with peotic fire whoever drank from it.

Aganippe (2) in Greek mythology, the name often given to the wife of ACRISIUS and mother of DANAË.

Agave a daughter of CADMUS, king of THEBES, and sister of SEMELE. She was the wife of ECHION (1), one of the SPARTI, and mother of PENTHEUS. For her abuse of Semele, who died when pregnant with DIONYSUS by ZEUS, she was driven mad by the gods and tore her son, Pentheus, to pieces. An exile from Thebes, she travelled to ILLYRIA where she married the king, Lycotherses. She later killed him so that her father, Cadmus, might become king of ILLYRIA. *See also* INO.

Agdistus *see* **Cybele**.

Agenor (1) in Greek mythology, a hero, king of Phoenicia and father of EUROPA and CADMUS, Phoenix, Cylix, THASUS and PHINEUS. When Europa was carried off by ZEUS, Agenor sent his sons in search of her and enjoined them not to return without her. As Europa was not to be found, none of them returned, and all settled in foreign countries.

Agenor (2) in Greek mythology, a brother of IASUS and PELASGUS. After their deaths he invaded their lands and thus became king of ARGOS.

Agenor (3) in Greek mythology, one of the bravest among the Trojans, slain by NEOPTOLEMUS.

ages of man *see* **races of man.**

Aglaia *or* **Aglaea** in Greek mythology, wife of HEPHAESTUS and one of the three GRACES, the other two being Euphrosyne and Thalia.

Agorious *see* **Oxylus.**

Agrianome *see* **Oicles; Oileus.**

Agrius *see* **Oeneus.**

Ajax in Greek mythology, son of TELAMON, a Greek hero and king of SALAMIS (1) who sailed with twelve ships to join the fight against TROY. He is represented by Homer as the boldest and handsomest of the Greeks after ACHILLES. He had more than one combat with HECTOR, against whom he was well matched. On the death of Achilles, when his arms, which Ajax claimed, were awarded to ODYSSEUS, he became insane and killed himself. This is the subject of Sophocles' tragedy *Ajax*. Shakespeare used him in *Troilus and Cressida*.

Ajax the Less in Greek mythology, son of OILEUS, king of Locris, and a champion on the Greek side in the TROJAN WAR. At the fall of TROY he entered the shrine of ATHENA and seized CASSANDRA. He lost his life during his homeward voyage, either by shipwreck or by a flash of lightning sent by Athena, who was offended at the violation of her temple.

Alba Longa a city of LATIUM, according to tradition built by ASCANIUS, the son of AENEAS, three hundred years before the foundation of ROME, at one time the most powerful city of Latium. It ultimately fell under the dominion of Rome, when the town was destroyed, it is said. *See also* HORATII.

Albula, River the ancient name of the River TIBER.

Alcaeus *see* **Electryon.**

Alcathous in Greek mythology, a son of PELOPS and Hippodamia, (1) brother of ATREUS and THYESTES, and father of Iphinoë,

Periboea, Automedusa and others. When MEGAREUS offered his daughter and his kingdom to whoever should slay the Cythaeronian lion, Alcathous undertook the task, conquered the lion and became king of Megara. He rebuilt the walls of MEGARA with the aid of APOLLO.

Alcestis in Greek mythology, wife of ADMETUS, king of THESSALY. Her husband was ill, and, according to an oracle, would die unless someone made a vow to meet death in his stead. This was secretly done by Alcestis, and Admetus recovered. After her death HERACLES brought her back from the infernal regions.

Alcidamea *see* **Bunus**.

Alcinous king of the PHAEACIANS, a son of NAUSITHOUS and grandson of POSEIDON. On their return from COLCHIS the ARGONAUTS came to the island where Alcinous lived with his queen, Arete, and were hospitably received. When the Colchians in their pursuit of the Argonauts also arrived and demanded that MEDEA be handed over to them, Alcinous declared that if she was still a virgin she would be restored to them, but if she was already the wife of JASON he would protect her. The Colchians were obliged, by the contrivance of Arete, to depart without their princess, and the Argonauts continued their voyage homewards. ODYSSEUS was shipwrecked on the island of Alcinous, and Homer's description of his palace and his dominions, the way in which Odysseus is received, the entertainments given to him, and the stories he related to the king about his own wanderings occupy a considerable portion of the *Odyssey*.

Alcmaeon in Greek mythology, a son of AMPHIARAUS and ERIPHYLE and brother of Amphilochus, Eurydice and Demonassa. Before Amphiaraus set out with the SEVEN AGAINST THEBES, he enjoined his sons to kill their mother as soon as they should be grown up. Alcmaeon commanded the EPIGONI and slew LAODAMUS. After the fall of Thebes he killed his mother, possibly with Amphilochus, for which deed he was made mad by the FURIES.

Alcmene *or* **Alcmena** in Greek mythology, the wife of

AMPHITRYON and the mother of HERACLES by ZEUS and of IPHICLES by Amphitryon. The love affair of Zeus and Alcmene has been the subject of comedies, notably by Plautus and Molière. HERA, jealous of Alcmene, delayed the birth of Heracles for seven days that EURYSTHEUS might be born first and thus be entitled to geater rights, according to a view of Zeus himself. After the death of Amphitryon, Alcmene married RHADAMANTHUS, son of Zeus.

Alecto in Greek mythology, one of the three FURIES, the others being Megaera and Tisiphone.

Alector in Greek mythology, king of Argos and father of IPHIS. He was consulted by POLYNICES as to the manner in which AMPHIARAUS might be compelled to take part in the expedition of the SEVEN AGAINST THEBES.

Aleus *see* **Lycurgus** (2); **Nauplius** (3).

Alexander *see* **Paris**.

Allcidocus *see* **Oxylus**.

Aloeus in Greek mythology, a son of POSEIDON and Canace. He married IPHIMEDEIA, the daughter of TRIOPAS (1), who was in love with Poseidon and had two sons by him, OTUS AND EPHIALTES.

Alope in Greek mythology, a daughter of Cercyon, king of ELEUSIS, who was seduced by the god POSEIDON to whom she bore a son, Hippothoon. She was afraid of what her father would do if he found out about the baby and so abandoned him. The child survived, being suckled by mares, and was found by shepherds. The shepherds were surprised at the magnificence of the child's clothing and took the child to the king. Cercyon recognized the clothing as having been made by his daughter and left the child to die, having killed Alope. Again the child was saved by being suckled by mares. On growing to manhood, Hippothoon asked THESEUS, king of Athens, to appoint him king of Eleusis. Theseus, who had already killed Cercyon in a quarrel in self-defence, agreed to the request. Like Hippothoon, Theseus was a son of Poseidon.

Alphaea *see* **Britomartis**.

Alpheias *see* **Alpheus**.

Alpheus *or* **Alpheius** (now Rufia) the largest river of PELOPONNESUS, flowing westwards into the IONIAN SEA. In Greek mythology, Alpheus appears as a celebrated river-god, like all the river-gods the son of OCEANUS and TETHYS. The fact that in its upper reaches the river flows underground probably gave rise to the fable that Alpheus flowed beneath the sea and attempted to mingle its waters with the fountain of ARETHUSA on ORTYGIA. Hence Ovid's name for Arethusa is Alpheias.

Althaea in Greek mythology, a daughter of Thestius and Eurythemis. She was the wife of her uncle, OENEUS, king of CALYDON, and the mother of MELEAGER and DEÏANEIRA. In the course of the CALYDONIAN BOAR Hunt, Meleager killed some of his mother's brothers in a quarrel. Althaea is said to have put a curse on her son and caused his death by burning a charred piece of wood, knowing that Meleager was doomed to die when it was burned to ashes. Having taken revenge on her son for her brothers' deaths, she then took her own life in remorse.

Alxior *see* **Oenomaus**.

Amarynceus *see* **Diores**.

Amazons in Greek mythology, the name of a community of women, who permitted no men to reside among them, who fought under the conduct of a queen, and who long constituted a formidable state. They were said to burn off the right breast so that it might not impede them in the use of the bow—a legend that arose from the Greeks supposing the name was from *a*, 'not', *mazos*, 'breast'. It is probably from *a*, 'together', and *mazos*, 'breast', the name meaning, therefore, 'sisters'. Several nations of Amazons are mentioned, the most famous being those who dwelt in PONTUS and who built EPHESUS and other cities. Their queen, HIPPOLYTA, was vanquished by HERACLES, who took from her the girdle of ARES. They attacked ATTICA in the time of THESEUS. They came to the assistance of TROY under their queen, Penthesilea, who was slain by ACHILLES.

Ambracia (modern Arta) a gulf, town and river in northwest

Greece. The town stands on the River Arta, which for a considerable distance above its mouth formed a part of the boundary between Greece and Turkey. In Greek mythology, the town was founded by Ambrax, son of Thesprotus, or by Ambracia, daughter of AUGEAS.

Amor in Roman mythology, a name for CUPID, the god of love, equivalent to the Greek EROS.

Amphiaraus a son of OICLES and Hypermnestra, the daughter of Thestius, he was a seer, descended on his father's side from the seer MELAMPUS. He was among the hunters of the CALYDONIAN BOAR and was said to have deprived it of one eye. He married ERIPHYLE, sister of ADRASTUS, and was the father of ALCMAEON, Amphilochus, Eurydice and Demonassa. When he married Eriphyle he swore that he would abide by her decision on any point in which he should differ in opinion from Adrastus. When he was asked by Adrastus, therefore, to join the SEVEN AGAINST THEBES, although he foresaw the outcome he was nevertheless persuaded by his wife to join his friends, Eriphyle having been enticed to induce her husband by the necklace of HARMONIA which POLYNICES had given her. On leaving ARGOS, Amphiaraus enjoined his sons to avenge his death on their heartless mother. During the war against Thebes, Amphiaraus fought bravely, but was pursued by Periclymenus and fled towards the river Ismenius. Here the earth opened up before he was overtaken by his enemy, and swallowed up Amphiaraus together with his chariot, but ZEUS made him immortal. He was worshipped as a hero and had a sancturary at Argos.

Amphidamus *see* **Lycurgus** (2).

Amphion in Greek mythology, son of ZEUS and ANTIOPE (1), daughter of NYCTEUS, and husband of NIOBE. He had miraculous skill in music, being taught by HERMES or, according to others, by APOLLO. In poetic legend he is said to have availed himself of his skill when building the walls of THEBES—the stones moving and arranging themselves in proper position at the sound of his lyre. He was assisted by his twin brother, Zethus.

Amphissa *see* **Echetus**.
Amphissus *see* **Dryope**.
Amphithamus *see* **Nasamon**.
Amphithea *see* **Deïpyle**; **Opheltes**.

Amphitrite in Greek mythology, daughter of OCEANUS and TETHYS, or of NEREUS and Doris, and wife of POSEIDON, represented as drawn in a chariot of shells by TRITONS, with a trident in her hand. In the Homeric poems she is the personification of the Sea, and her marriage to Poseidon is alluded to in a number of scenes depicted on ancient monuments.

Amphitryon in Greek mythology, king of THEBES, grandson of PERSEUS and husband of ALCMENE. During his absence from home in order to punish the murderers of his wife's brothers (*see* ELECTRYON), Alcmene was seduced by ZEUS in the disguise of Amphitryon, who himself returned home the next day.

Amulius in Roman mythology, a king of ALBA LONGA and brother of NUMITOR. In order to acquire the throne, he drove his brother from power, killed his nephews, and forced his niece REA SILVIA to be a Vestal Virgin (*see* VESTA) so that she would not bear sons to threaten his position. When twin sons, ROMULUS AND REMUS, were born to her by MARS, Amulius had them put in a basket on the Tiber so that they would die. However, they survived and later killed Amulius before restoring their grandfather Numitor to the throne.

Amyclae a town of ancient Greece, the chief seat of the Achaeans in Laconia, a short distance from SPARTA, by which it was conquered about 800 BC. It was one of the most celebrated cities of PELOPONNESUS in the heroic age. In Greek mythology, it was founded by AMYCLAS and was the home of TYNDAREUS and of CASTOR AND POLLUX, who are hence called *Amyclaei Fratres*.

Amyclas in Greek mythology, a son of LACEDAEMON and SPARTA, and father of HYACINTH by Diomede. He was king of LACONIA and was regarded as the founder of AMYCLAE.

Amycus *see* **Bebryces**.

Amymone *see* **Nauplius** (1).
Amythaon *see* **Bias**.
Anadyomene (Greek 'she who comes forth') a name given to APHRODITE when she was represented as rising from the sea.
Anaphe a small mountainous island in the south of the Greek Archipelago, east of THERA. In Greek legend, it was called Membliarus from the son of CADMUS of this name, who came to the island in search of EUROPA. It was celebrated for the temple of APOLLO, the foundation of which was acribed to the ARGONAUTS because Apollo had shown them the island as a place of refuge when they were overtaken by a storm.
Anaurus, River a small river in MAGNESIA, in THESSALY, flowing past IOLCOS into the Pagasean Gulf. According to legend, JASON lost one of his sandals in it.
Anaxabia *see* **Pylades**.
Anaxarete *see* **Iphis** (3).
Anaxo *see* **Electryon**.
Anchiale *see* **Dactyls**.
Anchises in Greek mythology, the father by APHRODITE of the Trojan hero AENEAS, who carried him off on his shoulders at the burning of TROY and made him the companion of his voyage to Italy. This voyage, which is not mentioned in the Homeric legend, is described by Virgil in his *Aeneid*. He died at Drepanum in Sicily.
Ancus Marcius according to Roman tradition, the fourth king of Rome, who succeeded TULLUS HOSTILIUS in 638 and died in 614 BC. He was the son of the daughter of NUMA POMPILIUS, and sought to imitate his grandfather by reviving the neglected observances of religion. He is said to have built the wooden bridge across the Tiber known as the Sublician, constructed the harbour at Ostia and built the first Roman prison.
Andraemon (1) in Greek mythology, the husband of GORGE, daughter of OENEUS, and father of THOAS. When TYDEUS delivered Oeneus, who had been imprisoned by the sons of Agrius, he gave the kingdom to Andraemon as he was already too old to rule.

Andraemon (2) a son of OXYLUS and husband of DRYOPE.

Andromache in Greek mythology, daughter of EËTION and wife of HECTOR, and one of the most attractive women of Homer's *Iliad.* The passage describing her parting with Hector, when he was setting out to battle, is well known and much admired. On the taking of TROY, her son was hurled from the wall of the city, and she herself fell to the share of NEOPTOLEMUS, who took her to EPIRUS where she bore him three sons. She afterwards married HELENUS, a brother of Hector.

Andromeda in Greek mythology, daughter of the Ethiopian king CEPHEUS and of CASSIOPEIA. Cassiopeia having boasted that her daughter surpassed the NEREIDES, if not HERA herself, in beauty, the offended goddesses prevailed on their father, POSEIDON to afflict the country with a horrid sea monster, which threatened universal destruction. To appease the offended god, Andromeda was chained to a rock but was rescued by PERSEUS and after death was changed into a constellation. The legend forms the subject of tragedies by Euripides and Sophocles, and Ovid introduced it into his *Metamorphoses*.

Antaea *see* **Stheneboea**.

Antaeus in Greek mythology, the giant son of POSEIDON and GE, who was invincible so long as he was in contact with the earth. HERACLES grasped him in his arms and stifled him suspended in the air, thus preventing him from touching the earth.

Antenor in Greek mythology, a Trojan hero who advised HELEN to return to MENELAUS.

Anteros in Greek mythology, the god of mutual love. According to some, however, Anteros is the enemy of love, or the god of antipathy. He was also said to punish those who did not return the love of others.

Antianeira *see* **Erchion** (2).

Anticleia *see* **Laertes**.

Antigone (1) in Greek mythology, the daughter of OEDIPUS and JOCASTA, celebrated for her devotion to her brother POLYNICES, for burying whom against the decree of King CREON she suffered death. She is the heroine of Sophocles' *Oedipus at Colonus* and his *Antigone*; also of Racine's tragedy *Les Frères Enemis*.

Antigone (2) in Greek mythology, a daughter of EURYTION of Phthia and wife of PELEUS, by whom she became the mother of POLYDORA. When Peleus had killed Eurytion and fled to ACASTUS at IOLCUS, he drew on himself the hatred of Astydamia, the wife of Acastus. As a result of this Astydamia sent a message to Antigone in which she lied that Peleus was on the point of marrying Sterope, a daughter of Acastus. When she heard this, Antigone hanged herself.

Antigone (3) in Greek mythology, a daughter of LAOMEDON and sister of PRIAM. She boasted of excelling HERA in the beauty of her hair and was punished for her presumption by being changed into a stork.

Antilochus in Greek mythology, a son of NESTOR, distinguished among the younger heroes who took part in the Trojan War by beauty, bravery and swiftness of foot. He was slain by MEMNON, but ACHILLES avenged his death.

Antimachus *see* **Deïphobus**.

Antinous *see* **Eupeithes**.

Antiope (1) in Greek mythology, daughter of NYCTEUS, king of THEBES. ZEUS was attracted by her beauty and came to her in the guise of a SATYR. Antiope conceived twin sons, AMPHION and ZETHUS, by this union and, scared of her father's wrath, when her condition became obvious she fled from Thebes and went to SICYON, where she married King EPOPEUS. Another version of the legend has it that Epopeus seduced and abducted Antiope.

Antiope (2) in Greek mythology, an Amazon, a sister of HIPPOLYTE, who married THESEUS. When Attica was invaded by the AMAZONS, Antiope fought with Theseus against them and died the death of a heroine by his side.

Aonia in ancient geography, a name for part of BOEOTIA in Greece, containing Mount HELICON and the fountain AGANIPPE, both haunts of the MUSES.

Aphaea *see* **Britomartis**.

Aphareus in Greek mythology, a son of the Messenian king PERIERES and GORGOPHONE. He had three sons, Peisus, LYNCEUS AND IDAS. He received NELEUS, the son of CRETHEUS, and Lycus, the son of PANDION (2), who had fled from their countries into his dominions. To the former he gave a tract of land in Messenia.

Aphrodite in Greek mythology, the goddess of erotic love and marriage, counterpart of the Roman VENUS. She was said to have sprung from the sea foam surrounding the severed parts of URANUS, although according to Homer she was the daughter of ZEUS and DIONE. A festival called Aphrodisia was celebrated in her honour in various parts of Greece, but especially in Cyprus.

Apollo in Greek mythology, son of ZEUS and LETO, who, being persecuted by the jealousy of HERA, after tedious wanderings and nine days' labour, was delivered of him and his twin sister, ARTEMIS, on the Island of DELOS. Skilled in the use of the bow, Apollo slew the serpent PYTHON on the fifth day after his birth. Afterwards, with his sister, Artemis, he killed the children of NIOBE. He aided Zeus in the war with the TITANS and the giants. He destroyed the CYCLOPS because they had forged the thunderbolts with which Zeus killed Apollo's son and favourite AESCULAPIUS. According to some traditions he invented the lyre, although this is generally ascribed to HERMES. The brightest creation of polytheism, Apollo is also the most complex, and many aspects of the people's life were reflected in his cult. He was originally the sun-god, and although in Homer he appears distinct from HELIOS (the sun), yet his real nature is hinted at even here by the epithet *Phoebus*, that is, 'the radiant' or 'beaming'. In later times the view was almost universal that Apollo and Helios were identical. From being the god of light and purity in a physical sense, he gradually became the god of moral and spiritual light and purity, the source of all intellectual, social, and political progress. He thus came to be regarded as the god of song and prophecy, the god that wards off and heals bodily suffering and disease, the institutor and guardian of civil and political order, and the founder of cities. His worship was introduced in Rome at an early period, probably in the time of the Tarquins. Among the ancient statues of Apollo that have survived, the most remarkable is the Apollo Belvedere in the Vatican at Rome. This statue was discovered at Frascati in 1455 and purchased by Pope Julian II, the founder of the Vatican museum. It is a copy of a Greek statue of the third century BC and dates probably from the reign of Nero.

Apollodorus a Greek writer who flourished about 140 BC. Among the numerous works he wrote on various subjects, the only one extant is his *Bibliothece,* which contains a concise account of the mythology of Greece down to the heroic age (*see* RACES OF MAN).

Apollonius of Rhodes (Apollonius Rhodius) a Greek rhetorician and poet, flourished about 230 BC. Of his various works only the *Argonautica* survives. It is an epic poem dealing with the story of the ARGONAUTS' expedition.

apple of discord *see* **Eris**; **golden apple**.

Apsyrtus *see* **Absyrtus**.

Apulia a region in the southeast of Italy on the Adriatic. In Greek mythology, it was settled by DIOMEDES (1), who founded its principal cities.

Aquarius *see* **Ganymede**.

Arachne in Greek mythology, a maiden from LYDIA who presumptuously challenged ATHENA to a weaving contest. Athena, out of jealousy, changed her into a spider.

Arcadia the central and most mountainous portion of the PELOPONNESUS, the inhabitants of which in ancient times were celebrated for simplicity of character and manners. Their occupation was almost entirely pastoral, and thus the country came to be regarded as typical of rural simplicity and happiness. In Greek mythology, the Arcadians derived their name from ARCAS, a son of ZEUS. The lyre is said to have been invented here by HERMES, and the syrinx, the musical instrument of the shepherds, was the invention of PAN, the tutelary god of Arcadia.

Arcas in Greek mythology, the ancestor and eponymous hero of the Arcadians, from whom ARCADIA and its inhabitants derived their name. He was the son of ZEUS by CALLISTO, a companion of ARTEMIS. After the death or metamorphosis of his mother, Zeus gave the child to MAIA. Arcas became afterwards by Leaneira or Meganeira, the father of ELATUS and Apheidas.

Arceisius *see* **Laertes**.

Arcesilaus *see* **Battus**.

Archemorus *see* **Opheltes**.

Arctophylax, Arctos *see* **Ursa Major**.

Ardea an ancient city of LATIUM, situated on a small river near the sea, south of Rome. According to one legend, it was founded by a son of ODYSSEUS and CIRCE, but others represent it as founded by DANAË, mother of PERSEUS. It appears in the story of AENEAS as the capital of the RUTULI.

Areas *see* **Oenomaus**.

Arene *see* **Gorgophone**; **Idas and Lynceus**.

Areopagus the oldest of the Athenian courts of justice, an assembly having a position more august than an ordinary court, and in its best days exercising a general supervision over public morals. It obtained its name from its place of meeting, on the Hill of ARES, near the Acropolis or citadel of Athens.

Ares in Greek mythology, the god of war whose Roman counterpart is MARS. The son of ZEUS and HERA, he is represented as terrible in battle but not as invulnerable, since he was wounded at various times by HERACLES, DIOMEDES, and ATHENA. He is represented as a youthful warrior of strong frame, either naked or clothed with the chlamys. He was a lover of APHRODITE, by whom he had several children, and of others. The chief seats of the worship of Ares were in THRACE and Scythia.

Arete *see* **Nausicaä**.

Arethusa in Greek mythology, a daugher of NEREUS and Doris and a nymph changed by ARTEMIS into a fountain in order to free her from the pursuit of the river-god ALPHEUS. This fountain was said to exist in the small Island of ORTYGIA, near Syracuse, and was fabled to have a subterranean connection with the River Alpheus in Greece.

Arge *see* **Opis.**

Argeia *see* **Polynices.**

Arges *see* **Cyclops; Titans.**

Argives *or* **Argivi** the inhabitants of ARGOS. It is a term used by Homer and other ancient authors as a generic appellation for all the Greeks.

Argo in Greek mythology, the ship of the ARGONAUTS.

Argolis *see* **Argos.**

Argonautica *see* **Apollonius of Rhodes.**

Argonauts in Greek mythology, fifty Greek heroes who performed a hazardous voyage to COLCHIS, a far-distant country at the eastern extremity of the BLACK SEA, in the ship *Argo* under the command of JASON. PELIAS, the usurping king of IOLCUS, to get rid of his nephew Jason, sent him to fetch the GOLDEN FLEECE that was preserved in Colchis suspended upon a tree and under the guardianship of a sleeplesss dragon. Jason caused ARGUS (3) to build a ship of fifty oars and gathered together the bravest heroes from all parts of Greece, including HERACLES, CASTOR AND POLLUX, MELEAGER, ORPHEUS and THESEUS. They sailed by LEMNOS, along the coast of THRACE, up the HELLESPONT and over the Black Sea, encountering many adventures, such as passing safely betwen the CLASHING ROCKS. When they arrived at Colchis, King AEËTES promised to give up the fleece on condition that Jason should yoke to a plough two fire-breathing bulls and should sow the dragon's teeth not already sown by CADMUS in THEBES. From the king's daughter MEDEA, who had fallen passionately in love with Jason, he obtained, under promise of marriage, a charm against fire and steel, which enabled him to destroy all the warriors who sprang up from the land sown with the dragon's teeth. With Medea's help he stupefied the guardian dragon, seized the fleece, and embarked in the *Argo* accompanied by Medea. Despite pursuit by Aeëtes and the charms of the SIRENS and of storms that drove them to Crete and elsewhere, the Argonauts arrived safely at Iolcus, and Jason dedicated the *Argo* to POSEIDON at CORINTH.

Argos a town of Greece, in the north-east of the PELOPONNESUS, between the Gulfs of AEGINA and NAUPLIA or ARGOS. The town and the surrounding territory of Argolis were famous from the legendary period of Greek history onwards. Here, besides Argos, was MYCENAE, where AGAMEMNON ruled. In the plain of Argos was the Lernean marsh, home of the HYDRA slain by HERACLES.

Argus (1) the third king of ARGOS, a son of ZEUS and NIOBE from whom Argos and Argolis derived their names.

Argus (2) *or* **Argus Panoptes** in Greek mythology, a fabulous being, said to have had a hundred eyes, placed by HERA to guard Io. Argus was slain by HERMES, who either stoned him or charmed him to sleep with the music of his flute and then cut off his head. Hera put his hundred eyes in the tail of the peacock, her favourite bird. From him comes the term 'argus-eyed', applied to one who is exceedingly watchful.

Argus (3) the builder of the ARGONAUTS' ship, *Argo*.

Ariadne in Greek mythology, a daughter of MINOS, king of Crete. She gave THESEUS a ball of thread to conduct him out of the labyrinth after his defeat of the MINOTAUR. Theseus promised to marry her but abandoned her on the island of Naxos, where she was found by DIONYSUS, who married her.

Arimaspians in Greek mythology, a people who lived in the extreme northeast of the ancient world. They were said to be one-eyed and to carry on a perpetual war with the gold-guarding griffins, whose gold they endeavoured to steal.

Arion (1) an ancient Greek poet and musician, born at Methymna, in LESBOS, flourished about 625 BC. He lived at the Court of Perinder of CORINTH, and afterwards visited Sicily and Italy. Returning from Tarentum to Corinth with rich treasures, the avaricious sailors resolved to murder him. APOLLO, however, having informed him in a dream of the impending danger, Arion in vain endeavoured to soften the hearts of the crew by the power of music. He then threw himself into the sea, when one of a shoal of dolphins, which had been attracted by his music, received him on his back and bore him to land. The sailors, having returned to Corinth, were confronted by Arion and convicted for their crime. The lyre of Arion and the dolphin that rescued him became constellations in the heavens. A fragment of a hymn to POSEIDON, ascribed to Arion, is extant.

Arion (2) in Greek mythology, a divine horse which POSEIDON, in the form of a horse, fathered on DEMETER while she was in the shape of a mare in order to escape from Poseidon's pursuit of her. Another story says the horse was created by Poseidon in his contest with ATHENA. From Poseidon the horse passed through the hands of ONCIUS, HERACLES and ADRASTUS. *See also* SEVEN AGAINST THEBES.

Aristeas in Greek mythology, a personage represented to have lived over many centuries, disappearing and reappearing by turns.

Aristomachus *see* **Oxylus**.

Arnaeus *see* **Irus**.

Artemis in Greek mythology, a divinity, identified with the Roman DIANA. She was the daughter of ZEUS and LETO and was the twin sister of APOLLO, born on the island of DELOS. She is variously represented as a huntress with bow and arrows; as a goddess of the nymphs, in a chariot drawn by four stags; and as the moon-goddess, with the crescent of the moon above her forehead. Probably originally a pagan fertility goddess, she became a maiden divinity, never conquered by love, except when ENDYMION made her feel its power. She demanded the strictest chastity from her worshippers, and she is represented as having changed ACTAEON into a stag, and caused him to be torn in pieces by his own dogs, because he had secretly watched her as she was bathing. The Artemisia was a festival celebrated in her honour at DELPHI. The famous temple of Artemis at EPHESUS was considered one of the wonders of the world, but the goddess worshipped there was very different from the huntress goddess of Greece, being of Eastern origin, and regarded as the symbol of fruitful nature.

Ascanius *or* **Iulus** in Greek mythology, the son of AENEAS and CREUSA, and the companion of his father's wanderings from TROY to Italy. *See also* IULUS.

Asclepius *see* **Aesculapius**.

Asia in Greek mythology, a daughter of OCEANUS and THETYS, who became by IAPETUS the mother of ATLAS, PROMETHEUS and EPIMETHEUS. According to some traditions, the continent of Asia derived its name from her.

Asopus the name of several rivers in Greece, of which the most celebrated is in BOEOTIA. The river-god Asopus, father of AEGINA, is associated with a river of PELOPONNESUS, which flows through Sicyonia to the Gulf of CORINTH.

asphodel a favourite plant among the ancients, who were in the habit of planting it round their tombs. In Greek religion it is associated with PERSEPHONE, the dead, and the underworld.

Assaracus *see* **Ilus** (2).

Asteria in Greek mythology, a daughter of the TITAN Coeus and PHOEBE (2). She was beloved by ZEUS, and in order to escape from him she metamorphosed into a quail, threw herself into the sea and was here metamorphosed into the island of Asteria or Ortygia, afterwards called DELOS.

Asterion (1) in Greek mythology, a Cretan king who married EUROPA after she had been carried to Crete by ZEUS. He also brought up her three sons by Zeus, MINOS, SARPEDON and RHADAMANTHUS.

Asterion (2) in Greek mythology, a river-god of the River Asterion in Argos

Asterope *see* **Oenomaüs**.

Astraea *or* **Astraia** in Greek mythology, the daughter of ZEUS and THEMIS and the goddess of justice. During the GOLDEN AGE she dwelt on earth, but on that age passing away she withdrew from the society of men and was placed among the stars, where she forms the constellation VIRGO. The name was given to one of the asteroids, discovered in 1845.

Astraeus *see* **Notus**.

Astydameia *see* **Acastus**; **Peleus**.

Astyoche *see* **Ialmenus**.

Atalanta *or* **Atalante** in Greek mythology, a famous huntress of ARCADIA who took part in the CALYDONIAN BOAR hunt. She was to be obtained in marriage only by him who could outstrip her in a race, the consequence of failure being death. Melanion, one of her suitors, obtained from APHRODITE three GOLDEN APPLES, which he threw behind him, one after another, as he ran. Atalanta stopped to pick them up and was not unwillingly defeated. There was another Atalanta belonging to BOEOTIA. In this case the suitor who won her was Hippomenes, but otherwise the two cannot be distinguished.

Ate in Greek mythology, the goddess of hate, injustice, crime and retribution, daughter of ZEUS according to Homer, but of ERIS according to Hesiod.

Athamas in Greek mythology, son of AEOLUS, brother of SISYPHUS and king of Orchomenus (2) in BOEOTIA. At HERA'S command, he married NEPHELE, who bore him two children, a son, PHRIXUS, and a daughter, HELLE. His second wife, INO, plotted against Phrixus, but Nephele was able to save them by using the ram with the GOLDEN FLEECE.

Athena *or* **Pallas Athene** a Greek goddess, identified by the Romans with MINERVA, the representative of the intellectual powers. She is one of the greater Greek divinities, forming with ZEUS and APOLLO the supreme triad in Greek mythology. According to the legend, Zeus, when he had attained supreme power after his victory over the TITANS, chose for his first wife Metis ('wisdom'), but being advised by both URANUS ('heaven') and GE ('earth'), he swallowed her when she was pregnant with Athena. When the time came that Athena should have been born, Zeus felt great pains in his head and caused

HEPHAESTUS to split it with an axe, whereupon Athena sprang forth with a mighty war shout and in complete armour. Her father was the greatest, her mother the wisest of the gods. She is literally born of both and so their qualities harmoniously blend in her. She is personified reason, the wisdom of the divine father, while Apollo, also beloved of Zeus, is his mouth, the revealer of his counsel. In her character of a wise and prudent warrior she was contrasted with the fierce ARES. In the war of Zeus against the giants she assisted her father with her counsel, killed the giant PALLAS (2) and buried ENCELADUS under the island of Sicily. In the wars of the mortals she aided and protected heroes distinguished for their wisdom as well as their valour. In the TROJAN WARS she favoured the Greeks. She is the patroness of agriculture, the inventor of the plough and rake, the first to introduce the olive into ATTICA, and (in harmony with her character as the personification of active wisdom) to teach men the use of almost all the implements of industry and art. Philosophy, poetry and oratory are also under her care. She was the special patroness of the state of Athens, protecting its liberties by her power and wisdom. She maintained the authority of law and justice in her courts, and was believed to have instituted the court of justice (the AREOPAGUS). In the images of the goddess she is always dressed, generally in a Spartan tunic with a cloak over it and wearing a gold helmet adorned with figures of different animals. Her aegis, the round Argolic shield, has in its centre the head of MEDUSA. Her face is beautiful, earnest and thoughtful, and the whole figure majestic.

Athens in ancient times the capital of ATTICA and centre of Greek culture, now the capital of Greece. It is situated in the central plain of Attica, near the Gulf of Aegina, an arm of the Aegean Sea running in between the mainland and the PELOPONNESUS. In mythology, it was founded by CECROPS, after whom it also bore the name Cecropia. The name of Athens is derived from ATHENA, who from earliest times was the city's patron goddess. The city was extended by THESEUS.

Atlantis a large mythical island which, according to Plato, existed in the Atlantic over against the Pillars of Hercules (Straits of Gibraltar), was the home of a great nation, and was finally swallowed up by the sea in an earthquake nine thousands years before his time, at the end of a long contest with the Athenians. The gardens of the HESPERIDES and the Islands of the Blessed were referred to the same region. The legend has been accepted by some as fundamentally true, but others have regarded it as the outgrowth of some early discovery of the New World.

Atlas in Greek mythology, son of the Titan IAPETUS and CLYMENE (1), and brother of PROMETHEUS and EPIMETHEUS. He was the father of the PLEIADES and the HYADES. As leader of the TITANS, he attempted to storm the heavens, and for this supreme treason was condemned by ZEUS to bear the vault of heaven on his head and hands in the neighbourhood of the HESPERIDES at the western extremity of the earth, where day and night meet, on the mountains in the northwest of Africa still called by his name. His name is given to a collection of maps and charts, because Gerard Mercator in the sixteenth century used the figure of Atlas bearing the globe on the title page of such a work.

Atreus in Greek mythology, a son of PELOPS and HIPPODAMIA, grandson of TANTALUS and elder brother of THYESTES. He was married first to Cleola, who bore him Pleisthenes, then to Aerope, who had been wife of his son Pleisthenes and who bore him AGAMEMNON and MENELAUS, and lastly to Pelopia, daughter of his brother Thyestes. Having to flee for the murder of his half-brother Chrysippus, he came with Thyestes to MYCENAE where he married Aerope, daughter of EURYSTHEUS, king of Mycenae, whom he succeeded. Aerope was seduced by Thyestes who, when banished for this outrage, sent Pleisthenes to kill Atreus, but Atreus killed the youth instead, unaware that he was his own son. In revenge Atreus gave a banquet ostensibly to celebrate the brothers' reconciliation at which Thyestes partook of the flesh of his own sons whom Atreus had killed. Thyestes fled in horror, and the vengeance of heaven, in the shape of famine, fell on Atreus for his atrocity. Advised by the oracle to call Thyestes back, he went in search of him, and at the court of King Thesprotus married his third wife, Pelopia, whom he believed to be a daughter of Thesprotus but who was really a daughter of Thyestes and at the time with child by him. This child, AEGISTHUS, afterwards slew Atreus when commissioned by the latter to slay his own father Thyestes. The tragic events connected with the family of Pelops provided plots for some of the great Greek dramatists.

Atropos *see* **Fates**.

Atthis *see* **Erechtheus**.

Attica one of the independent states of HELLAS, or ancient Greece, the capital of which was ATHENS. The territory was triangular in shape, with Cape Sounium (Colonna) as its apex and the ranges of Mounts CITHAERON and Parnes as its base. On the north these ranges separated it from BOEOTIA; on the west it was bounded by Megaris and the Saronic Gulf; on the east by the Aegean. Its most marked physical divisions consisted of the highlands, midland district. and coast district, with the two plains of ELEUSIS and Athens. The CEPHISSUS and ILISSUS, though small, were its chief rivers; its principal hills, Cithaeron, Parnes, Hymettus, Pentelicus, and Laurium. According to tradition the earliest inhabitants of Attica lived in a savage manner until the time of CECROPS, who came with a colony from Egypt, taught them all the essentials of civilization, and founded Athens. One of Cecrops' descendants founded eleven other cities in the regions around, and there followed a period of mutual hosility. THESEUS united these cities in a confederacy, with Athens as the capital. After this union of the several states, the whole of Attica shared in the fortunes of Athens.

Atys *or* **Attis** in classical mythology, the shepherd lover of CYBELE, who, having broken the vow of chastity which he made her, castrated himself.

Atys in Asia Minor a deity with somewhat the same character as ADONIS.

Auge *see* **Nauplius** (3); **Telephus.**
Augeas *or* **Augeias** in Greek mythology, son of PHORBAS or HELIOS and king of the Epeans in ELIS. He had 3,000 head oxen in his stables, which had not been cleaned for thirty year HERACLES was commissioned by EURYSTHEUS to cleanse th Augean stables in one day and was promised as payment a ten part of the oxen. He accomplished the task by turning th courses of the rivers Peneus and ALPHEUS through the stable Augeas refused to pay the stipulated wages, whereupo Heracles killed him.
Aurora in Roman mythology, the goddess of the dawn, th equivalent of the Greek EROS.
autochthones the earliest known or aboriginal inhabitants of country.
Automedusa *see* **Iolaüs; Iphicles.**
Autonoë *see* **Ino.**
Auxo *see* **Horae.**

B

bacchanalia *or* **dionysia** feasts in honour of BACCHUS or DIONYSUS, characterized by licentiousness and revelry, and celebrated in ancient Athens. In the processions were bands of BACCHANTES of both sexes, who, inspired by real or feigned intoxication, wandered about rioting and dancing. They were clothed in fawn-skins, crowned with ivy, and bore in their hands *thyrsi*, that is spears entwined with ivy, or with a pine-cone stuck on the point. These feasts passed from the Greeks to the Romans, who celebrated them with still greater dissoluteness till the Senate abolished them in 187 BC.

bacchants or bacchanals *see* **maenads**.

bacchante a person taking part in revels in honour of BACCHUS. *See also* BACCHANALIA; MAENAD.

Bacchus one of the names among the Greeks and the usual name among the Romans for DIONYSUS, the god of wine. Originally an epithet or surname, it did not occur in Greek writers until after the time of Herodotus, and its use is generally confined to the god in his more riotous aspects. His worship was introduced into Rome from Greece and was amalgamated with the worship of LIBER, an old Italian deity who presided over planting and fructification.

Balius *see* **Xanthus**.

Basalus *see* **Achemon**.

Bateia (1) in Greek mythology, daughter of TEUCER, king of the land which became known as TROY. She was married to DARDANUS, by whom she had two sons, ILUS and Erichthonius. The son of the latter, TROS, gave his name to Troy, and a town near Troy was named in Bateia's honour.

Bateia (2) *see* **Icarius** (1).

Baton in Greek mythology, the charioteer of AMPHIARAUS who with him was swallowed up by the earth after the battle of SEVEN AGAINST THEBES. He was worshipped as a hero and had a sanctuary at ARGOS.

Battus legendary founder of the Greek colony of CYRENE in Libya, about 650 BC. There were eight rulers of the family founded by him, bearing alternately the names Battus and Arcesilaus.

Baucis and Philemon in Greek mythology, an elderly husband and wife who were peasants of BITHYNIA. They entertained ZEUS and HERMES in their humble hillside hut after the two gods, in the guise of mortals, were refused hospitality by everyone else in the region. The gods sent a flood to cover the town at the foot of the hill to punish the inhabitants for their lack of hospitality. The peasants' hut was turned into a shrine by the gods and the old couple were asked to make a wish. Their wish was to spend the rest of their lives at the temple and that they should die together with neither of them outliving the other. Their wish was granted and when they died toether they were changed into two trees, an oak and a linden, which grew side by side.

Bear Mountain (now known as Kapidagi) a mountainous region on the Mysian coast of the Sea of MARMARA said in Greek mythology to have been inhabited by earthly monsters with six arms. They were killed by HERACLES and the ARGONAUTS after attacking the *Argo*.

Bebryces in Greek mythology, a tribe who lived towards the eastern side of the Sea of MARMARA and were noted for their warlike characteristics. In a dispute with the MARIANDYNIANS over ownership of the territory which divided their lands HERACLES sided with the Mariandynians for a time, and the Bebryces lost some of the land. However, on the departure of Heracles, they won some of it back again under the leadership of their king, Amycus. He was killed in a boxing match against Polydeuces when the ARGONAUTS visited the territory.

Bellerophon *or* **Hipponous** in Greek mythology, a hero who, having accidentally killed his brother, fled from CORINTH to PROETUS, king of Argos, whose wife, STHENEBOEA, fell in love with him. Being slighted by him, she persuaded her husband to send him to her father, IOBATES, king of LYCIA, with a letter urging him to put to death this man who had insulted his daughter. Iobates, not wishing to do so directly, imposed on him the dangerous task of conquering the CHIMAERA, a monster that was ravaging the Lycian countryside. Bellerophon, mounted on PEGASUS, a gift from ATHENA, overpowered the monster. Iobates then sent him on an expedition against his enemies, the Solymi, who were routed by Bellerophon and then against the AMAZONS. Once again Bellerophon was victorious, and Iobates, desperate to kill him, sent a band of his Lycian soldiers to ambush him. Bellerophon killed all of them, and as a reward Iobates gave up his attempt to kill Bellerophon and afterwards gave him his daughter Philonoë in marriage and shared his kingdom with him. Bellerophon attempted to soar to heaven on the winged horse Pegasus. ZEUS was angry at his arrogance and sent a gadfly to sting him and cause him to fall to the earth, where he wandered about blind, or lame (legends differ as to which) and alone, having been spurned by the gods, until he died.

Bellona in Roman mythology, the goddess of war and companion of MARS. She is described by the poets as being armed with a scourge, her hair dishevelled and a torch in her hand. She may originally have been a SABINE deity, worship of her being brought to Rome by Sabine settlers. In Rome a temple was erected to her at the Campus Martius.

Belus (1) in Greek mythology, a son of POSEIDON by Libya or Eurynome. He was a twin brother of AGENOR and father of AEGYPTUS and DANAUS. He was believed originally to be the ancestral hero and national god of several eastern countries who became mixed up with Greek myths.

Belus (2) in Greek mythology, the father of DID. He conquered Cyprus and then gave it to TEUCER.

Bia in Greek mythology, the personification of might and force, represented as the offspring of STYX and the Titan PALLAS, held in some legends to be a son, in others to be a daughter. Together with his brother CRATOS, the personification of strength, Bia helped HEPHAESTUS to nail PROMETHEUS to a cliff. Bia and Cratos together were a symbol of the absolute power of ZEUS, and in company with their brother and sister, ZELUS and NIKE, were always beside ZEUS.

Bias in Greek mythology, son of Amythaon and Idomene and brother of MELAMPUS. He married PERO, daughter of NELEUS. Her father had stipulated that anyone who married his daughter would first have to bring him the oxen of IPHICLES and Melampus arranged this on behalf of his brother. Melampus is also said to have acquired for Bias a third of the kingdom of ARGOS. Bias's second wife was IPHIANASSA.

Bistonians *or* **Bistones** a Thracian tribe, said by some legends to have been located on the south shore of THRACE east of the River Nestos, where they gave their name to Lake Bistonis, and by others to have been located in the Thracian Chersonese with Polymestor having been one of their kings.

Bithynia an ancient territory in the northwest of Asia Minor, on the Black Sea and Sea of MARMARA, at one time an independent kingdom, afterwards a Roman province. The legend of BAUCIS AND PHILEMON is based in Bithynia.

Black Corcyra an island named after CORCYRA, daughter of the Phliasian river-god ASOPUS, as was Corcyra, now Corfu. Situated off the Croatian coast the island is now called Korcula.

Black Sea a sea situated between Europe and Asia and connected with the Mediterranean by the BOSPORUS, Sea of MARMARA and HELLESPONT. The Black Sea was called Euxine by the ancients and the area is rich in myth. COLCHIS lay at the eastern end of the Black Sea, and the Crimean Peninsula was the home of the TAURIANS. The ARGONAUTS entered the Black Sea through the Bosporus and escaped from it by sailing up the Ister, now the Danube.

Boeotia one of the independent states of Hellas, or ancient

Greece, lying between ATTICA and PHOCIS, and bounded east and west by the Euboean Sea and the Gulf of CORINTH respectively. The whole country is surrounded by mountains, on the south Mounts CITHAERON and Parnes, on the west Mount HELICON, on the north Mount PARNASSUS and the Opuntiuan Mountains, which also closed it in on the east. The northern part is drained by the CEPHISSUS, the waters of which formed Lake Copais (in ancient times also called Cephissus); the southern by the ASOPUS, which flows into the Euboean Sea. The inhabitants were AEOLIANS, and most of the towns formed a kind of republic, of which THEBES in the southeast was the chief city. The other major city was ORCHOMENUS on the northwest on the shore of Lake Copais. Since refinement and cultivation of mind never made such progress in Boeotia, 'Boeotian' was used by the neighbouring Athenians as a synonym for dullness.

Bona Dea in Roman mythology, a goddess worshipped from earliest time exclusively by women. A prophetic deity with a sanctuary in the Aventine, she revealed her oracles only to women, and men were not even allowed to know her name. Bona Dea means 'good goddess', and the goddess was also called FAUNA. Legend has it that she was related to the god FAUNUS, but the legends differ as to whether she was his sister, wife or daughter. She is variously depicted as being connected with chastity, fertility and healing.

Boötes *or* **Philomelus** in Greek mythology, the son of DEMETER and IASION who, being robbed of all his possessions by his brother, invented the plough and cultivated the soil. He was translated to heaven with the plough and yoke of oxen under the name of Boötes ('ox-driver'), which is still borne by a constellation beside the Great Bear (or Wain). According to others, Boötes was the son of CALLISTO (*see* URSA MAJOR) and to yet others the winemaker ICARIUS (2).

Boreades an epithet meaning 'sons of BOREAS'. ZETES AND CALAÏS are often referred to by it.

Boreas in mythology, the name of the north wind as personified by the Greeks and Romans and said to be the son of Astraeus and Eos. His home was in THRACE in a cave in Mount HAEMUS. He carried off and married OREITHYIA, a daughter of ERECHTHEUS, who would have opposed the match since the Athenians hated the Thracians. Later, during the Persian war he showed favour to the Athenians by destroying the Persian ships and saving the Athenians from invasion. He had two winged sons, ZETES AND CALAIS, and two daughters, CLEOPATRA (2), who became the wife of PHINEUS, and Chione. He is also supposed to have fathered twelve stallions by mares belonging to Erichthonius, a king of TROY. Boreas is sometimes represented in art as having serpent tails instead of feet, especially when depicted as carrying off Oreithyia.

Borus in Greek mythology, a son of PERIERES who married POLYDORA, daughter of PELEUS.

Bosporus *or* **Bosphorus** the strait joining the BLACK SEA with the Sea of MARMARA, called also the Strait of Constantinople. The Cimmerian Bosporus was the ancient name of the strait that leads from the BLACK SEA into the Sea of AZOV. There was also in ancient times a kingdom of the name of Bosporus situated on both sides of the strait.

Brasiae a town on the coast of northern LACONIA connected with one of the legends relating to the birth of DIONYSUS. According to this legend, SEMELE, having been seduced by ZEUS, gives birth to Dionysus and is locked with her baby in a chest by her father CADMUS, king of THEBES, who did not believe the story of the seduction. The chest was flung into the sea and was washed up at Brasiae where Semele was found to be dead but the baby alive. INO is then said to have reached Brasiae in the course of her wanderings and takes care of the infant Dionysus in a cave.

Brass Race *see* **Races of Man**.

Brauron a town in eastern ATTICA, whose name was derived from the ancient hero of the name Brauronian. ARTEMIS was worshipped here, the ancient statue of the goddess supposedly being the one stolen from the TAURIANS by ORESTES and IPHIGENEIA.

Brazen Race *see* **Races of Man**.

Briareus *or* **Aegaeon** in Greek mythology, a giant with a hundred arms and fifty heads, who aided ZEUS in the great war waged with the TITANS and was rewarded by Cympola, daughter of ZEUS. He was the son of POSEIDON or GE and URANUS. *See also* ETNA.

Briseïs in Greek mythology, the concubine of ACHILLES who abducted her from LYRNESSUS after he had plundered the city and killed her husband, parents and brothers. AGAMEMNON, on the loss of his own concubine, Chryseïs, took Briseïs from Achilles, thereby starting a quarrel between Achilles and Agamemnon, which led to Achilles refusing to fight with the the Greeks. On the death of PATROCLUS, Achilles relented and agreed to fight and Briseïs was returned to him.

Britomartis a Cretan goddess and the daughter of ZEUS and Carme, daughter of Eubulus. She was associated with hunting and with fishermen. There were several points of resemblance between her and ARTEMIS, who loved her and is said to have assumed her name. Thus in some legends the two goddesses have become identified. Britomartis was loved by MINOS, king of Crete, who pursued her relentlessly. Weary of his advances, she threw herself into the sea. Legends differ as to whether she was saved by falling into the nets of some fishermen or whether she died and became immortal, being made a goddess by Artemis. As a goddess in Crete she was given the name DICTYNNA, a name which was also later sometimes given to Artemis. She was also worshipped by AEGINA where she was known as Aphaea.

Bromios in Greek mythology, a name given to DIONYSUS, meaning 'thunderer'.

Brontes *see* **Cyclops**; **Titans**.

Broteas (1) in Greek mythology, a son of TANTALUS (1), king of Phrygia, who is supposed to have carved the oldest image of CYBELE on a rock named Coddinus which was north of Mount Sipylus. ARTEMIS drove him mad because of his refusal to worship her, and he leapt into a fire and died, believing himself in his madness to be immune to flames. According to some legends Broteas was the father of TANTALUS (2), the first husband of CLYTEMNESTRA.

Broteas (2) in Roman mythology, a son of VULCAN and MINERVA who was so upset by taunts about his exteme ugliness that he burned himself.

Brygeians *or* **Brygi** in Greek mythology, a tribe in EPIRUS who with the support of ARES defeated the Thesprotians led by ODYSSEUS.

Bull of Minos *see* **Minotaur**.

Busiris a mythical Egyptian king, a son of POSEIDON and Lysinianassa, daughter of EPAPHUS. In the course of a severe drought he sacrificed strangers to his land to ZEUS on the advice of a seer. He was defeated and killed by HERACLES.

Butes (1) in Greek mythology, a son of BOREAS. His father forced him into exile because of his hostile treatment of his stepbrother, LYCURGUS (1), king of THRACE, and he went to the island of Strongyle, later called Naxos, with a band of followers. Having no women in their party they tried to carry off a group of women who were celebrating a festival of DIONYSUS at THESSALY. Butes took Coronis, who complained to Dionysus. The god then drove Butes mad, and he leapt into a well and was killed.

Butes (2) in Greek mythology, an ARGONAUT and son of Teleon or POSEIDON and ZEUXIPPE, daughter of the river-god ERIDANUS. When the ARGONAUTS passed by the SIRENS on their homeward journey, Butes leapt overboard and swam towards them as they sang on the island of Anthemoessa. APHRODITE took pity on him and saved him by taking him to Lilybaeum in Sicily where she bore him a son, ERYX.

Butes (3) in Greek mythology, a son of PANDION (1), king of Athens, and ZEUXIPPE, he has become confused with BUTES (2) the Argonaut and may be the same person. He was a twin brother of ERECHTHEUS, and he married his brother's daughter, Chthonia.

After the death of Pandion he obtained the office of priest of ATHENA and of Poseidon Erechtheus.

Buthrotum a port in EPIRUS opposite the island of CORCYRA founded by the Trojan HELENUS who was taken there after the fall of TROY by NEOPTOLEMUS.

Byblis and Caunus in Greek mythology, Byblis was a daughter of MILETUS and Eidothea or Cyaneë and twin sister of Caunus. There are two different versions of the legend relating to brother and sister. According to one, Caunus had feelings of love for Byblis which were more than brotherly and went away to Lycia when he could not get over these. His sister went to look for him and finally killed herself by hanging herself on her girdle when she could not find him. From her tears sprang the well Byblis. According to another legend Byblis had feelings of passion for her brother and confessed these to him. He was horrified and fled to the country of Leleges, and Byblis hanged herself. There are various variations on these legends. The Phoenician city of BYBLUS is said by some to be named after Byblis.

Byblus *or* **Byblos** (now called Jebail) an ancient maritime city of Phoenicia, a little north of Beirut. It was famous as the birthplace of ADONIS or Tammuze, of whose worship it became the centre.

C

Cabiri *or* **Cabeiri** deities or deified heroes worshipped in the ancient Greek islands of LEMNOS, Imbros and SAMOTHRACE, and also on the neighbouring coast of TROY in Asia Minor.

Cadmus in Greek mythology, the son of AGENOR (1) and Telephassa, grandson of POSEIDON and brother of EUROPA. When Europa was carried off by ZEUS, he was sent by Agenor in quest of her and told not to return without her. His search was in vain, and the oracle at DELPHI told him to abandon it and instead to follow a cow of a certain kind which he would meet and build a city where it would lie down. Cadmus found the cow in PHOCIS, followed her to BOEOTIA and built there the city of THEBES. Intending to sacrifice the cow to ATHENA, he sent some men to the nearby well of ARES for water, but they were killed by the dragon, a son of Ares, who guarded it. Cadmus then slew the dragon and sowed its teeth in the ground. From these sprang up armed men who slew each other until only five were left. They became the SPARTI, the progenitors of the Theban families. Athena assigned to Cadmus the government of Thebes, and Zeus gave him HARMONIA for his wife. All the gods of OLYMPUS were at the marriage, and Cadmus gave Harmonia a peplus and necklace that he had received from HEPHAESTUS or Europa. They had one son, POLYDORUS, and four daughters, INO, SEMELE, Autonoë and AGAVE. Subsequently Cadmus and Harmonia left Thebes and conquered ILLYRIA. Other legends ascribe the introduction of the Phoenician alphabet into Greece to Cadmus. The solar mythologists identify him with the sun-god. *See also* AGAVE.

caduceus the winged staff of HERMES, which gave the god power to fly. Originally a simple olive branch, its stems were afterwards formed into two snakes twisted round it, and several tales were devised by mythologists to explain this, as that Hermes having found two snakes fighting, divided them with his rod and thus they came to be used as an emblem of peace. It was the staff or mace carried by heralds and ambassadors in time of war. It was not used by the Romans. Many magical virtues were ascribed to the caduceus. In Homer, Hermes touches the souls of the dead with it and so lulls them to sleep before carrying them to the underworld. It is also seen in the hands of ARES, DIONYSUS, HERACLES, DEMETER and APHRODITE. The rod represents powers; the serpents, wisdom; and the two wings, diligence and activity.

Caenis *or* **Caenus** *see* **Elatus** (2).

Calaïs *see* **Zetes**.

Calchas in Greek mythology, a seer, son of Thestor, who was attached to the Greek forces during the TROJAN WAR. His reputation was such that AGAMEMNON went to him in person to persuade him to join their expedition. He is said to have foretold the length of the siege and to have predicted that Troy could not be won without the help of ACHILLES while Achilles was still a child. When the fleet was detained at Aulis by adverse winds, he demanded the sacrifice of IPHIGENEIA. He is said to have died at Colophon from chagrin at being surpassed in soothsaying by one Mopsus.

Calliope in Greek mythology, one of the MUSES. She presided over eloquence, heroic poetry, and knowledge in general. She is said to have been the mother of ORPHEUS by APOLLO or OEAGRUS.

Callirrhoë *see* **Ganymede**; **Ilus** (2).

Callisto in Greek mythology, a huntress and companion of ARTEMIS, who was loved by ZEUS and was mother of ARCAS by him. To hide his liaison from HERA, Zeus metamophosed Callisto into a bear, and she was slain by Artemis during a hunt. Zeus gave Arcas to MAIA to be brought up, and Callisto was placed among the stars as Arctos (*see* URSA MAJOR).

Calydon the ancient capital city of Aetolia in northern Greece, ruled by Oeneus and celebrated in Greek mythology on account of the ravages of the Calydonian Boar.

Calydonian Boar in Greek mythology, a terrible boar sent by Artemis to lay waste Calydon, the land of Oeneus, who had omitted a sacrifice to her and who was absent on the Argonauts' expedition. No one dared to face the monster until Meleager, the son of Oeneus, with a band of heroes pursued and slew him. The Curetes laid claim to the head and hide, but were driven off by Meleager. Later accounts make Meleager summon to the hunt heroes from all parts of Greece, among them Atalanta, who gave the monster the first wound.

Calypso in Greek mythology, a nymph, a daughter of Atlas, who inhabited the wooded island of Ogygia, on the shores of which Odysseus was shipwrecked. She promised him immortality if he would consent to marry her, but after a seven years' stay she was ordered by the gods to permit his departure. Calypso bore Odysseus two sons, and on his departure died of grief.

Camenae in Roman mythology, goddesses or nymphs identified with the Muses. They were worshipped from early times.

Canis Major ('the greater dog') a constellation of the southern hemisphere containing Sirius, the brightest star. **Canis Minor** ('the lesser dog') is a constellation in the northern hemisphere, immediately above Canis Major, the chief star in which is Procyon. The dog represented in the larger constellation is said to have been the hound of Orion, or Maera, the dog of Icarius (2). Alternatively, Maera is sometimes held to have been the dog repesented in the smaller constellation.

Capaneus in Greek mythology, one of the Seven against Thebes. He scaled the walls of Thebes during the siege and said that he would set fire to the city even if Zeus opposed it. As a punishment for his arrogance, Zeus sent a thunderbolt to kill him. His son, Sthenelus (2) was one of the Epigoni.

Capys *see* **Ilus** (2).

Caria an ancient country in the southwest corner of Asia Minor.

The original inhabitants may have been LELEGIANS, who were subjects of Crete and manned the ships of MINOS. Later it was partly settled by Greek colonists, chiefly Dorians. Cnidus, Halicarnassus and MILETUS were among the chief towns.

Carme *see* **Britomartis**.

Carmenta *see* **Evander**.

Carnabos *see* **Ophiuchus**.

Carpo *see* **Horae**.

Carthage a Phoenician city on the north coast of Africa, the capital of one of the great empires of the ancient world, situated on a peninsula at the northeast corner of the region now known as Tunis. In mythology, it was founded by DIDO.

Cassandra in Greek mythology, a daughter of PRIAM and HECUBA and twin sister of HELENUS. The two children were left one night in the sanctuary of APOLLO, and during their sleep their ears were touched and purified by two snakes so that they could understand the meaning of the language of birds and thus know the future. Cassandra afterwards attracted the love of Apollo by her beauty, and he taught her the secrets of prophecy, but, displeased by her rejection of his suit, he laid upon her the curse that her prophecies should never be believed. She frequently foretold the fall of TROY and warned her countrymen in vain against the stratagem of the horse. When Troy was taken, she fled to the temple of ATHENA, but was torn from the altar by AJAX THE LESS and ravished in the temple. She fell, as part of his share of the booty, to AGAMEMNON, who, in spite of her warnings, carried her with him as his slave to MYCENAE, where they were both murdered by CLYTEMNESTRA. The name is now often used of one who takes gloomy views of the political or social future.

Cassiopeia a conspicuous constellation in the northern hemisphere, situated next to CEPHEUS and often called the Lady in her Chair. It was said to represent Cassiopeia, the wife of Cepheus, king of Ethiopia, in a chair but on her back and with her feet in the air. This was meant to be a punishment for her pride in thinking that either she or her daughter, ANDROMEDA was more beautiful than the NEREIDES.

Castalia a fountain on the slope of PARNASSUS, a little above DELPHI, in PHOCIS, sacred to APOLLO and the MUSES. Those who visited the temple at Delphi would wash their hair in the fountain but those who needed to be purified from murder bathed their whole body. Its waters were supposed to give poetic inspiration to those who drank from it. The name was due to Castalia daughter of ACHELOUS, who threw herself into the fountain to escape the pursuit of Apollo.

Castor and Pollux (also called **Dioscuri**, 'sons of Zeus') in Greek mythology, twin divinities, sons of TYNDAREUS, king of SPARTA, and LEDA, and so brothers of HELEN of TROY. According to a later tradition, they were the sons of ZEUS and Leda. Castor was mortal, but Pollux was immortal. The former was particularly skilled in breaking horses, the latter in boxing and wrestling. Both received divine honours at Sparta as patrons of mariners. One story tells that when Castor, the mortal, was killed, Pollux prayed Zeus to let him die with him, and was permitted either to live as his immortal son in OLYMPUS or to share his brother's fate and live one day in heaven with the gods, the other among the shades. Zeus placed the brothers among the stars as Gemini, and their names are attached to the principal stars in that constellation.

Castra *see* **Idas and Lynceus**.

Catalogues of Women *or* **Eoiae** a fragmentary catalogue of Greek mythological heroines. It has been pieced together from brief passages quoted or summarized by ancient writers.

Catreus *see* **Nauplius** (3).

Caunus *see* **Byblis**.

Cebren *see* **Oenone**.

Cecrops in Greek mythology, the founder of ATHENS and the first king of ATTICA, sometimes represented as half man and half dragon. He was said to have taught the savage inhabitants religion and morals, made them acquainted with the advantages of social life and instituted marriage and the worship of the gods, and introduced agriculture, navigation and commerce. By the later Greeks he was represented as having led a colony to Attica from Egypt about 1440 or 1500 BC.

Cedalion *see* **Orion**.

Celaeno *see* **Nycteus**.

Celeus in Greek mythology, a king of ELEUSIS and husband of METANEIRA, by whom he had two sons, DEMOPHON and TRIPTOLEMUS. *See also* ELEUSINIAN MYSTERIES.

Centaurs in Greek mythology, beings represented as half man, half horse. The earliest references to them, however, merely represent them as a race of wild and savage men inhabiting the mountains and forests of THESSALY. The most ancient account of the Hippocentaurs, sometimes considered as distinct but more often confused with the Centaurs, is that they were the offspring of Magnesian mares and Centaurus, himself the offspring of IXION and a cloud. Mythology relates the combat of the Centaurs with the LAPITHS, which arouse at the marriage feast of PEIRITHOUS and took place in Thessaly or ARCADIA. This fight is sometimes put in connection with a combat of HERACLES with the Centaurs. It ended in the Centaurs being expelled from their country and taking refuge on Mount Pindus on the frontiers of EPIRUS. The most famous Centaur was CHIRON, the teacher of ACHILLES and other heroes. The Centaur NESSUS is also famous in ancient mythology. Chiron and Pholus are the good Centaurs, while the others are represented as lustful and savage. In art, the Centaurs were represented as men from the head to the loins, with the rest of the body that of a horse.

Centaurus *see* **Centaurs**.

Cephalonia *or* **Kephallenia** a mountainous island of Greece, the largest of the IONIAN ISLANDS, west of the Morea, at the entrance of the Gulf of Patras. Its earliest inhabitants were probably Taphians, and it is said to have derived its name from CEPHALUS, who made himself master of the island with the help of AMPHITRYON.

Cephalus in Greek mythology, a son of DEION, ruler of PHOCIS, and and husband of PROCRIS. Eos was in love with Cephalus, but he resisted her because of a vow that he and Procris had made to remain faithful to each other. Eos advised Cephalus not to break his vow until Procris had broken hers. She then metamorphosed Cephalus into a stranger bearing rich gifts with which to tempt Procris, who was induced by these to break the vow. When she recognized her husband, she fled to Crete where either ARTEMIS or MINOS made her a present of a dog, LAELAPS, and a spear, which were never to miss their object. Procris returned home disguised as a youth and went out hunting with Cephalus. When he saw the excellence of her dog and spear, he tried to buy them from her, but she refused to part with them for any price except love. When he promised to love her, she revealed herself to him and they were reconciled. As, however, she still feared the love of Eos, she always jealously watched Cephalus when he went out hunting, and on one occasion he killed her by accident with the never-erring spear. Subsequently AMPHITRYON came to Cephalus and persuaded him to give up his dog to hunt the Teumessian vixen which was ravaging the Cadmean territory. Cephalus is said to have committed suicide by leaping into the sea from Cape Leucas, on which he had built a temple of APOLLO, in order to atone for having killed his wife.

Cepheus (1) in Greek mythology, a king of Ethiopia and husband of CASSIOPEIA, father of ANDROMEDA and father-in-law of PERSEUS. His name was given to a constellation of stars in the nothern hemisphere surrounded by Cassiopeia, URSA MAJOR, Draco and Cygnus.

Cepheus (2) in Greek mythology, a son of Aleus, brother of LYCURGUS (2) and an ARGONAUT from TEGEA in ARCADIA, of which he was king. He had twenty sons and two daughters. Nearly all his sons perished in an expedition that they had undertaken with HERACLES.

Cephissus, River the name of two rivers in Greece. The Cephissus in ATTICA rises on the western slope of Mount Pentelicus and the southern side of Mount Parnes and flows past Athens into the Saronic Gulf. The Cephissus in Boetia flows into Lake Copais. The river-god Cephissus was the father of Narcissus by the nymph Leirope.

Cerberus in Greek mythology, a son of Echidna and Typhon, the dog-monster that guarded Hades, variously described as having a hundred, fifty, and three heads, with a serpent's tail and a mane consisting of the heads of various snakes. Homer mentions him simply as the dog of Hades. Orpheus charmed him with the magic of his lyre, and he was subdued by Heracles, who, as the last test of his strength, snatched Cerberus from the halls of Hades.

Cercopes in Greek mythology, a band of dwarf-like creatures who lived in Lydia. They were noted for their habit of stealing. and were either killed or captured by Heracles. The ancient Greeks believed monkeys to be degraded men. The Cercopes were changed into monkeys for attempting to deceive Zeus.

Cercyon *see* **Alope**.

Ceres in Roman mythology, a goddess corresponding to the Greek Demeter. She was the daughter of Saturn and Rhea, and the mother of Proserpine and Bacchus. She was the goddess of the earth from the aspect of bringing forth fruits, and she especially watched over the growth of grain and other plants. The Romans celebrated in her honour the festival of the Cerealia (12th to 19th April) with games in the circus. Ceres was always represented in full attire, her attributes being ears of corn and poppies, and her sacrifices consisting of pigs and cows.

Cerynes *see* **Deïphontes**.

Cerynitian hind in Greek mythology, a golden-horned deer which was sacred to Artemis. One of the tasks of Heracles was to capture it alive.

Cestus in Greek mythology, a girdle worn by Aphrodite or Venus, endowed with the power of exciting love towards the wearer. It was borrowed by Hera when she desired to win the love of Zeus.

Ceto in Greek mythology, a sea monster, the daughter of GE and PONTUS and mother of the GORGONS.

Cetus (The Sea-Monster or The Whale) a constellation. It was said to represent the monster sent by POSEIDON to devour ANDROMEDA as a punishment for her mother's arrogance (*see* CASSIOPEIA).

Chalciope *see* **Aeëtes**; **Eidyia**.

Chalybes a tribe inhabiting a part of the southern coast of the BLACK SEA. They were famous for their work in iron and were warlike.

Chaos in old theories of the earth, the void out of which sprang all things or in which they existed in a confused, unformed shape before they were separated into kinds. Some ancient writers make it the original source of all; others mention along with it GE, TARTARUS and EROS, the rough outlines of heaven and earth proceeding from Chaos while the organization and perfecting of all things was the work of Eros. Later writers represent it as that confused shapeless mass out of which the universe was formed into a cosmos, or harmonious order. One writer makes Chaos the mother of EREBUS and NYX.

Chariclo *or* **Naïs** *see* **Chiron**.

Charites the Greek name for the GRACES.

Charon in Greek mythology, the son of EREBUS and NYX. It was his task to ferry the dead over the rivers of the infernal regions, for which he received an obolus, or farthing, which accordingly was usually put into the mouth of the deceased. If this rite was neglected, Charon refused to convey the soul across, and it was doomed to wander restlessly along the shores of ACHERON. He was represented as an old man, with a gloomy aspect, matted beard and tattered garments.

Charybdis an eddy or whirlpool in the Strait of MESSINA, celebrated in ancient times and regarded as the more dangerous to navigators because in endeavouring to escape it they ran the risk of being wrecked upon SCYLLA, a rock opposite to it.

Cheiron *see* **Chiron**.

Chimaera in Greek mythology, a fire-breathing monster, the foreparts of whose body were those of a lion, the middle of a goat, and the hind part of a dragon. She was the daughter of ECHIDNA and TYPHON, and devastated Lycia until killed by BELLEROPHON. The name has come to be used for something imaginary.

Chione *see* **Boreas**; **Oreithyia**..

Chios *or* **Scio** an island belonging to Greece, in the AEGEAN SEA, separated from the coast of Asia Minor by a channel. It is one of the places that contended for the honour of having given birth to Homer.

Chiron *or* **Cheiron** in Greek mythology, son of CRONOS and PHILYRA, and husband of Naïs or Chariclo, the most famous of the CENTAURS. He lived at the foot of Mount PELION in THESSALY, and was famous throughout all Greece for his wisdom and acquirements, particularly for his skill in healing, hunting, music and prophecy. The greatest heroes of the time—DIONYSUS, JASON, HERACLES, ACHILLES, etc—were represented as his pupils. He died by being accidentally wounded by one of the poisoned arrows of his friend Heracles.

Chloris *see* **Neleus**; **Pero**.

Chlorus *see* **Pelasgus**.

Chromius *see* **Neleus**.

Chryseïs *see* **Briseïs**; **Homer**.

Chrysomallus *see* **golden fleece**.

Chrysopeleia in Greek mythology, a wood NYMPH who was one day in great danger as the oak tree which she inhabited was undermined by a mountain torrent. ARCAS, who was hunting in the neighbourhood, discovered the situation, led the torrent in another direction and secured the tree by a dam. Chrysopeleia became by Arcas the mother of ELATUS (1) and Apheidas.

Chryssipus *see* **Laius**.

Chthonia *see* **Butes** (3).

chthonian deities in Greek mythology, spirits of the earth or underworld.

Chthonius *see* **Nycteus; Sparti.**
Ciconian Women *see* **Hebrus.**
Cilicia in ancient geography, the region of Asia Minor between Pamphylia and Syria, lying south of Mount Taurus. In early ages it was ruled by its own kings, the people, who were probably akin to Syrians and Phoenicians, being notorious pirates.
Cinna *see* **Niobe** (2).
Circe in Greek mythology, a sorceress, the daughter of HELIOS and the ocean nymph PERSE. She lived in the Island of Aeaea and around her palace were numbers of human beings whom she had changed into the shapes of wolves and lions by her drugs and incantations. She changed twenty-two of the companions of ODYSSEUS into swine after making them drink enchanted wine. Odysseus, protected by the herb MOLY that HERMES had given him, remained uninjured by her drugs and compelled her to restore his companions. Odysseus remained with her for a year, and when he departed, she instructed him how to avoid the dangers that he would encounter on his homeward voyage. Ovid relates how, when Circe was jealous of SCYLLA, whose love was sought by GLAUCUS, she poured the juice of poisonous herbs into that part of the sea where her rival was accustomed to bathe and so changed her into a hideous monster.
Cithaeron, Mount (modern Elatea) a mountain of Greece, which, stretching northwest, separates BOEOTIA from MEGARIS and ATTICA. On its northern slope stood the city of Plataea.
Clashing Rocks two rocks on either side of the northern entrance of the Bosporus. They were called the Symplegades and were sometimes called the Cyanean ('dark blue') Rocks. They were said to clash together when the wind blew strongly. The ARGONAUTS with the help of ATHENA successfully negotiated them.
Cleio *see* **Clio.**
Cleola *see* **Atreus.**
Cleopatra (1) *or* **Alcyone** in Greek mythology, a daughter of

IDAS and Marpessa and wife of MELEAGER. She is said to have hanged herself after her husband's death or to have died of grief.

Cleopatra (2) in Greek mythology, daughter of BOREAS and OREITHYIA, and the first wife of PHINEUS.

Clio *or* **Cleio** in Greek mythology, one of the nine MUSES, a daughter of ZEUS and MNEMOSYNE. The Muse of history and epic poetry, she is represented as sitting with a half-opened scroll in her hand and a casket for holding manuscripts at her feet.

Clonio *see* **Nycteus**.

Clotho in Greek mythology, that one of the three FATES, or Parcae, whose duty it was to put the wool for the thread of life round the spindle, while that of LACHESIS was to spin it, and that of ATROPOS to cut it when the time had come.

Clymene (1) in Greek mythology, a daughter of OCEANUS and THETYS, and the wife of IAPETUS, by whom she became the mother of ATLAS, PROMETHEUS and others.

Clymene (2) in Greek mythology, a daughter of Minyas (*see* MINYANS) and the wife of PHYLACUS, by whom she became the mother of IPHICLUS and Alcimede.

Clymene (3) in Greek mythology, the daughter of King Catreus of Crete who sold her to NAUPLIUS (3), who married her.

Clytemnestra in Greek mythology, a daughter of King TYNDAREUS and LEDA, and wife of AGAMEMNON. During the absence of her husband in the TROJAN WAR, she became the mistress of AEGISTHUS, and with him murdered Agamemnon on his return from Troy. Together with her lover she governed MYCENAE for seven years. Her son ORESTES killed them both.

Clytoneus *see* **Nauplius** (2).

Cocytus, River a river of ancient EPIRUS, a tributary of the ACHERON, in Greek mythology, supposed to be connected with the lower world. Homer makes it a branch of STYX; Virgil makes the Acheron flow into the Cocytus.

Codrus in Greek mythology, the last king of ATHENS. Having learned that the enemies of his country would be victorious, according to the declaration of an oracle, if they did not kill the Athenian king, he voluntarily entered their camp, provoked a quarrel, and was slain. The grateful Athenians abolished the royal dignity, substituting that of archon, regarding no one worthy to be the successor of Codrus. His son Medon was the first archon, chosen for life.

Coeus *see* **Phoebe** (2); **Titans**.

Colchian Dragon *see* **Echidna**.

Colchis the ancient name of a region at the eastern extremity of the BLACK SEA, resting on the Caucasus, famous in Greek mythology as the destination of the ARGONAUTS, and the native country of MEDEA. The principal coast town was Dioscurias (the Roman Sebastopolis).

Corcyra in Greek mythology, a daughter of the river god ASOPUS, with whom POSEIDON fell in love. He carried her off to the most northerly of the Ionian Islands, which was called Corcyra after her.

Corinth a once celebrated city-state on the isthmus of the same name which unites PELOPONNESUS with northern Greece. It commanded an advantageous position, and its citadel, the Acrocorinthus, rendered it a strong fortress. Originally a Phoenecian colony, according to legend an Aeolian dynasty was founded there by SISYPHUS, whose cunning and love of gain may typify the commercial enterprise of the early maritime population who replaced the original inhabitants. Under the sway of Sisyphus and his descendants, Corinth became one of the richest and most powerful cities in Greece. Sisyphus had two sons, GLAUCUS (3) and Ornytion. From the line of Glaucus came BELLEROPHON, who was worshipped with heroic honours at Corinth, and whose exploits were a favourite subject among the Corinthians. The figure of the winged horse PEGASUS, which Bellerophon caught at the fountain of Peirene on the Acrocorinthus, is constantly found on the coins of Corinth and her colonies. Bellerophon settled in Lycia, and the descendants of

Ornytion continued to rule at Corinth until overthrown by the DORIANS.

Corinth, Gulf of *or* **Gulf of Lepanto** a beautiful inlet of the Mediterranean between the PELOPONNESUS and northern Greece, having the Isthmus of Corinth closing it in on the east.

Coronis (1) in Greek mythology, a daughter of PHLEYGAS and mother of AESCULAPIUS by APOLLO. She became the lover of ISCHYS while she was pregnant, so Apollo, wishing to punish her faithlessness, caused ARTEMIS to kill her and Ischys.

Coronis (2) *see* **Butes** (1).

Corybants in Greek mythology, male attendants of CYBELE. Their rites included dances during which they clashed spears and shields.

Corycian Cave *see* **Delphyne**.

Cos *or* **Kos** an island in the AEGEAN SEA, on the coast of Asia Minor.

Cottus *see* **Hundred-handed**.

Cranaus *see* **Erechtheus**.

Cratos in Greek mythology, the personification of strength, a son of URANUS and GE and brother of BIA, NIKE and ZELUS.

Creon the brother of JOCASTA and successor to OEDIPUS as king of THEBES.

Cretan Bull in Greek mythology, a bull that was sacred to POSEIDON. MINOS prayed to Poseidon for his assistance when he claimed the throne of Crete. Poseidon sent a bull from the sea with instructions that Minos should sacrifice it to him. Minos sacrificed a less fine bull in its place. As an act of vengeance, Poseidon caused the wife of Minos, PASIPHAË, to give birth to a monster by the bull, the MINOTAUR. After this the bull roamed CRETE. Capturing it alive was the seventh labour of HERACLES.

Crete a large mountainous island in the Mediterranean, north of the African coast. High mountains, covered with forests, run through the whole length of the island in several ranges. The island was colonized at a very early period by Egyptians and Anatolians and was the 'cradle' of pre-Greek or Aegean civilization, which has two phases, Minoan and Mycenaean. Minoa refers to the island culture and is named after Minos, whil Mycenaean, a late phase of Minoan, is so called because it i well represented at Mycenae. About 1400 BC the palace c Knossos was sacked, probably by Mycenaeans aided b Achaeans, and the dynasty of Minos ended. Large numbers c Cretans appear to have migrated. A colony of them settled i Cyprus, and it may be that the classical legend of the expeditio of Minos to Sicily, and the subsequent Cretan expedition t avenge his death, refer to attempts made to found colonial se tlements in Sicily and Italy. The king of Crete who fought in th Trojan War was evidently subject to Mycenae. The chief d vinity of Crete appears to have been the mother goddess wh had links with Rhea, Demeter, Athena and Aphrodite. Offe ings were made to her in cave sanctuaries. The dove and serpe were connected with her cult. There was also a group of thre goddesses. A double-axe symbol of a deity was honoured, an in late times it was connected with the son of the mother goc dess, the 'Cretan Zeus' or 'Zeus of the Double-axe'.

Cretheus *see* **Iolcus; Neleus.**

Creusa (1) in Greek mythology, the daughter of Erechtheu wife of Xuthus and mother of Achaeus and Ion. She is also sai to have been loved by Apollo, who is sometimes said to be th father of Ion.

Creusa (2) in Greek mythology, a daughter of Priam an Hecuba, and the wife of Aeneas and mother of Ascanius an Iulus. She was lost in their flight from Troy. When Aeneas re turned to seek her, she appeared to him as a ghost, console him, revealed to him his future fate and told him she was kep back the great mother of the gods and was obliged to let hi depart alone.

Creusa (3) *see* **Glauce.**

Crius *see* **Titans.**

Crommyonian Sow in Greek mythology, a wild pig name Phaea, said to have been the offspring of Echidna and Typho which ravaged the town of Crommyon on the Isthmus of CORINTH until it was destroyed by THESEUS.

Cronos, Cronus *or* **Kronos** in Greek mythology, a son of URANUS and GE (Heaven and Earth) and youngest of the TITANS. He was the ruler of the world after Uranus was deprived of it, and was in turn deposed by ZEUS in the War of the Titans. Cronos was considered by the Romans as identical with their SATURN.

Cumean Sibyl *see* **sibyl**.

Cupid *or* **Amor** in Roman mythology, the god of love, corresponding to the Greek EROS. He is variously said to be the son of VENUS by MARS, JUPITER or MERCURY. He is represented as a winged boy, naked, armed with a bow and a quiver full of arrows. His eyes are often covered so that he shoots blindly. His darts could pierce the fish at the bottom of the sea, the birds in the air, and even the gods in OLYMPUS.

Curetes in Greek mythology, the attendants of RHEA. They were supposed to have saved the infant ZEUS from his father CRONOS, and then to have become a sort of bodyguard of the god. Their number is sometimes given as ten, although in Greek art only three are usually represented. The ceremonies in connection with the cult of the Curetes consisted principally in performing the Pyrrhic dance, a kind of war dance. The ancients themselves confused the Curetes with other rather similar beings—the CORYBANTES and CABEIRI—and modern research has been unable to clear up the confusion. *See also* TITANS.

Curiatii *see* **Horatii**.

Cyanean Rocks *see* **Clashing Rocks**.

Cyaneë *see* **Byblis and Caunus**.

Cyathus *or* **Eunomus** *see* **Oeneus**.

Cybele, Agdistis *or* **Dindymeme** originally a goddess of the Phrygians, the Great Mother Deity, and, like Isis, the symbol of the moon. From Asia Minor her cult spread to THRACE and the islands, and finally to Greece and to Rome. Her worship was celebrated with a violent noise of instruments and rambling through fields and woods, and her priests were eunuchs in memory of ATYS. The Greeks identified her with their ancient earth goddess RHEA, whose worship seems to have originated in CRETE where she is associated with the CURETES. Among the Romans she was considered as identical with OPS, the wife of SATURN and mother of JUPITER. The Roman priests of Cybele were often called Galli. In later times she was represented as a matron seated on a throne adorned with a mural crown (in reference to the improved condition of men arising from agriculture and their union into cities) with lions crouching to the right and left, or sitting in a carriage drawn by lions.

Cyclades *or* **Kyklades** the principal group of islands in the Greek Archipelago, so named from lying round the sacred island of DELOS in a circle. The largest islands of the group are Andros, Paros, Mykonos, NAXOS, Melos, and Thera (or Santorini). They are of volcanic formation and generally mountainous.

Cyclops *or* **Cyclopes** (literally 'round-eyed', in English the word is used as a singular or a plural) a fabled race of one-eyed giants, variously described in Greek mythology. According to Homer, they were a wild, lawless and impious race of giants inhabiting the sea coasts of SICILY, the most prominent of whom is POLYPHEMUS. Although Homer does not directly call them one-eyed, he expressly describes Polyphemus as such, and later writers attribute this peculiarity to the rest. Another version has them as the three Cyclops, Brontes, Steropes and Arges, each with an eye in the middle of his forehead. These are the three sons of URANUS and GE (Heaven and Earth), belonging to the TITANS, who forged thunderbolts for ZEUS. Hurled into TARTARUS by their father, they were saved by their mother. They helped CRONOS to usurp the government of heaven, but Cronos threw them back to Tartarus, from which they were again released by Zeus, whose servants they now became. Finally they were slain by APOLLO because they forged the thunderbolt with which Zeus killed AESCULAPIUS. Later tradition placed their workshop in Mount ETNA or in the volcanoes of LEMNOS and Lipari, and made them the slaves of HEPHAESTUS.

Cyllen in Greek mythology, a son of ELATUS (1), from whom Mount Cyllene was believed to have received its name.

Cyllene (modern Ziria) a mountain of Arcadia in southern Greece. It is the fabled birthplace of HERMES.

Cympola *see* **Briareus**.

Cynortas *see* **Oebalus**.

Cynthia, Cynthius surnames respective of ARTEMIS and APOLLO, from Mount Cynthus on the island of DELOS, on which they were born.

Cyprus an island lying on the south of Asia Minor, and the most easterly in the Mediterranean. The chief features of its surface are two mountain ranges, both stretching east and west. The Cypriot or Paphian goddess, answering to the Phoenician Astarte or Ashtaroth, was worshipped by the Greeks as APHRODITE. DIDO stopped at Cyprus and carried off from there eighty virgins to be the wives of her followers in their new home at CARTHAGE.

Cyrene (1) in Greek mythology, a nymph of Mount PELION who was loved by APOLLO. He carried her to Libya, where CYRENE derived its name from her. She became by Apollo the mother of IDMON.

Cyrene (2) *see* **Diomedes** (1).

Cyrene in ancient times a celebrated city in Africa, near the north coast, founded by BATTUS and named after CYRENE (1).

Cythera *or* **Kithera** a Greek island in the Mediterranean, south of the Morea, from which it is separated by a narrow strait. It is mountainous and barren, although some of the valleys are fertile. In Greek mythology ancient Cythera is mentioned as the sacred abode of APHRODITE.

Cyzicus *see* **Doliones**.

D

Dactyls in Greek mythology, beings whose name means literally 'fingers'. Their number is variously given as three, five, ten or even a hundred. Born on Mount Ida in Crete and said to be the sons of the nymph Anchiale, they are credited with the discovery of iron and the art of smelting. They are connected with the worship of Rhea and that of Cybele.

Daedalus (literally the 'cunning worker') in Greek mythology, an architect and sculptor, said to have lived three generations before the Trojan War. An Athenian of royal race, he killed his nephew and pupil, Talus (2), in envy at his growing skill and had to flee to Crete, where he is credited with building for Minos the famous labyrinth to confine the Minotaur. He was imprisoned by Minos but escaped with the help of Queen Pasiphaë and invented wings for himself and his son Icarus with which to fly across the sea. He himself flew safely across the Aegean, but Icarus foolishly flew too near the sun, the heat of which melted the wax that fastened his wings to him and he was drowned in the Icarian Sea. Daedalus himself made his way to Sicily. Some accounts made him first alight at Cumae, where he dedicated his wings to Apollo and built a temple to the god.

daimon *or* **daemon** in mythology, a kind of spirit usually associated with a particular place or object, such as a tree, stream, mountain, etc. Numbered among the daimons are nymphs, satyrs, river-gods and penates.

Damastes *see* **Procrustes**.

Danaë in Greek mythology, daughter of Acrisius, king of Argos. She was shut up by her father in a tower, as there was a prophecy that her son would kill her father. Zeus, who loved her, descended to her in a shower of gold and thus gained access to her. She bore him a son, PERSEUS. Acrisius next put both mother and child into a chest and set it adrift on the sea. The chest, however, drifted ashore on the island of SERIPHOS in the CYCLADES, and Danaë and her child were saved. She remained on the island until Perseus had grown up and become a hero famous for his exploits, then she accompanied him to Argos. On his arrival, Acrisius fled, but was subsequently slain accidentally by Perseus at Larissa. Correggio, Rembrandt and Titian have made the story of DANAË'S union with Zeus the subject of famous paintings.

Danaïdes in Greek mythology, the fifty daughters of DANAUS, who were all condemned with the exception of one (Hypermnestra) eternally to pour water into a vessel full of holes. Hypermnestra allowed her husband, LYNCEUS (1), to escape. This was their punishment for murdering their husbands, the sons of AEGYPTUS, on their wedding night.

Danaus in Greek mythology, the son of BELUS and twin brother of AEGYPTUS, originally ruler of Libya. Fearing his brother, he fled to ARGOS with his fifty daughters, the DANAÏDES. Here he became king of Argos, after a dispute with Gelanor which was settled by the people of Argos in favour of Danaus after a wolf rushed among a herd of cattle and killed an ox, which they took to be an omen. The fifty sons of Aegyptus followed Danaus to Argos and under the pretence of friendship sought the hand of his daughters in marriage. Danaus consented, but on the wedding night he gave his daughters each a dagger and urged them to murder their bridegrooms in revenge for the treatment he had received from Aegyptus. All did so, except one.

Daphne the Greek name for laurel, in Greek mythology a NYMPH loved by APOLLO. Deaf to the wooing of the god and fleeing from him, she beseeched ZEUS to protect her. Her prayer was heard, and at the moment Apollo was about to encircle her in his arms she was changed by her mother, GE, into a laurel, a tree thereafter consecrated to the god.

Dardania the area around or including TROY. It was called after DARDANUS (1), who became ruler of the land and who was the son-in-law of TEUCER (1), the first king.

Dardanus (1) in Greek mythology, son of ZEUS and ELECTRA (3), the daughter of ATLAS. He was the mythical ruler of DARDANIA and the Dardanians, who are identified with the Trojans, and is regarded as being the ancestor of the Trojans. Originally a king in ARCADIA, he migrated to SAMOTHRACE and from there to Asia where TEUCER (1) gave him the site of his town, Dardania. He married BATEIA, a daughter of Teucer, and his grandson was the eponymous hero TROS, who removed his grandfather's PALLADIUM to TROY.

Dardanus (2) in Greek mythology, a king of the Scythians and father of IDAEA (2), whom he condemned to death because of crimes that she committed against her stepsons.

Dascylus (1) in Greek mythology, a king of the MARIANDYNIANS who received assistance from HERACLES in defeating his enemies.

Dascylus (2) in Greek mythology, son of LYCUS (4), king of the MARIANDYNIANS, and grandson of DASCYLUS (1). He acompanied the ARGONAUTS on their journey as far as the Thermodon so that they would be treated in a friendly manner by the allies of the Mariandynians.

Dawn in Roman mythology was represented as AURORA and in Greek mythology as EOS.

Death *see* **Thanatos**.

Degmenus *see* **Oxylus**.

Deïaneira in Greek mythology, a daughter of ALTHAEA and OENEUS, king of CALYDON, and sister of MELEAGER. She was the wife of HERACLES. She killed herself after she accidentally killed him with a poisoned potion which she believed to be a harmless love potion given to her by the centaur NESSUS.

Deïdameia (1) in Greek mythology, a daughter of BELLEROPHON and wife of EVANDER, by whom she became the mother of SARPEDON.

Deïdameia (2) in Greek mythology, a daughter of LYCOMEDES in the island of Scyros. When ACHILLES was concealed there in woman's dress, Deïdamia became by him the mother of NEOPTOLEMUS and, according to others, also of Oneirus.

Deïdameia (3) in Greek mythology, the wife of PEIRITHOUS, who is commonly called Hippodamia.

Deion *or* **Deïoneus** in Greek mythology, a son of AEOLUS and Enarete, king of PHOCIS and husband of DIOMEDE (1), by whom he became the father of Asteropeia, Aenetus, Actor, PHYLACUS and CEPHALUS. After the death of his brother, Salmoneus, he took his daughter TYRO into his house and gave her in marriage to Creutheus.

Deioneus *see* **Dia**.

Deïphobus in Greek mythology, son of PRIAM, king of TROY, and HECUBA, who married HELEN after the death of PARIS. On the fall of Troy to the Greeks, he is said in some legends to have been killed by MENELAUS. According to other legends he was killed by Helen or was killed in battle.

Deïphontes in Greek mythology, son of Antimachus and husband of Hyrnetho, daughter of Temenus, a leader of the HERACLIDS who became king of Argos. The sons of Temenus were jealous of Deïphontes and his influence on their father. They overthrew Temenus and tried to kidnap their sister from her husband. In the ensuing struggle Deïphontes killed one of the brothers, Cerynes, but Hyrnetho was acidentally killed by her brother, Phalces. Deïphontes erected a sanctuary to her memory in an olive grove in EPIDAURUS, where he had lived with her.

Deïpyle in Greek mythology, a daughter of ADRASTUS and Amphithea, wife of TYDEUS and mother of DIOMEDES (2).

Delia in Greek mythology, a surname sometimes applied to ARTEMIS and formed from the island of DELOS, her birthplace.

Delos an island of great renown among the ancient Greeks. In Greek mythology, it was at first a floating island, but was fixed to the bottom of the sea by ZEUS in order that it might become a safe place for LETO for the birth of APOLLO and ARTEMIS. It was centre of the worship of Apollo and the site of a famous oracle It is the central and smallest island of the CYCLADES, in th AEGEAN SEA. At first the island, occupied by the IONIANS, ha kings of its own, who also held priestly office. It subsequentl became the common treasury of the Greeks. Its festivals wer visited by strangers from all parts of Greece and Asia Minor.

Delphi an ancient Greek town, originally called Pytho, the sea of the famous oracle of APOLLO. It was situated in PHOCIS, on th southern side or PARNASSUS, north of the Gulf of CORINTH. Th oracles were delivered through the mouth of a priestess wh was seated on a tripod above a subterranean opening, fron which she received the vapours ascending from beneath, an with them the inspiration of the Delphian god. The oracular re plies were always obscure and ambiguous but they served, i earlier times, in the hands of the priests, to regulate and uphol the political, civil and religious relations of Greece. The oracl was celebrated as early as the ninth century BC, and continued t have importance till long after the Christian era, being at las abolished by the Emperor Theodosius. People came to consul it from all quarters, bestowing rich gifts in return. The spendi temple thus possessed immense treasures, and the city wa adorned with numerous statues and other works of art.

Delphinus (The Dolphin) a small constellation that in Gree mythology is identified with the dolphin that saved the life o ARION and with his lyre.

Delphinius in Greek mythology, a surname or epithet applied t APOLLO. It is derived either from the fact that he is said to hav killed the dragon DELPHYNE or from the fact that he is said t have assumed the shape of a dolphin to lead Cretan colonists t DELPHI.

Delphyne a mythical monster who was half serpent and hal woman and who was given the task of guarding the sinews o ZEUS in the Corycian Cave after TYPHON had severed these HERMES and Aegipan succeeded in stealing the sinews from th cave to give them back to Zeus. Delphyne is said to have been killed by Apollo.

Deluge *see* **Deucalion**.

Demeter *or* **Deo** in Greek mythology, one of the twelve principal deities, the great mother-goddess, goddess of corn or of the earth and its fruitfulness. By the Romans she was called Ceres. She was the daughter of Cronos and Rhea, but her main claim to fame is as the mother of Persephone by Zeus. While gathering flowers in the Nysian plain, Persephone was carried off by Hades. Demeter wandered for some time in search of her daughter, and when she learned where she had been taken, she left Olympus in anger and dwelt on earth among men, bringing blessings in her train. At length Zeus sent Hermes to bring Persephone back, and both mother and daughter returned to Olympus. As Persephone had eaten part of a pomegranate in the underworld, she was obliged to spend one-third of the year in her husband's gloomy kingdom, returning to her mother for the rest of the year.

demigod *see* **Races of Man**.

demon a spirit or immaterial being of supernatural but limited powers, especially an evil or malignant spirit. Among the ancient Greeks the name was given to beings similar to those called angels in the Bible.

Demonice *or* **Demodoce** in Greek mythology, daughter of Agenor and Epicaste who was the mother of several children by Ares.

Demophon *or* **Demophoön** (1) in Greek mythology, a son of Theseus and Phaedra and brother of Acamas. Legend has it that the two brothers went to the Trojan war on the side of the Greeks and, while there, rescued their grandmother, Aethra (1), who had been previously abducted to become a servant of Helen. According to another legend, Demophon was going to marry Phyllis, the daughter of the Thracian king, Sithon. While he was on a journey to Attica she is said to have assumed that he had abandoned her and to have taken her own life and become a tree which grew buds and leaves when Demophon returned and pressed it to his bosom. Demophon is also presented as having defended the family of HERACLES against EURYSTHEUS.

Demophon *or* **Demophoön** (2) in Greek mythology, a son of CELEUS and METANEIRA who was brought up by DEMETER. She fed him with her own milk and ambrosia and gave him no human food. She also placed him in a fire every night so that he would become immortal. The story goes on to relate that his mother disturbed the goddess one night, protesting at the treatment of the child, and Demophon burned to death.

Dendrites in Greek mythology, an epithet applied to DIONYSUS indicating his connnection with trees.

Deo another name for DEMETER.

Despoina in Greek mythology, the daughter of DEMETER and POSEIDON, conceived while Demeter had turned herself into a mare while being pursued by Poseidon. He became a stallion and mounted her. Despoina means 'mistress' or 'ruling goddess' and occurs as the epithet of several goddesses, such as APHRODITE and PERSEPHONE.

Deucalion (1) in Greek mythology, a son of PROMETHEUS. He was the king of PHTHIA and was the husband of PYRRHA. When ZEUS sent a flood to destroy mankind Deucalion took his father's advice and built a ship and stocked it with stores of provisions. Deucalion and Pyrrha were saved from the flood and sailed around for nine days before reaching Mount PARNASSUS. They felt very lonely and asked the oracle of THEMIS to help them restore mankind. They were advised to throw the bones of their mother behind them and correctly interpreted this as an instruction to throw the stones of mother-earth behind them. The stones thrown by Deucalion became men and those thrown by Pyrrha became women. Deucalion and Pyrrha were the parents of HELLEN, ancestor of the HELLENES.

Deucalion (2) in Greek mythology, a son of MINOS and PASIPHAË, and one of the ARGONAUTS and one of the hunters of the CALYDONIAN BOAR. He was the father of IDOMENEUS.

Dexames in Greek mythology, a king of OLENUS and father of DEÏANEIRA, who married HERACLES after having been saved by him from a forced marriage to the Centaur, EURYTION (2).

Dia (1) *or* **Eioneus** in Greek mythology, a daughter of Deioneus and mother of PEIRITHOUS by her husband, IXION, according to one legend, or according to another, by ZEUS. Peirithous is said to have received his name from the fact that Zeus when he attempted to seduce Dia ran around her in the form of a horse.

Dia (2) in Greek mythology, an epithet given to HEBE or GANYMEDE.

Dia an early name of the island Naxos.

Diana in Roman mythology, an ancient Italian goddess, in later times identified with the Greek ARTEMIS, with whom she had various attributes in common, being the virgin goddess of the moon and of the hunt, and as such associated with the crescent moon, bow, arrows, and quiver. The name is a feminine form of JANUS. She seems to have been originally the patron divinity of the SABINES and LATINS. She was worshipped especially by women, as presiding over births, no man being allowed to enter her temple.

Dicte, Mount a mountain in CRETE in which the infant ZEUS is said to have been sheltered. It is also said to have been the home of the HARPIES.

Dicte a NYMPH from whom Mount DICTE is said to have received its name.

Dictynna in Greek mythology, an epithet applied to the Cretan goddess, BRITOMARTIS, thought by some to mean 'lady of the nets', by others to mean 'she of mount Dicte'.

Dictys in Greek mythology, a fisherman who became king of SERIPHOS, brother of POLYDECTES and son of MAGNES (1).

Dido *or* **Elissa** in Greek mythology, the reputed founder of CARTHAGE. She was the daughter of a king of TYRE, called by some BELUS, by others Metten or Matgenus. After her father's death, her brother murdered her husband, SICHAEUS, with the intention of obtaining his wealth. However, Dido, accompanied by many Tyrians of her party, fled with all the treasure over the sea, and landed on the coast of Africa, not far from the Phoenician colony of Utica, where she built a citadel called Byrsa ('the hide of a bull') on a piece of ground which she had bought from the Numidian king, IARBAS. The meaning of the word Byrsa gave rise to the legend that Dido bought as much land as could be encompassed with a bullock's hide. Once the agreement was concluded, she cut the hide into small thongs, and thus enclosed a large piece of ground, on which she built the city of CARTHAGE. To avoid being compelled to marry Iarbas, she stabbed herself on a funeral pile, and after her death was honoured as a deity by her subjects. The story is told by Virgil, with many inventions of his own, in the *Aeneid*. He ascribes the death of Dido to her unrequited passion for AENEAS, but many of the ancient writers realized that he had committed an anachronism in making her contemporary with the Trojan prince. More than three hundred years separated the fall of TROY (1184 BC) from the founding of Carthage (853 BC).

Dike *see* **Virgo**.

Dindymene *see* **Cybele**.

Dindymus, Mount a mountain near the ancient city of Gordium and a place much favoured by the goddess CYBELE who was called DINDYMENE in recognition of this fact. The ARGONAUTS sacrificed to her on the mountain.

Diomede (1) *see* **Deion**.

Diomede (2) *see* **Diomedes** (2).

Diomedes (1) in Greek mythology, the son of ARES and Cyrene, and king of the BISTONES in THRACE, who fed his horses on human flesh, and used to throw all strangers who entered his territories to those animals to be devoured. He was killed by HERACLES, who carried off the horses.

Diomedes (2) *or* **Diomede** in Greek mythology, one of the heroes at the siege of TROY, the son of TYDEUS and DEÏPYLE, and king of ARGOS, one of the suitors of HELEN. He was one of the EPIGONI, and after Helen was carried off, he took part in the expedition against Troy, in which his courage and the protection of ATHENA rendered him one of the most distinguished heroes. He was the bravest, after ACHILLES, of all the Greeks who took part in the TROJAN WAR. He vanquished in fight HECTOR and AENEAS, and even APHRODITE and ARES, when they took the field on the Trojan side, were attacked and wounded by him. Three times he attacked APOLLO. In the games instituted by Achilles in honour of PATROCLUS, he gained the prize in the chariot race and worsted AJAX in single combat. By carrying off the horses of RHESUS from the enemies' tents, by aiding ODYSSEUS in the removal of PHILOCTETES from LEMNOS and carrying off the PALLADIUM on which the fate of Troy depended, he fulfilled three of the conditions on which alone Troy could be conquered. Finally he was one of the heroes concealed in the WOODEN HORSE by which the capture of Troy was at length accomplished. Different accounts were given of his life thereafter. According to one, on returning to Argos, to the crown of which he had succeeded after the death of ADRASTUS, he found that his wife had been unfaithful in his absence, whereupon he sailed to Italy and there married the daughter of DAUNUS and lived to a good old age.

Dione in Greek mythology, a female TITAN, a daughter of OCEANUS and TETHYS or perhaps of URANUS and GE. She is held in some legends to be the mother of APHRODITE, daughter of ZEUS.

dionysia *see* **bacchanalia**.

Dionysus the original Greek name of the god of wine, the name BACCHUS, by which he was also called both by the Greeks and the Romans, being at first a mere epithet or surname. The worship of Dionysus, who was originally the god of vegetation and not until the time of Homer the god of wine, was borrowed by the Greeks from the Thracians. When adopted as a Greek god he was naturally made the son of ZEUS, the sky from which falls the rain that makes vegetation grow. His mother, SEMELE, was destroyed before his birth because of her folly in begging Zeus to visit her in all his majesty of thunder and lightning. Dionysus was born from the thigh of Zeus, making his paternity doubly sure, so he was called the 'twice born'. When wine became known it was regarded as the gift of Dionysus, and from that came his title as god of wine. He was said to be the first to teach the cultivation of the vine and the preparation of wine. To spread the knowledge of his invention he travelled over various countries, receiving honours as he went. Drawn by lions (some say panthers, tigers, or lynxes), he began his march, which resembled a triumphal procession. Those who opposed him were severely punished, but on those who received him hospitably he bestowed rewards. His love was shared by several, but only ARIADNE, whom he found deserted upon NAXOS, became his wife and a sharer of his immortality. In art he is represented with the round, soft, and graceful form of a maiden rather than with that of a young man. His long waving hair is plaited behind in a knot and wreathed with sprigs of ivy and vine leaves. He is usually naked; sometimes he has a loose mantle hung negligently round his shoulders; sometimes a fawn-skin hangs across his breast. He is often accompanied by SEILENUS, BACCHANTES, SATYRS, etc. *See also* BACCHANALIA.

Diores in Greek mythology, a son of Amarynceus who was killed by the Thracian leader Pieros during the TROJAN WAR.

Dioscuri *see* **Castor and Pollux**.

Dirae in Roman mythology, one of the names under which the FURIES were known to the Romans.

Dirce in Greek mythology, daughter of HELIOS and wife of LYCUS, a king of THEBES. AMPHION and ZETHUS, sons of ANTIOPE, tied Dirce to a bull because of her cruel treatment of their mother. She was killed by the bull, and in the spot where she died on Mount CITHAERON DIONYSUS, of whom she was a devoted follower, caused a spring to burst forth in her memory.

Dis in Roman mythology, a contraction of **Dives**, a name sometimes given to PLUTO, god of the underworld.

Dius in Greek mythology, a king of ELIS who resisted OXYLUS's usurpation but failed to keep his throne.

Dodona a celebrated place of ancient Greece, in EPIRUS, where one of the most ancient Greek oracles was located. It was a seat of ZEUS (surnamed the Pelasgian), whose communications were announced to the priestesses in the rustling of the leaves on its oak tree and the murmuring of water which gushed forth from the earth.

Doliche *see* **Icaria**.

Doliones a Mysian tribe who, in Greek mythology, gave hospitality to the ARGONAUTS. Their king, Cyzicus, was killed when the Argonauts attacked the Doliones by mistake and his subjects renamed their capital city after their dead king.

Dolius in Greek mythology, an elderly slave of PENELOPE given by her father to her on her marriage to ODYSSEUS, and who was her gardener. When Odysseus returned from his travels Dolius and six of his sons were faithful to him and took his side against the Ithacan relatives of the suitors. His seventh son, MELANTHEUS, took the side of the relatives and was killed.

Dolon in Greek mythology, the son of Eumedes, who was a Trojan herald. He spied for the Trojans on the Greeks hoping to be rewarded by the chariot and horses of ACHILLES. He was soon captured by ODYSSEUS and DIOMEDES and gave them information about the Trojan camp to ensure his safety but they killed him.

Dolphin, The *see* **Delphinus**.

Dorians one of the three great branches of the Greek nation who migrated from THESSALY southwards, settling for a time in the mountainous district of DORIS in Northern Greece and finally in PELOPONNESUS. Their migration to the latter was said to have taken place in 1104 BC, about eighty years after the fall of TROY, and as among their leaders were Temenus, Cresphontes and Aristodemus, three descendants of HERACLES, it was known as 'the return of the Heraclidae' ('descendants of Heracles'), who had come to recover the territory taken from their ancestors by EURYSTHEUS. The Dorians ruled SPARTA with great renown as a strong and warlike people, although less cultivated than the other Greeks in arts and letters. Their laws were severe and rigid, as typified in the codes of the great Doric legislator MINOS.

Doris *see* **Galatea** (1); **Nereides.**

Doris in ancient times a small and mountainous region of northern Greece, at one time the home of the DORIANS.

Dorus (1) in Greek mythology, the ancestor of the DORIANS, said to have been a son of HELLEN and the nymph Orseis. When Hellen divided the Greek lands among his three sons, Dorus, AEOLUS (2) and XUTHUS, Dorus received the region around PARNASSUS.

Dorus (2) son of APOLLO. With his brothers, Laodocus and POLYPOETES, he was killed by AETOLUS when he invaded their country.

Doso in Greek mythology, a name given to DEMETER.

Drepane the island which was home to the PHAEACIANS. The name means 'sickle', and legend has it that the island's name comes from the sickle with which CRONOS castrated his father, URANUS. Another legend has it that the name derives from the sickle of DEMETER, the goddess of corn, who had once lived on the island and who had taught the TITANS to plant corn.

Dryad in Greek mythology, a wood NYMPH, supposed to be a deity of trees. Each particular tree or wood was the home of its own special dryad.

Dryas *see* **Lycurgus** (1); **Tereus.**

Dryope in Greek mythology, a daughter of King Eurytus. APOLLO took the shape of a tortoise and then of a serpent in order to seduce her. Soon afterwards she married ANDRAEMON (2)but bore Apollo a son, Amphissus.

Dryopians *or* **Dryopes** a people who originally lived in the valley of the River SPERCHEIUS. They were called after Dryops, a son either of the river-god Sperchius or of APOLLO. They were driven from their land by HERACLES, some emigrating to Asine and later to MESSENIA. Others settled in Styra.

E

Earth-born Monsters *or* **Gegenees** in Greek mythology, a tribe of giants each of whom had six arms. They lived on BEAR MOUNTAIN on the Mysian coast and mounted an attack on the ARGONAUTS, who destroyed them.

Echemus in Greek mythology, son of Aeropus and grandson of of CEPHEUS. He succeeded LYCURGUS (2) to the throne of ARCADIA. He was the husband of Timandra, daughter of TYNDAREUS and LEDA, but she deserted him to go off with PHYLEUS after bearing Echemus a son, Laodocus. Echemus, while helping the Arcadian forces defend the PELOPONNESUS against the HERACLIDS, killed Hyllus, the son of HERACLES, in single combat, after which the Heraclids undertook not to repeat their attempted invasion of Peloponnesus within the next fifty or a hundred years.

Echetus in Greek mythology, a king of Epirus who was noted for his terrible cruelty. Such was his cruelty that he blinded his own daughter, Metope or Amphissa, and compelled her to grind grains of bronze in a dungeon as a punishment for having taken a lover. He promised his daughter that he would restore her sight if she could grind the bronze into flour. Her lover Aechmodicus was cruelly mutilated.

Echidna in Greek mythology, a daughter of TARTARUS and GE, or of CETO and PHORCYS, or of STYX and Peiras. She was a monster, being half-maiden and half serpent, who lived in a cave and ate passers-by. By TYPHON she became the mother of CHIMAERA, the HYDRA, CERBERUS and the many-headed dog ORTHUS. She was also the mother of the SPHINX, the NEMEAN LION, the Colchian dragon and perhaps SCYLLA (2). She was not immortal although she never grew old and was killed in her sleep by ARGUS PANOPTES.

Echion (1) in Greek mythology, one of the SPARTI, the five survivors of the group of armed men that sprang up from the teeth of ARES' sacred dragon at Thebes sown by CADMUS. He was the husband of AGAVE, daughter of Cadmus, and the father by her of PENTHEUS, who succeeded Cadmus to the throne.

Echion (2) in Greek mythology, son of HERMES and Antianeira and twin brother of Erytus, with whom he took part in the CALYDONIAN BOAR hunt and in the expedition of the ARGONAUTS in which he acted as a spy.

Echo in Greek mythology, a mountain NYMPH (one of the Oreads). Legend relates that by her talking she detained HERA, when the latter sought to surprise ZEUS among the mountain nymphs. To punish her the goddess deprived her of speech, unless first spoken to. She subsequently fell in love with NARCISSUS, and because he did not reciprocate her affection, she pined away until nothing was left but her voice.

Ectenes in ancient Greece, a tribe native to the region of THEBES which was completely wiped out by a terrible plague. Their king was OGYGUS.

Edonians *or* **Edoni** a tribe of Thracia who lived in the region of Mount PANGAEUS. Their king, LYCURGUS (1), persecuted DIONYSUS and his followers. He was subjected to a terrible punishment—such as being torn apart by horses—when his subjects were told by an oracle that the severe drought which affected their land had been sent by the gods because of the crimes of their king.

Eëtion in Greek mythology, a king of Hypoplacian Thebes in the Troad and father of ANDROMACHE and Podes. He was an ally of the Trojans, and he and his seven sons were killed by ACHILLES in one day.

Egeria in Roman mythology, a nymph who received divine honours. NUMA POMPILIUS is said to have received from her the laws which he gave to the Romans.

Egypt the country around the river Nile named after AEGYPTUS, a son of King BELUS (1), the scene of many Greek myths.

Eidothea *see* **Byblis and Caunus**.

Eidyia *or* **Idyia** in Greek mythology, a daugter of OCEANUS and TETHYS, who married AEËTES, king of AEA (COLCHIS), and mother of MEDEA and Chalciope and possibly ABSYRTUS.

Eileithyia in Greek mythology, daughter of ZEUS and HERA, who became the goddess of childbirth, although there is some confusion with ARTEMIS here. When she was kindly disposed she would hasten a birth, but when she was angry she delayed the birth and protracted labour.

Eioneus (1) in Greek mythology, a son of MAGNES (1) and one of the suitors of HIPPODAMIA. He was slain by OENOMAUS.

Eioneus (2) *see* **Dia**.

Elatus (1) in Greek mythology, a son of ARCAS possibly by the nymph CHRYSOPELEIA. He married Laodice and was the father of STYMPHALUS, Aepytus, CYLLEN, and Pereus. He is often called the father of ISCHYS, the lover of CORONIS, but this is probably from confusion with ELATUS (2). Elatus received Mount CYLLENE as his share of his father's kingdom. He protected the Phocians and the Delphic sanctuary against the Phlegyans. He founded the town of Elateia.

Elatus (2) in Greek mythology, a Lapith prince and father of Caenis (later Caenus) and POLYPHEMUS (2), both of whom took part in the expedition of the ARGONAUTS. He is sometimes confused with ELATUS (1), and there is in particular confusion as to which one was the father of ISCHYS.

Elba an island off the west coast of Italy, known in classical times as Aethalia or Ilva. It was a stopping point of the ARGONAUTS on their return journey.

Electra (1) in Greek mythology, a daughter of AGAMEMNON and CLYTEMNESTRA. After the murder of her father by her mother and her mother's lover, AEGISTHUS, she helped her brother ORESTES and PYLADES to kill Clytemnestra and Aegisthus. She married Pylades and bore him two sons, Medon and Strophius. One legend has it that Electra was told that her sister, IPHIGENIA, had sacrificed their brother Orestes to ARTEMIS, and she snatched up a firebrand with the intention of putting out her sister's eyes. Fortunately Orestes appeared at that point alive and well. Electra is the principal character in a number of classical tragedies, such as Sophocles's *Electra* and Euripides's *Electra*.

Electra (2) in Greek mythology, a sister of CADMUS from whom the Electrian gate at Thebes was said to have received its name.

Electra (3) in Greek mythology, daughter of ATLAS and Pleione. She was one of the PLEIADES and lived on the island of Samothrace. By ZEUS she was the mother of DARDANUS (1) and possibly of HARMONIA (3), and one legend has it that the dim star among the Pleiades constellation is Electra, who lost her brilliance with grief either when her son Dardanus was killed or when TROY was sacked.

Electra (4) in Greek mythology, daughter of OCEANUS and TETHYS and the wife of THAUMAS, a Titan, by whom she bore IRIS and the HARPIES.

Electris a mythical island of Greece said to have been named for ELECTRA (3).

Electryon in Greek mythology, son of PERSEUS and ANDROMEDA who inherited the throne of MYCENAE from his father. He married Anaxo, the daughter of Alcaeus, by whom he had a daughter, ALCMENE, and several sons. He also had a son, LICYMNIUS, by Midea, a Phrygian woman. While his sons were tending their father's herd they were attacked by a party of TAPHIANS, the sons of Pterelaus, a descendant of Electryon's brother, Mestor. Only Licymnius and Everos, who was guarding the Taphian ships, survived. Electryon was killed in a quarrel with his son-in-law, AMPHITRYON, either accidentally or deliberately, and STHENELUS (1) banished Amphitryon and seized the throne. Amphitryon avenged Electryon's sons on the Taphians.

Eleusinian Mysteries the sacred rites observed in ancient Greece at the annual festival of DEMETER or CERES, so named from their original seat in ELEUSIS. According to the Homeric hymn to Demeter, the goddess, while wandering in search of PERSEPHONE, came to Eleusis, where she was hospitably received by King Celeus. He directed the establishment of a temple in her honour, and showed the use of grain to TRIPTOLEMUS and other princes. As a preparation for the greater mysteries celebrated at Athens and Eleusis, lesser Eleusinia were celebrated at Agrae on the Ilissus. The greater Eleusinia were celebrated September-October, beginning on the fifteenth of the month and lasting nine days. The celebrations, which were varied each day, consisted of processions between Athens and Eleusis, torch-bearing and mystic ceremonies attended with oaths of secrecy. They appear to have symbolized the old conceptions of death and reproduction, and to have been allied to the orgiastic worship of DIONYSUS (Bacchus).

Eleusis next to ATHENS, the most important town of ancient ATTICA, on the Bay of Eleusis, opposite Salamis. It was famous as the chief seat of the worship of CERES, whose mystic rites were performed here with great pomp and solemnity from earliest times. *See also* ALOPE.

Elis a maritime state of ancient Greece in the west of the PELOPONNESUS, bordering on ACHAEA, ARCADIA and MESSENIA, and watered by the Rivers ALPHEUS and Peneus. It was famed for the excellence of its horses. Of its capital Elis (now Kloskopi) there are few traces. OLYMPIA, where the famous games were held, was near the Alpheus.

Elissa *see* **Dido**.

Elysium *or* **Elysian Fields** in Greek and Roman mythology, the regions inhabited by the blessed after death. They are placed by Homer at the extremities of the earth. Plato located them at the antipodes, and others in the Fortunate Islands (the Canaries). They were at last supposed to be in the interior of the earth, where Virgil described them as being. In the *Odyssey*, Homer describes Elysium as a place where the blessed led a life of tranquil enjoyment in a perfect summer land, where the heroes, freed from all care and infirmities, renewed their favourite sports. In the *Iliad*, however, he gives a sombre view of the state of the departed souls. ACHILLES, although in Elysium, is made to envy the life of the meanest hind on earth.

Enarete *see* **Magnes** (1); **Sisyphus**.

Enceladus in Greek mythology, a son of TARTARUS and GE, and one of the hundred-armed giants who made war upon the gods. He was killed, according to some, by ZEUS, by a flash of lightning and buried under Mount ETNA. According to others he was killed by the chariot of ATHENA. In this flight Athena threw the island of Sicily on him.

Endymion in Greek mythology, a huntsman, a shepherd, or a king of Elis, who is said to have asked of ZEUS, or to have received as a punishment, eternal sleep. Others relate that SELENE or ARTEMIS conveyed him to Mount Latmos in Caria, and threw him into a perpetual sleep in order that she might enjoy his society whenever she pleased. Endymion is also supposed to be a personification of the sun, or of the plunge of the setting sun into the sea, as in Keats's *Endymion*.

Enna *see* **Athena**.

Eoiae *see* **Catalogues of Women**.

Eos in Greek mythology, the goddess of the dawn. *See* AURORA.

Epaphus in Greek mythology, a son of ZEUS and Io, who was born on the River Nile after the long wanderings of his mother. He was then hidden by the CURETES, at the request of HERA, but Io afterwards found him in Syria. He subsequently became king of Egypt, married MEMPHIS or, according to others, CASSIOPEIA, and built the city of Memphis in Egypt. He had one daughter, Libya, from whom the African country received its name.

Epeirus *see* **Epirus**.

Epeius *see* **wooden horse**.

Ephesus an ancient Greek city of LYDIA, in Asia Minor. It was a sacred city from an early period and became famous for its temple of ARTEMIS, called Artemision, the largest and most perfect model of Ionic architecture and reckoned one of the seven wonders of the world.

Ephialtes *see* **Otus**.

Epicasta *see* **Jocasta**.

Epidaurus a town and seaport of ancient Greece, situated in ARGOLIS, in the PELOPONNESUS, particularly celebrated for its magnificent temple of AESCULAPIUS, which stood on an eminence not far from the town. It had also temples of ARTEMIS, DIONYSUS, APHRODITE, and HERA.

Epigoni ('heirs' or 'descendants') in Greek mythology, the sons of the SEVEN AGAINST THEBES, who ten years later conducted a war against Thebes to avenge their fathers. This is called the war of the Epigoni. According to some traditions, this war was undertaken at the request of ADRASTUS, the only survivor of the seven heroes. Those who took part were AEGIALEUS (1), son of Adrastus, DIOMEDES (2), son of Tydeus, Promachus, son of Parthenopaeus, STHENELUS (2), son of CAPANEUS, THERSANDER, son of POLYNICES, and Eurylus, under the command of ALCMAEON and supported by a considerable band of ARGIVES. A Theban force under Laodamas protecting the city was defeated, with the death on the Argive side of Aegialeus, and the city put under siege. TEIRESIAS persuaded the Thebans to quit the town with their wives and children, and the Argives took possession of it and razed it to the ground. The Epigoni sent a portion of the booty and Manto, the daughter of Teiresias, to Delphi and then returned to Peloponnesus.

Epimetheus in Greek mythology, the son of IAPETUS, brother of PROMETHEUS and ATLAS, and husband of PANDORA. Epimetheus may be translated as 'afterthought', and Prometheus as 'forethought'.

Epirus *or* **Epeirus** the ancient name of a part of northern Greece, extending between ILLYRIA and the Ambracian Gulf and from the Ionian Sea to the chain of Pindus. The ACHERON was one of its principal rivers, and the chief towns were DODONA and AMBRACIA.

Epistrophus *see* **Iphitus** (1).

eponym a mythical person created to account for the name of a tribe or people. Thus Tros is the eponymous hero of Troy, Italus was assumed as ancestor of the Italians, etc.

Epopeus in Greek mythology, a son of Poseidon who went from Thessaly to Sicyon where he succeeded in the kingdom. He carried away from Thebes the beautiful Antiope (1), the daughter of Nycteus, who therefore made war on Epopeus. The two hostile kings died of the wounds that they received in the war.

Erato in Greek mythology, one of the nine Muses, whose name signifies 'loving' or 'lovely'. She presided over lyric and especially amatory poetry, and is generally represented crowned with roses and myrtle, and with the lyre in the left hand and the plectrum in the right in the act of playing.

Erebus in Greek mythology, the son of Chaos (darkness) and father of Aether and Hemera (day). The name Erebus was also given to the infernal region.

Erechtheus *or* **Erichthonius** in Greek mythology, an Attic hero, said to have been the son of Hephaestus and Atthis, daughter of Cranaus, the son-in-law and successor of Cecrops. He was brought up by Athena, who placed him in a chest, which was entrusted to the three daughters of Cecrops. In defiance of orders, they opened the chest, and discovering a child entwined with serpents, were seized with madness and threw themselves down the most precipitous part of the Acropolis. When Erechtheus became king of Athens, he instituted the Panathenaea, and in his honour a fine temple, the Erechtheum, was built on the Acropolis. In some representations of him he is depicted as half snake, so that he was one of the autochthones, the earthborn ancestors of the Athenians.

Erichthonius (1) *see* **Erechtheus**.

Erichthonius (2) *see* **Bateia** (1); **Boreas**.

Eridanus the name of various rivers in ancient Greece and Europe, including the River Po. In Greek mythology, the river-god associated with this river is a son of Oceanus and Tethys and father of Zeuxippe. He is called the king of rivers, and on its banks amber was found.

Erigone (1) in Greek mythology, a daughter of Icarius (2). She was seduced by Dionysus when he came into her father's house.

Erigone (2) in Greek mythology, a daughter of Aegisthus and Clytemnestra, and by Orestes the mother of Penthilus.

Erinyes *see* **Furies**.

Eriopis *see* **Oileus**.

Eriphyle in Greek mythology, the wife of Amphiaraus, whom she betrayed for the sake of the necklace of Harmonia.

Eris in Greek mythology, the goddess of discord, the sister of Ares, and, according to Hesiod, daughter of Nyx (night). Not being invited to the marriage of Peleus, she revenged herself by means of the golden apple of discord.

Eros in Greek mythology, the god of love, whom the Romans called Cupid.

Erysichthon *see* **Triopas** (1).

Erytus *or* **Eurytus** a son of Hermes and Antianeira and brother of Echion (2). He was one of the Argonauts.

Erytus *or* **Eurytus** *see* **Echion** (2).

Eryx (modern San Giuliano) an ancient city and a mountain in the west of Sicily. The mountain rises direct from the plain. On the summit in ancient times stood a temple of Venus said to have been built by Eryx, son of Aphrodite by Butes (2). Eryx is also said to have received Heracles on his visit to this part of Sicily and to have taken part in a wrestling match with him, in which he was defeated.

Eteocles and Polynices in Greek mythology, two heroes, sons of Oedipus, king of Thebes and brothers of Antigone (2). After their father's banishment from Thebes, Eteocles usurped the throne to the exclusion of his brother, an act which led to an expedition by Polynices and six others against Thebes. This war is known as the Seven against Thebes, and forms the basis of Aeschylus's *The Seven against Thebes*. The two brothers fell by each other's hand.

Eteoclus in Greek mythology, a son of Iphis and one the Seven

AGAINST THEBES. He had to make the attack upon the Neïtian gate. He was killed by a Theban champion.

Ethiopia *or* **Aethipia** in ancient geography, the country lying to the south of Egypt, but its limits were not clearly defined. It was vaguely spoken of in Greek and Roman accounts as the land of the Ichthyophagi or 'fish-eaters', the Macrobii or 'long-livers', the Troglodytes or 'dwellers in caves', and of the Pygmies or 'dwarf races'. In ancient times its history was closely connected with that of Egypt.

Etna *or* **Aetna, Mount** the greatest volcano in Europe, a mountain in Sicily that dominates the whole northeast part of the island. In mythology, the remarkable phenomena exhibited by Etna were ascribed to the struggles of the giant TYPHON (or ENCELADUS according to others), who had been buried under the mountain by Zeus after the defeat of the giants. Others assigned it as the workshop of VULCAN (HEPHAESTUS), although more ordinary traditions placed this in the AEOLIAN ISLANDS. The mountain was supposed to have received its name from a nymph, Aetna, the daughter of Uranus and Ge, or, according to others, of BRIAREUS. In some accounts it was consecrated to Zeus, but at a later period to Vulcan.

Etruria the name given in ancient times to that part of Italy which corresponds partly with modern Tuscany and was bounded by the Mediterranean, the Apennines, the River Magra, and the TIBER. The name of Tusci or Etrusci was used by the Romans to designate the race of people inhabiting this country, but the name by which they called themselves was Rasena (or perhaps more correctly Ta-rasena). After a long struggle with Rome, Etruscan power was completely broken by the Romans in a series of victories. The Etruscans were specially distinguished by their religous institutions and ceremonies, which reveal gloomy and mystic tendencies. Their gods were of two orders, the first nameless, mysterious deities, exercising a controlling influence in the background on the lower order of gods, who manage the affairs of the world. At the head of these is a deity resembling the Roman JUPITER (in Etruscan Tinia). VULCAN was Sethlans, BACCHUS Phuphluns, and MERCURY Turms.

Etruscans *see* **Etruria**.

Euboea a Greek island, the second largest island of the AEGEAN SEA. It is separated from the mainland of Greece by the narrow channels of Egripo and Talanta. It was peopled in early historic times chiefly by tribes from Thessaly and by Ionic Greeks, and afterwards by colonists from Athens. It was believed to have derived its name from Euboea, a daughter of ASOPUS.

Eubulus *see* **Britomartis**.

Eumedes *see* **Dolon**.

Eumenides *see* **Furies**.

Euneus in Greek mythology, a son of JASON by HYPSIPYLE, in LEMNOS, from where he supplied the Greeks with wine during the TROJAN WAR. He purchased Lycaon, a Trojan prisoner, from PATROCLUS for a silver urn.

Eunomus *or* **Cyatheus** *see* **Oeneus**.

Eupeithes in Greek mythology, a nobleman of Ithaca, father of Antinous. Once when he had attacked the Thesprotians, the allies of the Ithacans, ODYSSEUS protected him from the anger of the Ithacan people. When Odysseus returned home after his long wanderings, Eupeithes wanted to avenge the death of his son, who had been one of PENELOPE'S suitors and was slain by Odysseus. He accordingly led a band of Ithacans against Odysseus but died in the struggle, killed by LAERTES.

Euphorbas *see* **Patroclus**.

Euphorion *see* **Helen**.

Euphrosyne in Greek mythology, one of the GRACES.

Euripides the last of the three great Greek writers of tragedies, the others being AESCHYLUS and SOPHOCLES. He was born about 480 BC and died 406 BC. Seventeen tragedies have survived. His most notable plays are *ALCESTIS*, *MEDEA*, *ORESTES* and *The Trojan Women*, the last of which describes the fate of the captive Trojan women after the Greek victory over Troy. Euripides adopted a more rationalist, questioning approach to the gods and their divine affairs than his great predecessors and was clearly more concerned with the business of everyday human beings.

Euripus in ancient geography, the strait between the Island of Euboea and Boeotia in Greece.

Europa in Greek mythology, the daughter of AGENOR, king of the Phoenicians, and the sister of CADMUS.Tradition relates that she was abducted by ZEUS, who for that occasion had assumed the form of a white bull and swam with his prize to the island of Crete. Here Europa bore him three sons, MINOS, SARPEDON (1), and RHADAMANTHUS.

Europa in ancient geography the known world around the Mediterranean, named after EUROPA.

Eurotas in Greek mythology, a son of Myles and grandson of Lelex. He was the father of SPARTE, the wife of LACEDAEMON, and is said to have carried the waters stagnating in the plain of Lacedaemon into the sea by means of a canal and to have called the river that arose there from after his own name.

Eurybia *see* **Ge**.

Eurydice (1) in Greek mythology, the wife of ORPHEUS.

Eurydice (2) in Greek mythology, one of the DANAIDES.

Eurydice (3) in Greek mythology, daughter of ADRASTUS and wife of ILUS, mother of Themiste and LAOMEDON.

Eurydice (4) in Greek mythology, a daughter of LACEDAEMON and wife of ACRISIUS.

Eurydice (5) in Greek mythology, a daughter of Clymenus and wife of Nestor.

Eurydice (6) in Greek mythology, the wife of LYCURGUS (3) and mother of Archemorus.

Eurydice (7) in Greek mythology, the wife of CREON, king of THEBES.

Euryganeia *see* **Ismene** (1).

Eurylus *see* **Epigoni**.

Eurynome in Greek mythology, a daughter of OCEANUS. When HEPHAESTUS was expelled by HERA from OLYMPUS, Eurynome and Thetis received him in the depths of the sea. Before the time of CRONOS and RHEA, Eurynome and OPHION had ruled in OLYMPUS over the TITANS, but after being conquered by CRONOS, she had sunk down into TARTARUS or Oceanus. By ZEUS she was the mother of the GRACES or of ASOPUS.

Eurystheus in Greek mythology, a king of Mycenae and persecutor of HERACLES. When Heracles killed his wife and children in a fit of madness, he was compelled by the Delphic oracle to serve Eurystheus for twelves years and perform a series of tasks or labours. Eurystheus chose the most difficult tasks that he could think of since he wished to get rid of Heracles.

Euryte *see* **Oeneus**.

Eurythemis *see* **Althaea**.

Eurytion (1) in Greek mythology, king of PHTHIA. When PELEUS was expelled from his dominions, he fled to Eurytion, who purified him and whose daughter ANTIGONE (2) he married, but in shooting at the CALYDONIAN BOAR, Peleus inadvertently killed his father-in-law.

Eurytion (2) in Greek mythology, a Centaur who fled during the fight of HERACLES with the CENTAURS. He was later killed by Heracles in the dominions of Dexamenus, whose daughter, DEXAMES, Eurytion was on the point of making his wife.

Eurytion (3) *see* **Orthus**.

Eurytus (1) in Greek mythology, a son of Melaneus and Stratonice and king of Oechalia. He was a skilful archer and married to Antioche. He was proud of his skill with the bow and is said to have instructed HERACLES in the art. He organized an archery contest for the hand of of his daughter IOLE, which Heracles won.

Eurytus (2) *see* **Dryope**.

Eurytus (3) *see* **Erytus**.

Euryvale (1) *see* **Gorgons**.

Euryvale (2) *see* **Orion**.

Euterpe in Greek mythology, one of the MUSES, considered as presiding over lyric poetry, the invention of the flute being ascribed to her. She is usually represented as a virgin crowned with flowers, having a flute in her hand.

Euxine Sea (*Pontus Euxinus*) the ancient name for the BLACK SEA.

Evadne *see* **Iphis**.

Evander in Greek mythology, son of HERMES by an Arcadian NYMPH, called by the Romans Carmenta or Tiburtis. About sixty years before the TROJAN WAR he is said to have led a Pelasgian colony from ARCADIA to Italy, and to have landed on the banks of the TIBER and near the foot of the Palatine Hill. Here he built a town, naming it Pallantium after the one in Arcadia. Virgil represents him as being still alive when AENEAS arrived in Italy after the sack of Troy and as having sent him aid under his son Pallas, who was killed by TURNUS.

Evarete *see* **Oenomaus**.

Evenus *see* **Idas and Lynceus**.

Everos *see* **Electryon**.

F

Fates in Greek and Roman mythology, the inexorable sisters who were engaged in spinning the thread of human life. In Greek mythology, the name Clotho ('the spinner') was probably at first common to them all, constituting an ultimate monotheistic element—the vague Unity binding together and dominating the crowd of Olympian deities. To Homer, who in every instance save one speaks of Fate in the singular, Fate was not a deity but merely a personification, the destinies of men being determined by the will of the gods. According to later Greek writers the gods too were subject to the control of the Fates, and they were three in number: Clotho, the spinner of the thread of life; Lachesis, who determines the lot of life; Atropos, the inevitable, all three referring to the same subject from different points of view. The Fates knew and predicted what was yet to happen. They were usually represented as young women of serious aspect, Clotho with a spindle, Lachesis pointing with a staff to the horoscope of man on a globe, and Atropos with a pair of scales, or a sundial, or an instrument to cut the thread of life.

Fauna in Roman mythology, the female complement of Faunus, also called Bona Dea. Her name is now used to designate animals of a particular region or of a particular geological period. Flora is the term used for vegetation.

Fauns in Roman mythology, rural deities or demi-gods, inhabiting forests and groves and differing little from satyrs. Their form was principally human, but with a short goat's tail, pointed ears, projecting horns and sometimes also with cloven feet. All terrifying sounds and appearances were ascribed to them.

Faunus in Roman mythology, an ancient king who instructed his subjects in agriculture and the management of flocks and was afterwards worshipped as the god of fields and of shepherds, somewhat like Pan, with whom he became associated and whose attributes he acquired. He was the son of Picus and the grandson of Saturn. Fauna was his female counterpart.

Faustulus in Roman mythology, the chief shepherd of Amulius, uncle of Rea Silvia, the mother of Romulus and Remus. It was he who found the twin boys when they had been put in a basket on the Tiber and had been tended by a wolf. He took them home to his wife, Larentia, who reared them.

Fishes, The *see* **Pisces.**

Flora in Roman mythology, the goddess of flowers and spring and also of exuberant youthful vitality, whose worship was established at Rome from earliest times. Her festival, the Floralia was celebrated at the end of April with much licentiousness. She is represented as a flower-crowned maiden in the full bloom of beauty. Her name is now used to designate the plant species of a particular region or of a particular geological period. Fauna is the term used for animals.

Fortuna in Roman mythology, the goddess of chance or success corresponding to the Greek Tyche. She was the daughter of Oceanus or a sister of the Fates. She differed from the Fates in that she worked without rule, giving or taking away at her own pleasure and dispensing joy or sorrow indifferently. Greek artists generally depicted her with a rudder, emblem of her guiding power, or with a globe, or wheel or wings as a symbol of her mutability. The Romans proudly declared that when she entered their city she threw away her globe and put off her wings and shoes to indicate that she meant to dwell with them for ever. Later she is represented with a bandage over her eyes and a sceptre in her hand, and sitting or standing on a wheel or globe.

Furies in Roman mythology, three winged maidens who dwell in the depths of Tartarus, daughters of Earth or of Night (called Erinyes or Eumenides in Greek mythology). They were originally personifications of the curses pronounced upon guilty criminals. The crimes which they punished were failing to honour father and mother, perjury, murder, and violation of the laws of hospitality or of the rights of suppliants. They were supposed to be able to destroy all peace of mind, and to be able to make their victim either childless or have ungrateful or wicked children. They were regarded also as goddesses of Fate, somewhat like the FATES, and they had a share in the grim providence which led the doomed into the way of calamity. A part of their function was also to hinder man from acquiring too much knowledge of the future. Their number is usually three, and their names Alecto, Megaera and Tisiphone, but sometimes they appear as one, and in the *Eumenides*, the concluding play of AESCHYLUS's *Oresteia*, there is a chorus of twelve furies on the stage. This describes the reconciliation between the older gods and the newer ones, and ends with the Furies consenting to share a sanctuary with ATHENA. Aeschylus describes them as being dressed in black, having serpents in their hair, and blood oozing from their eyes. Later poets and sculptors represented them in the form of winged virgins wearing hunting garb, bearing torches in their hands and with a wreath of serpents round their heads. Gradually they came to be considered goddesses of the infernal regions, who punished crimes after death but seldom appear on earth. In Athens their worship, which, like that of the other infernal deities, was conducted in silence, was held in great honour. The sacrifices offered to them consisted of black sheep and a mixture of honey and water, no wine being offered. The turtle dove and the narcissus were sacred to them.

G

Gabii a town east of Rome which the mythical king Lucius Tarquinus conquered without a single battle. This was because of the treachery of his son Sextus.

Gaea *see* **Ge**.

Galanthis in Greek mythology, a Theban attendant present at the birth of Heracles. The goddess Eileithyia was preventing the birth from taking place and Galanthis tricked her into lifting the spell that was responsible for this. In revenge the goddess turned Galanthis into a weasel.

Galatea (1) in Greek mythology, the daughter of Nereus and Doris, who rejected the suit of the Cyclops Polyphemus and gave herself to the Sicilian shepherd Acis. The monster, having surprised them, crushed Acis beneath a rock.

Galatea (2) in Greek mythology, a daughter of Eurytius and wife of Lamprus at Phaestus in Crete. Her husband, wanting a son, ordered that if she should give birth to a daughter she must kill the infant. Galatea did give birth to a daughter but could not comply with her husband's cruel command and instead disguised the child as a boy under the name of Leucippus. When the child had grown up, Galatea, dreading the discovery of the secret and her husband's anger, took refuge with her daughter in a temple of Leto and prayed to the goddess to change the girl into a youth. Leto granted the request.

Galatea (3) in Roman mythology, the name of a statue said to have been endowed with life by Venus in answer to the prayer of the sculptor Pygmalion. The story, which is derived from Ovid's *Metamorphoses*, is the subject of comedies by W. S. Gilbert and George Bernard Shaw.

Galli *see* **Cybele**.

Ganymede *or* **Ganymedes** in Greek mythology, an exeptionally handsome youth who was the son of TROS and of Callirrhoë, daughter of SCAMANDER. ZEUS sent his eagle to carry him off from Mount IDA to OLYMPUS, where he held the office of cup-bearer to the gods in succession to HEBE. Zeus gave Tros a pair of divine horses as a compensation for his loss, and comforted him by informing him that Ganymede had become immortal and free from all earthly ills. He was later also represented as the god of the fertilizing and life-giving Nile. Greek astronomers placed him among the stars under the name of Aquarius ('the water-bearer'). Ganymede was a favourite subject of ancient art.

Ge *or* **Gaea** in Greek mythology, the earth or the earth goddess. The equivalent in Roman mythology was TELLUS or Terra. Ge is said to have been born from CHAOS, having as siblings TARTARUS and EROS. Although she did not have a mate, she gave birth to URANUS, Ourea and PONTUS, respectively the sky, the mountains and the sea. Thereafter she married Uranus and gave birth to the CYCLOPS, the TITANS, and the HUNDRED-HANDED (or Hecatoncheires). Because of their extreme strength and their extreme ugliness Uranus very much disliked Cyclops and the Hundred-handed and hid them in Ge's body, thereby giving her intense pain. She was very angry and persuaded one of her sons, the Titan CRONOS, to castrate Uranus as she lay with him with a sickle which she had made for the purpose. From the drops of the blood of Uranus which fell to the earth Ge bore the FURIES, the GIANTS and the MELIAE or Ash NYMPHS. Later she gave birth to NEREUS, Thaumas, PHORCYS, CETO and Eurybia, their father being Pontus. Many of the offspring of Ge were monsters, different legends ascribing different monstrous offspring to her. For example she gave birth to Echidna and TYPHON by her brother Tartarus. Typhon became a formidable enemy of ZEUS.

Gegeneës *see* **Earth-born monsters.**

Gelanor *see* **Danaus**.

Gemini (the Twins), the third sign of the Zodiac. The constellation Gemini was supposed to represent CASTOR AND POLLUX, the two brights stars of the constellation being named Castor and Pollux. Another versions says that they are IASION and TRIPTOLEMUS.

Genii in Roman mythology, the protecting spirits who were supposed to accompany every created thing from its origin to its final decay. They belonged not only to people, but to all things animate and inanimate, and especially to places. Not only had every individual his genius, but also the whole people. The statue of the national genius was placed in the vicinity of the Roman forum and is often seen on the coins of the emperors Hadrian and Trajan. The genius of an individual was represented as a figure in a toga, with the head veiled and the cornucopia or patera in the hands, while local genii appear under the figure of serpents eating fruit set before them.

Gerenia a city in Messenia or Laonia on the southern coast of Messenia, whose people were renowned horse-breeders. NESTOR, son of the king of Pylus, NELEUS, was reared by them and so was saved from the fate experienced by his brothers at the hands of HERACLES.

Geryon *or* **Geryones** in Greek mythology, a king of Erytheia who had three heads or the body of three men from the waist down. He was the son of the Gorgon MEDUSA. He had herds of man-eating cattle, and was killed when trying to retrieve them from HERACLES who had driven them off.

Giants in Greek mythology, beings of monstrous size, with hideous countenances and with the tail of a dragon. They lived in volcanic districts, having been banished there after an unsuccessful attempt upon heaven, when the gods, with the assistance of Heracles, imprisoned them under Etna and other volcanoes. They are said to have been of mingled heavenly and earthly descent and to have sprung from the blood that fell from the slain URANUS upon the earth, GE, which was their mother

Their reputed origin, like where they live, points to the idea of the electrical and volcanic convulsions of nature, which they obviously typify.

Glauce *or* **Creusa** in Greek mythology, the daughter of CREON, king of Corinth. She was to marry JASON but at the wedding she was killed when she tried on a poisoned robe that Jason's jealous divorced wife, MEDEA, had sent as a present.

Glaucus (1) in Greek mythology, a son of MINOS and PASIPHAË, who as a child drowned in a large jar of honey. The seer Polyidus of Argos revived him with the aid of a serpent, which revealed a herb effective for the purpose.

Glaucus (2) in Greek mythology, a minor sea-god who gave good advice to the ARGONAUTS. He was originally a fisherman who was transformed into a sea-god after eating a strange herb. He fell in love with SCYLLA, who was then beautiful. When she rejected him, he asked CIRCE for help, but she fell in love with him. On being rejected by him she was furious and poisoned the water in which Scylla as a sea-nymph often swam. Because of this Scylla was turned into a terrible monster.

Glaucus (3) in Greek mythology, a son of SISYPHUS and MEROPE, and a king of Ephyra (Corinth), who married Eurynome, daughter of NISUS. Sisyphus was hated by ZEUS, who swore that although Sisyphus would rear children he would never father his own. As a result of this Sisyphus reared BELLEROPHON who was unbeknownst to him the result of a union between EURYNOME and POSEIDON. He was eaten by his horses after losing a chariot race to IOLAUS and his ghost scared horses in Corinth in revenge.

Glaucus (4) in Greek mythology, captain, with SARPEDON (2), of the Lycian forces at TROY, noted for his bravery. He was the son of Hippolochus and was killed by AJAX while trying to retrieve the corpse of ACHILLES. When he was about to be engaged in combat with DIOMEDES (2), the Greek general, he and his enemy discussed their ancestors before embarking on the fight. On discovering that OENEUS, grandfather of Diomedes, had once entertained BELLEROPHON, grandfather of Glaucus, the two abandoned the fight and exchanged armour as an act of friendship the relationship of guest/host being important in Greek mythology.

Golden Age that early mythological period in the history of almost all races, depicted as having been of primeval innocence and enjoyment, in which the earth was common property, and brought forth spontaneously all things necessary for happy existence, in which people did not engage in warfare. while beasts of prey lived at peace with other animals. The Romans referred this time to the reign of SATURN.

golden apple in Greek mythology, a prize for beauty which was to be awarded to a goddess by PARIS. It had its origins in the wedding of PELEUS to THETIS, which all the gods attended except ERIS, goddess of strife, who was not invited because of her propensity for making trouble. When she went to it without invitation she was not allowed to enter and in spite she threw a golden apple, inscribed 'for the fairest', into the wedding group. Immediately it was claimed by three of the goddeses, HERA, ATHENA and APHRODITE, each of whom considered herself the fairest and each of whom assumed that the apple was meant for her. As Eris had planned, a quarrel broke out, and ZEUS ordered HERMES to turn the problem over to Paris, son of PRIAM, king of Troy and thought to be the most handsome man in the world, who was tending a flock of sheep on Mount Ida. It was assumed that he would be impartial, but each of the goddesses immediately tried to bribe him with tempting rewards if he would select her as the fairest. Hera promised to make him ruler of the world Athena promised him that he would always be the victor in war and Aphrodite, goddess of love, promised him the love of the most beautiful woman in the world. Paris decided to accept Aphrodite's bribe and declare her the fairest. The woman who was considered to be the most beautiful woman in the world was HELEN, daughter of TYNDAREUS, the former king of SPARTA and married to MENELAUS. Paris persuaded Helen to go off with him and the event gave rise to the TROJAN WAR.

golden bough in Greek mythology, a magical bough of a tree near Cumae. AENEAS took this bough from the tree, having taken the advice of the Cumaean SIBYL, before his descent into the Underworld so that it would help him gain access to it. It was intended as a gift for PERSEPHONE. The phrase was used as the title of a comprehensive work by Sir James Frazer on comparative religion.

golden fleece in Greek mythology, the fleece made of gold of the ram Chrysomallus. The ram had rescued PHRIXUS from death as a youth and had flown through the air with him to AEA, the capital of COLCHIS, a land situated at the farthest end of the BLACK SEA. Phrixus sacrificed the ram and nailed its fleece to a tree in a grove sacred to ARES, where the fleece was guarded by a dragon that never slept. Whoever wished to take the fleece would not only have to get past the dragon but would have to persuade AEËTES, the king of Colchis, to allow the golden fleece to leave the country. The king had been warned by an oracle that he would hold the throne of Colchis only as long as the golden fleece remained in the sacred grove. It was in quest of this golden fleece that JASON undertook the ARGONAUTS' expedition to Colchis, he having been tricked into acquiring the golden fleece by PELIAS, who had deposed Jason's father as king of THESSALY. When the Argonauts came to Colchis for the fleece, MEDEA put the dragon to sleep and Jason carried the fleece away. Medea was in love with Jason at the instigation of HERA, who hated Pelias and wanted him destroyed. She thought that Medea was the most likely to be able to undertake this destruction but knew that she would be unwilling to make the long journey to Thessaly. Medea did make the journey as Jason's wife and did help Jason destroy Pelias.

Golden Race *see* **Races of Man**.

Gordius in Greek mythology, a peasant who became king of PHRYGIA. The Phrygians were seeking a king and were informed by the oracle at DELPHI that they were to choose the first person they met riding on an ox cart towards the temple of Zeus. That person was Gordius, who was duly elected king. He afterwards dedicated his cart and yoke to Zeus in the acropolis of Gordium (a city named after himself) and tied the knot of the yoke in so skilful a manner that an oracle declared that whoever should unloose it would be ruler of all Asia. When Alexander the Great came to Gordium, he cut the knot in two with his sword and applied the prophecy to himself. From this legend comes the phrase 'to cut the Gordian knot', i.e. to solve a problem or end a difficulty in a vigorous or drastic way.

Gorge in Greek mythology, a daughter of Oeneus and Althaea who married Andraemon and became the mother of Thoas leader of the Aetolian forces during the Trojan War. According to some legends she was also the mother of Periboea by Oeneus, her own father, this having been brought about because Zeus had decreed that Oeneus should fall in love with his daughter.

Gorgons in Greek mythology, three monsters whose names were Stheno, Euryale and Medusa, daughters of Phorcys and Ceto. They were all immortal, except Medusa. Their hair was said to be entwined with serpents, their hands were of brass, their bodies were covered with impenetrable scales, their brazen teeth were as long as the tusks of a wild boar, and they turned to stone all those who looked upon them. According to later legends Medusa was originally a very beautiful maiden. Having become a mother by Poseidon in one of Athena's temples, the virgin goddess changed her hair into serpents, which gave her so fearful an appearance that whoever looked on her was turned to stone. Medusa was killed by Perseus, and her head was afterwards placed on the aegis of Athena. From her blood the winged horse Pegasus is supposed to have sprung.

Gorgophone in Greek mythology, the only daughter of Perseus and Andromeda. A great deal of confusion is attached in legend to the question of her husbands. She is supposed to have married Perieres, to whom she bore Aphareus and Leucippus, and

OEBALUS, king of Sparta, to whom she bore three sons, TYNDAREUS, HIPPOCOÖN and ICARIUS, and two daughters, Arene and Peirene. She was the grandmother of CLYTEMNESTRA.

Graces in Greek mythology, the divine personifications of grace, gentleness and beauty, usually described as daughters of ZEUS and EURYNOME and as being three in number, AGLAIA (brilliancy), Thalia (the blooming) and Euphrosyne (mirth). The earliest conception seems to have been but one aspect of APHRODITE, the divsion into a plurality of beings coming later. Homer mentions them in the *Iliad* as handmaidens of HERA (Juno), but in the *Odyssey* as those of APHRODITE (Venus), who is attended by them in the bath, etc. He conceived them as forming a group of goddesses, whose duty it was to make sure that the gods and goddesses were happy. The three Graces are usually represented slightly draped or entirely nude, either locked in each other's embrace, or hand in hand.

Graeae in Greek mythology, the grey women, two hags called Enyo and Pemphredo or Pephredo, who were the daughters of of PHORCYS and CETO and sisters of the GORGONS and of ECHIDNA and Ladon. Their name derives from the fact that they had grey hair from birth. They had only one eye and one tooth between them and these were stolen by PERSEUS. According to some legends the hags were three in number, the third being called Deino.

Gratioe the Roman name for the GRACES.

Great Mother *see* **Cybele**; **Rhea**.

Greek mythology the ancient religion of the Greeks with a great number of divinities, many of whom were personifications of natural powers, or of phenomena of the external world, or personified feelings. Thus there were gods corresponding to Earth and Heaven, the Ocean and Night. The Romans, when they became acquainted with the literature and religion of the Greeks, identified the Greek deities with those of their own pantheon. In this way the Greek and Roman deities came to be confused, and the names of the latter even came to supersede those of the former. The supreme ruler among the gods was ZEUS (Roman JUPITER), the son of CRONOS (Roman SATURN), who, after the subjugation of the TITANS and GIANTS, ruled in OLYMPUS while his brother PLUTO reigned over the lower world (HADES) and POSEIDON (NEPTUNE) ruled in the sea. Similar reverence was paid to HERA (JUNO), the sister and wife of Zeus and the queen of Heaven, to the virgin ATHENA (MINERVA), to the two children of LETO (LATONA), namely, APOLLO, the leader of the MUSES, and his sister, the huntress ARTEMIS (DIANA), the goddess of the moon, to the beautiful daughter of Zeus, APHRODITE (VENUS), the goddess of love, to ARES (MARS), the god of war, HERMES (MERCURY), the herald of the gods, and others. In addition, there was an innumerable host of inferior deities (NYMPHS, NEREIDES, TRITONS, SIRENS, DRYADS, etc) who presided over woods and mountains, fields and meadows, rivers and lakes. There was also a race of heroes or demigods, such as HERACLES (HERCULES) and PERSEUS, tracing their origin from Zeus and forming a connecting link between gods and men, while on the other hand the SATYRS formed a connecting link between the race of men and the lower animals.

The priests were keepers of sacred things, of rites, symbols and images. They showed how a god was to be worshipped, but it was not their office to teach theological doctrine, or even as a rule to exhort people to religious duty. The true teachers of religion were the poets and other writers (see Aeschylus, Hesiod, Homer, Euripides, Sophocles). No degree of consistency is to be found in them, however, the personality and local origin of a writer largely moulding his views. A belief in the justice of the gods as manifested in the punishment of all offences against them was central. The man himself might escape, but his children would suffer, or he might be punished in a future state. The gods are also represented as being holy and truthful, although they are in innumerable other passages described as being themselves guilty of the grossest vices, and likewise as prompting humans to sin and deceiving them to their own destruction

In their general attitude towards humans, the gods appear as inspired by a feeling of envy or jealousy. Hence they had constantly to be appeased, and their favour won by sacrifices and offerings. Certain classes were, however, under the peculiar protection and favour of the gods, especially strangers and suppliants.

The Greeks believed that the gods communicated their will to humans in various ways, but above all by means of ORACLES, the chief of which were those of Apollo at DELPHI, and of Zeus at DODONA. Dreams ranked next in importance to oracles, and divination by birds, remarkable natural phenomena, sneezing, etc, was also practised.

griffin *or* **gryphon** a fabulous monster commonly represented with the body, the feet, and claws of a lion, and the head and wings of an eagle. The native country of the griffins was supposd to be India or Scythia, and it was alleged that they guarded the gold in the mountains. Amongst the Greeks it appears on antique coins and as an ornament in classical architecture.

Gyes *see* **Hundred-handed**.

H

Hades in Greek mythology, originally the name of the king of the lower or invisible world, afterwards called PLUTO (*see also* PERSEPHONE), but in later times, it is applied to the region itself. According to the belief of the ancients, the departed spirits of good and bad alike went to the halls of Hades.

Haemon in Greek mythology, a son of PELASGUS and father of Thessalus. The ancient name of THESSALY, Haemonia or Aemonia, was believed to have been derived from him.

Haemones *see* **Iolcus**.

Haemus in Greek mythology, a son of BOREAS and OREITHYIA, who was married to RHODOPE, by whom he became the father of HEBRUS. As he and his wife presumed to assume the names of ZEUS and HERA, both were metamorphosed into mountains.

Haemus, Mount the range of mountains in THRACE, now called the Balkans. The name is derived from the Greek word for blood (*haima*), the explanation being that TYPHON is said to have lost a great deal of blood there when ZEUS pelted him with thunderbolts.

hamadryads in mythology, NYMPHS who presided over woods and trees.

Hare, The *see* **Lepus**.

Harmonia in Greek mythology, daughter of ARES and APHRODITE, or of ZEUS and ELECTRA (3), and wife of CADMUS. On her marriage, she received a necklace worked by HEPHAESTUS from Cadmus, or it may have been given to her by Aphrodite or ATHENA. POLYNICES inherited the necklace and gave it to ERIPHYLE to induce her to persuade her husband, AMPHIARAUS, to accompany the SEVEN AGAINST THEBES.

Harpies in Greek mythology, ancient goddesses who were considered as ministers of the vengeance of the gods. Their parentage, ages, appearance, names and number are very differently given by the poets. In the Homeric poems they are ministers of untimely death, 'snatchers', and personfications of the angry winds. Others represent them as two young virgins of great beauty, called Aëllo and Ocypete, daughters of THAUMAS and ELECTRA (4), and sisters of IRIS. Three are sometimes recognized by later writers, who call them variously daughters of POSEIDON or of TYPHON and vie with each other in depicting them under the most hideous forms, covered with filth and polluting everything in contact with them. They are often represented as being birdlike with female faces. The most celebrated tradition regarding the Harpies is connected with the blind PHINEUS, whose meals they carried off as soon as they were spread for him, a plague from which he was delivered by the ARGONUATS, on his engaging to join in their quest. ZETES AND CALAÏS attacked the Harpies, but spared their lives on their promising to cease molesting Phineus. In Roman mythology, Virgil locates them in the Strophades.

Harpius *see* **Oenomaüs**.

Hebe in Greek mythology, the goddess of youth, and the cupbearer to the gods, until replaced by GANYMEDE. She was a daughter of ZEUS and HERA, who, according to one version of the legend, gave her as a wife to HERACLES after he was deified, to whom she bore two sons, Alexiares and Aniketos. According to Homer she remained a virgin. In the arts she presents the nectar, under the figure of a charming young girl, her dress adorned with roses, and wearing a wreath of flowers. In Rome she was worshipped as Juventas, personifying the eternal youth of the city. She is represented in art as caressing an eagle.

Hebrus, River the ancient name of an important river in THRACE, now the boundary between Greece and Turkey. In Greek mythology, the river-god Hebrus was the son of HAEMUS and RHODOPE. When ORPHEUS was killed by the Ciconian women his head and lyre floated down the Hebrus.

Hecabe *see* **Hecuba**.

Hecate in Greek mythology, an ancient goddess whose powers were various. She could bestow wealth, victory and wisdom; good luck on sailors and hunters; prosperity on youth and on flocks. She was afterwards confused with other divinities, such as DemetER, ARTEMIS and PERSEPHONE (Proserpina), and finally became especially an infernal goddess and was invoked by magicians and witches. Dogs, honey and black female lambs were offered to her at places where three roads met. She was often represented with three bodies or three heads, with serpents round her neck. Her festivals were celebrated annually at AEGINA (2). One legend says she is the mother of MEDEA.

Hecatoncheires *see* **Hundred-handed**.

Hector in Greek mythology, the eldest son of PRIAM and HECUBA, the bravest of the Trojans, whose forces he commanded. His wife was ANDROMACHE. His exploits are celebrated in the *Iliad*, where he is portrayed as the ideal of a warlike hero, brave to the last degree, yet faithful and tender alike as husband, father and son. One of the finest passages in the Iliad describes his parting with Andromache. He holds the same rank among the Trojans as Achilles does among the Greeks. After bearing the main burden of the war, he was slain by Achilles, enraged at the death of his beloved friend PATROCLUS. The body of Hector was dragged at the chariot wheels of the conqueror round the tomb of Patroclus, but afterwards it was delivered to Priam for a ransom. Priam gave it a solemn burial.

Hecuba *or* **Hecaba** in Greek mythology, the second wife of PRIAM, king of TROY, to whom she bore nineteen children, including HECTOR, PARIS, CASSANDRA, CREUSA (2)and TROILUS. During the TROJAN WAR she witnessed the destruction of all her sons, with the exception of HELENUS, and at last saw her husband murdered before her eyes by Pyrrhus (*see* NEOPTOLEMUS). After the fall of Troy she was given as a slave to ODYSSEUS, and, according to one form of the legend, in despair leaped into the HELLESPONT. EURIPIDES and others describe her as a tender mother, a noble princess and a virtuous wife, exposed by fate to the most cruel sufferings.

Heleius *or* **Helius** in Greek mythology, son of PERSEUS and ANDROMEDA. He joined AMPHITRYON in war against the Teleboans and received from him the islands of the TAPHIANS. He founded the city of Helos in Argolis.

Helen *or* **Helena** in Greek mythology, the most beautiful woman of her age. She was daughter of ZEUS by LEDA, wife of the Spartan king, TYNDAREUS, and owed her more than mortal loveliness to her divine origin. At the age of ten she was carried off by THESEUS and PEIRITHOUS, but was soon recovered by her brothers CASTOR AND POLLUX, of whom the latter was half an immortal like herself. She was sought in marriage by all the noblest Greek princes. By the advice of ODYSSEUS, her suitors were bound by oath to respect her choice of husband, and to maintain it even by arms. She chose MENELAUS and bore him the fair HERMIONE. When she was carried off by PARIS, son of PRIAM of TROY, through the connivance of APHRODITE, Menelaus mustered all the Greek princes to revenge the wrong and thus the ten years' TROJAN WAR began. After the death of Paris, not long before the fall of the city, she married his brother Deiphobus, and she is said to have betrayed him to Menelaus and so regained her husband's love. On the fall of Troy she returned to Sparta with Menelaus. There they lived the rest of their lives and were buried together at Therapnae in Laconia, although, according to a prophecy in the Odyssey, they were not to die but to be translated to ELYSIUM. Another story makes Helen survive Menelaus and be driven out of the Peloponnesus by his sons. She fled to Rhodes and was there tied to a tree and strangled by Polyxo, a crime expiated only by the Rhodians building a temple to her under the name of Helena Dendritis. Yet another tradition makes her marry ACHILLES on the island of Leuce and bear him a son, Euphorion.

Helenus in Greek mythology, a Trojan soothsayer, son of PRIAM and HECUBA, twin brother of CASSANDRA, and husband of

ANDROMACHE after HECTOR's death. He foretold the destiny of AENEAS, and welcomed the latter in Epirus, where he ruled after the death of NEOPTOLEMUS.

Helice in Greek mythology, the wife of ION. The town of Helice in Achea on the gulf of Corinth was founded by Ion, who named it after her.

Helicon, Mount (now Sagara) a mountain range of Greece, in the west of Boeotia, in some sense a continuation of the range of PARNASSUS. It was the favourite seat of the MUSES, who, with APOLLO, had temples here. In it also were the fountains of AGANIPPE (1) and HIPPOCRENE, whose waters were reputed to give poetic inspiration.

Helios in Greek mythology, the god of the sun (the Roman Sol), son of the Titan HYPERION and THEIA, and brother of Eos and SELENE. He was said to dwell with Eos in the ocean behind Colchis, from which he issued in the morning and to which he returned at night. He later began to be identified with APOLLO, but the identification was never complete. His worship was widely spread, and he had temples in CORINTH, ARGOS, Troezen and ELIS, but particularly in RHODES, the Colossus of which was a representation of Helios. The island of Trinacria (Sicily) was also sacred to Helios, and here his daughters, Phoetusa and Lampetia, kept his flocks of sheep and oxen. It was customary to offer up white lambs or boars on his altars. The animals sacred to him were horses, wolves, cocks and eagles.

Hellas the Greek name for Greece ('Greece' being the Roman name).

Helle in Greek mythology, sister of PHRIXUS. She left her home with him on the back of a miraculous ram that could fly and that had a GOLDEN FLEECE. They were escaping from their stepmother, Io, who was trying to persuade their father to sacrifice Phrixus. Helle lost her grip on the ram as they flew over the strait between Europe and Asia, and she fell into the water. Thereafter the stretch of water was called HELLESPONT, 'sea of Helle'.

Hellen in Greek mythology, son of DEUCALION and Pyrrha, and founder by his three sons, DORUS, AEOLUS and XUTHUS, of the four great branches of the Greek people, or HELLENES.

Hellenes the people of Greece. The earliest inhabitants of Greece were the Pelasgians, of whom little is known. They were succeeded by the Hellenes, or Greeks proper, who may have been a Pelasgian tribe. To the early period of their occupation of Greece belongs its mythology. The Hellenes were divided into four chief tribes—the AEOLIANS, occupying the northern parts of Greece (THESSALY, BOEOTIA, etc); the DORIANS, occupying originally a small region in the neighbourhood of Mount Eta; the ACHAEANS, occupying the greater part of the PELOPONNESUS; and the IONIANS, occupying the northern strip of the Peloponnesus and Attica. Of the four, the Ionians were most influential in the development of Greece. The distribution of the Hellenic tribes was greatly altered by the migration of the Dorians.

Hellespont the ancient name for the Dardanelles, the strait between the Aegean Sea and the Sea of Marmara. It gained its name from the legend of HELLE.

Hemera in Greek mythology, day and the goddess of day. She was born from EREBUS (darkness) and NYX (night). She emerged from TARTARUS as Nyx left it and returned to it as he was emerging from it.

Hephaestus *or* **Hephaistos** in Greek mythology, the son of HERA, the god of fire and smithying, patron of all those who worked in iron and metals, identified by the Romans with their VULCAN. He is represented by Homer as lame, walking with the aid of a stick. His character is good-tempered, affectionate and compassionate. There is also an element of the comic connected with him. His gait and ungainly figure provoked the laughter of the gods, yet he was himself given to practical jokes. He fixed his residence in LEMNOS, where he built himself a palace, and raised forges to work metals. The CYCLOPS of Sicily were his workmen and attendants, and with him they manufactured not only the thunderbolts of ZEUS, but also arms for the gods and the most celebrated heroes. His forges were supposed to be under ETNA. APHRODITE was the wife of Hephaestus, although according to the *Iliad*, he was married to AGLAIA, one of the GRACES. He was concerned in the myths of the birth of the first woman, PANDORA, and the birth of ATHENE, and ERECHTHEUS claimed Hephaestus as his father.

Hera in Greek mythology, an ancient goddess, identified by the Romans with their Juno, the sister and wife of ZEUS (Jupiter), and daughter of CRONOS and RHEA. She was the goddess of marriage, childbirth and menstruation. The poets represent Zeus as an unfaithful husband and Hera as an obstinate and jealous wife, the result of which was frequent strife between them. As the goddess of lawful marriage, she persecuted the illegitimate offspring of her consort Zeus, such as HERACLES and DIONYSUS. She conspired against Zeus, who made reprisal by hanging her up from heaven with golden fetters on her hands and a couple of anvils on her feet. In consequence she subsequently preferred to thwart him secretly rather than defy him openly. She took the part of the Greeks in the TROJAN WAR as she hated the Trojans because PARIS awarded the fatal GOLDEN APPLE of discord to APHRODITE. She is the mother of HEPHAESTUS, the god of fire, of ARES, the god of war, of EILEITHYIA, of HECATE and of HEBE. She was worshipped in all Greece, but her principal seats were at ARGOS and SAMOS. The companions of Hera were the NYMPHS, GRACES and HORAE. IRIS was her particular servant. Among animals, the peacock, the goose, and the cuckoo were sacred to her. Her usual attribute is a royal diadem on her head. The festivals in her honour were called Heaea. The principal ones were those celebrated every fifth year at Argos, which city was considered to be especially under her protection.

Heracles in Greek mythology, the most celebrated hero or semidivine personage of Greek mythology, called Hercules by the Romans. He was the son of ZEUS by ALCMENE, the wife of AMPHITRYON. The name Heracles is explained as 'renowned through HERA'. He was brought up at THEBES, and before he had completed his eighth month strangled two snakes sent by the jealous HERA to devour him. His tutor was the Centaur CHIRON. Early in life he had, at the command of Zeus, to subject himself for twelve years to the will of EURYSTHEUS, king of Argos, on the understanding that after he had acquitted himself of this duty he should be counted among the gods. He therefore went to MYCENAE, and performed at the bidding of Eurystheus the tasks known as the twelve labours of Heracles. These were: (1) to kill a lion which ravaged the country near Mycenae; (2) to destroy the Lernaean HYDRA; (3) to capture, alive and unhurt, a stag famous for its incredible swiftness, its golden horns, and brazen feet; (4) to capture alive a wild boar which ravaged the neighbourhood of Erymanthus; (5) to clean the stables of AUGEAS, where 3000 oxen had been confined for many years; (6) to kill the birds which ravaged the country near the Lake Stymphalus, in Arcadia, and ate human flesh; (7) to bring alive into Peloponnesus the CRETAN BULL, which laid waste the Island of Crete; (8) to obtain the mares of DIOMEDES (1), which fed upon human flesh; (9) to obtain from HIPPOLYTE, the queen of the Amazons, a girdle which she had received from ARES (Mars); (10) to kill the monster GERYON, king of Gades, and bring to Argos his numerous flocks, which fed upon human flesh; (11) to obtain apples from the garden of the HESPERIDES; (12) the last and most dangerous of all, to bring from the infernal regions the three-headed dog CERBERUS. Besides these labours, he also achieved of his own accord others equally celebrated. He killed a sea monster that ravaged TROY, and when the mares promised him as reward for killing the monster were denied him he destroyed Troy. His love of horses also led him to kill IPHITUS, although his guest. He assisted the gods in their wars against the GIANTS, and it was through him alone that Zeus obtained the victory. Having attempted to plunder the temple at DELPHI, he became engaged in conflict with APOLLO, and was punished by being sold to OMPHALE, queen of LYDIA, as a slave. She eventually freed him and married him. On his return to Greece, he became the husband of DEÏANEIRA, who unwittingly brought about his death by giving him a tunic poisoned with the blood of the Centaur NESSUS, which she innocently believed would retain for her Heracles's love. The poison took effect when the garment was put on, and was fatal. Therefore Heracles placed himself on a burning pile on Mount ETA, was received up into heaven, and being there reconciled to Hera, received her daughter HEBE in marriage. In ancient works of art Heracles is generally represented as naked, with strong and well-proportioned limbs, He is sometimes covered with the skin of the Nemaean lion, and holds a knotted club in his hand, on which he often leans. The myth of Heracles is believed by many writers to represent the course of the sun through the twelve signs of the zodiac. His marriage with Hebe was explained even by the ancients as symbolic of the renewing of the sun's course after its completion.

Heraclids *or* **Heracleidae** in its widest sense, all 'the descendants of HERACLES', but more particularly applied to those who, founding their claims on their supposed descent from the great hero (to whom ZEUS had promised a portion of the land), were said to have joined the DORIANS in the conquest of the PELOPONNESUS. Several expeditions were undertaken for this purpose, the last and greatest occurring eighty years after the Trojan War. The chiefs of the invaders defeated Tisamenus, son of ORESTES and grandson of AGAMEMNON, and took possession of the Peloponnesus.

Heraean Games in ancient Greece, games held specifically for women every four years at OLYMPIA. The contestants took part in the race wearing a dress with one shoulder bared and their hair hanging loose. The prizes were crowns of wild olive and portions of a cow sacrificed to HERA. The Heraean Games are thought to be older than the OLYMPIC GAMES and to have been inaugurated by HIPPODAMIA in honour of Hera in gratitude to the goddess for assisting her in getting PELOPS as her husband.

Hercules the Roman name for HERACLES.

Hermaphroditus in Greek mythology, the son of HERMES and

APHRODITE, born on Mount Ida and brought up by NAIADS. He rejected the love of the nymph Salmacis, but the latter, embracing him, prayed to the gods to unite her to her lover for ever. The two finally formed a being half male and half female.

Hermes in Greek mythology, the son of ZEUS and MAIA, the daughter of ATLAS. He was born in ARCADIA, and soon after his birth left his cradle and invented the lyre by stringing the shell of a tortoise with three or seven strings. The lyre, however, he accorded to APOLLO, with whom it was ever after identified. Hermes also invented the the flute and syrinx. The ancients represent Hermes as the herald and messenger of the gods. He conducted the souls of the departed to the lower world and had the closely related function of bringing dreams to mortals. He was the ideal embodiment of grace, dignity and persuasiveness, but also of prudence, cunning, fraud, perjury, theft, and robbery. His cunning was frequently of service both to the gods and the heroes, and even to Zeus himself. Later writers ascribe to him the invention of dice, music, geometry, etc. He was worshipped in all the cities of Greece, but Arcadia was the chief place of his worship, his festivals being called Hermoea. In monuments he is represented as in the flower of youth, or in the full power of early manhood. He often appears with small wings attached to his head and to his ankles. Among his symbols are the cock, the tortoise, a purse, etc, and especially his winged rod, the CADUCEUS. The Romans identified Hermes with their own MERCURY.

Hermione in Greek mythology, the daughter of MENELAUS and HELEN. She was nine years old when her mother left her to go off with PARIS to Troy. She is said to have been promised in marriage both to NEOPTOLEMUS and ORESTES. According to one legend she married Neoptolemus and then married Orestes after his death.

Hero in Greek mythology, a priestess of APHRODITE at Sestos, on the coast of Thrace. She was loved by Leander, whose home was at Abydos, across the HELLESPONT. Hero's office and her parents' will forbade their union, but Leander every night swam across the Hellespont, guided by a lamp that burned on the top of a tower on the seashore. One stormy night the light was blown out and Leander was drowned, and his body washed ashore. Hero, when she saw his dead body at daybreak, was overcome with anguish and threw herself down from the tower into the sea and perished.

heroes in Greek mythology, the kings, princes, generals, leaders, all brave warriors, and men who excelled in strength, courage, wisdom and experience. Many of these had, on account of such qualities, an origin half human, half divine, and were honoured after their death with a kind of adoration or inferior worship. These heroes and demigods were recognized as the special patrons or protectors of particular countries, cities or families, and temples and altars were raised to them.

Heroic Age *see* **Races of Man**.

Hesiod the father of Greek didactic poetry, who lived probably in the eighth century BC. His most important work is *Works and Days*, which contains many well-known passages, such as the story of PANDORA. The *Theogony* is an attempt to systematize mythology, and gives an account of the creation, a history of Zeus and Cronos and a list of women who married gods. It also deal with the war between the gods and TITANS.

Hesione in Greek mythology, a daughter of LAOMEDON and sister of PRIAM. When Troy was visited by a plague and a monster because of Laomedon's breach of promise, in order to get rid of these calamities, Laomedon chained Hesione to a rock in accordance with the command of an oracle, where she was to be devoured by wild beasts. HERACLES, on his return from the expedition against the AMAZONS, promised to save her if Laomedon would give him the horses that he had received from ZEUS as a compensation for GANYMEDE. Laomedon again promised but did not keep his word. Hesione was afterwards given as a slave to TELAMON, by whom she became the mother of TEUCER (2). Priam sent ANTENOR to claim her back, and the refusal on the part of the Greeks is mentioned as one of the causes of the TROJAN WAR.

Hesperides in Greek mythology, certain NYMPHS who lived in gardens, of rather uncertain locality, as guardians of the golden apples that grew there and which HERA had recieved from GE on her marriage with ZEUS. They were assisted in the charge by a dragon, Ladon. Some legends place the gardens in an island of the ocean far to the west. It was the eleventh labour of HERACLES to kill the dragon and bring the golden apples of the Hesperides, but they were afterwards restored by ATHENA.

Hestia in Greek mythology, the hearth and the goddess of the hearth. The equivalent Roman goddess was VESTA. Hestia was the goddess associated with general household activities and the community generally. She was a daughter of CRONOS and RHEA.

Hiarbas *see* **Iarbas**.

Hippocentaurs *see* **Centaurs**.

Hippocoön in Greek mythology, a king of Sparta, son of OEBALUS and GORGOPHONE, who refused to purify HERACLES after he murdered IPHITUS. He caused further offence by killing OEONUS, a relative of Heracles. In revenge Heracles killed Hippocoön and his twelve sons.

Hippocrene ('The Horse's Fountain') a spring on Mount HELICON, a mountain in BOEOTIA, consecrated to the MUSES, the waters of which possessed the power of poetic inspiration. It is said to have risen from the ground when struck by the hoofs of PEGASUS.

Hippodamia (1) in Greek mythology, the beautiful daughter of OENOMAÜS, king of Pisa in ELIS. It had been predicted to her father that he should be slain by his future son-in-law. He therefore stipulated that every suitor of his daughter should run a chariot race with him, and that death should be the consequence of defeat. At length PELOPS bribed the king's charioteer and thus succeeded in reaching the goal before Oenomaus, who, in despair, killed himself. Hippodamia became by Pelops the mother of ATREUS and THYESTES.

Hippodamia (2) *see* **Deïdameia.**

Hippolochus *see* **Glaucus** (4).

Hippolytus in Greek mythology, son of THESEUS and ANTIOPE (2), queen of the AMAZONS. His stepmother, PHAEDRA, fell in love with him and made accusations about him to his father in order to revenge herself for his indifference. Theseus cursed his son and requested POSEIDON to destroy him. One day, therefore, when Hippolytus was riding his chariot along the coast, Poseidon sent a bull from the sea. The horses were frightened, upset the chariot and dragged Hippolytus until he was dead. His innocence was afterwards established, and Phaedra killed herself. Hippolytus was restored to life by AESCULAPIUS, and according to Italian traditions, ARTEMIS placed him, under the name of VIRIBUS, under the protection of the nymph EGERIA in the grove of Aricia in LATIUM where he was honoured with divine worship.

Hippomedon *see* **Seven against Thebes.**

Hippomenes *see* **Atalanta**; **Megareus**; **Onchestus.**

Hipponous (1) in Greek mythology, the original name of the hero BELLEROPHON. He received the name Bellerophon because he had killed Bellerus, a distinguished Corinthian.

Hipponous (2) *see* **Oeneus; Olenus.**

Hippothoon *see* **Alope.**

Hodoedocus *see* **Oileus.**

Homer the name given by the Greeks to the (traditionally blind) author of the two great Greek epics, the *Iliad* and the *Odyssey*. Of Homer's date and birthplace nothing was known to the Greeks. Many cities claimed to be his birthplace, mostly in the islands and in early Greek colonies in Asia, and it is probable that he was born on Chios and lived in the eighth century BC. The *Iliad* deals with an episode of the TROJAN WAR: the wronging of ACHILLES by AGAMEMNON in the matter of the captive maiden Chryseïs, the wrath which Achilles feels and shows at that, and the consequences and final appeasement of his wrath. The Greeks suffer disaster through his withdrawing himself from the Trojan fight. PATROCLUS, his close friend, is slain by the Trojan champion, HECTOR, son of PRIAM. Achilles was roused to slay Hector in revenge, and the poem ends with the ransoming of Hector's body by his father. The *Odyssey* tells of the wanderings and adventures of ODYSSEUS in the course of his return to Ithaca after the capture of Troy, and of what had meanwhile gone on in his house, where PENELOPE, his wife, was besieged by suitors. Finally, it relates how Odysseus and his son TELEMACHUS, whom he had left an infant when he set out for Troy, encountered and slew the suitors, and how husband and wife were reunited. The capture of Troy is related. incidentally. The *Iliad* breaks off before that point is reached.

Horae in Greek mythology, the goddesses of the seasons and the order of nature. At Athens they were originally two: Thallo and Carpo. Elsewhere they were at first three, Thallo, Carpo and Auxo, and afterwards their number increased to four. They are represented as maidens carrying the different products of the seasons.

Horatii in Roman mythology, three brothers who, in the reign of TULLUS HOSTILIUS, were selected to fight three Alban brothers (the Curiatii), the champions of ALBA Longa, in order to decide the supremacy between Rome and Alba. Victory went to Rome, and the only surviving Horatius was triumphantly conducted back to the city. His sister, however, had been betrothed to one of the Curiatii, and her obvious grief so enraged Horatius that he stabbed her in the heart. For this he was condemned to death, but his father and the people begged him off. He lived to destroy Alba and carry its inhabitants to Rome. The myth points to the close relationship that existed between Rome and Alba Longa and to the internecine struggle that probably took place before the latter was incorporated in the political organization of the former.

Horatius Cocles in Roman mythology, a hero of ancient Rome and descendant of the surviving HORATII, who, with Titus Herminius and Spurius Lartius, formed the 'dauntless three' who in 507 BC held the Sublician bridge against the army of Lars Porsena of Latium while the Romans broke it down behind them. When this was nearly finished, Horatius sent his two companions back, and as the bridge fell he plunged into the Tiber with his armour and safely reached the opposite bank.

Hundred-handed *or* **Hecatoncheires** in Greek mythology, three giants each with fifty heads and one hundred arms. Their names were BRIAREUS, Gyes and Cottus. Their father, URANUS, was jealous of their supreme strength and hid them within their mother, GE, to her great pain. When Ge persuaded CRONOS to castrate Uranus, the god kept the Hundred-handed locked up in TARTARUS with the CYCLOPS. They were released temporarily to help ZEUS fight the TITANS but were returned to Tartarus to be guardians of the Titans now imprisoned there.

Hyacinth *or* **Hyacinthus** in Greek mythology, a son of AMYCLAS, king of Sparta, and Diomede, or of Perius and the Muse CLIO. He was an extremely handsome young man and the first man to be loved by another man. The bard Thamyris fell in love with Hyacinth. APOLLO and ZEPHYRUS were also in love with him. Zephyrus became jealous because Hyacinth favoured Apollo and caused Apollo's quoit to strike and kill the youth while they were at play. A flower sprang up from the blood of the dying youth, and the flower was called hyacinth.

Hyades in Greek mythology, daughters of ATLAS and the nurses and guardians (three, five or seven in number) of the young DIONYSUS. ZEUS converted them into stars and transplanted them to the heavens where they form the head of the constellation TAURUS. Their rising with the sun was held in Greece to mark the beginning of the rainy season.

Hydra in Greek mythology, a celebrated monster which infested the neighbourhood of Lake Lerna in Argolis in the PELOPONNESUS. Some writers make it the offspring of STYX and the TITAN PALLAS (1), and others of ECHIDNA and TYPHON. Some accounts give it a hundred heads, others fifty, others nine, with an equal number of mouths that discharged a subtle and deadly venom.

As soon as one of these heads was cut off, two immediately grew up if the wound was not stopped by fire. It was one of the labours of HERACLES to destroy this monster, and this he effected with the assistance of IOLAUS, who applied a burning iron to the wounds as soon as one head was cut off.

Hygieia in Greek mythology, the goddess of health, daughter of AESCULAPIUS. Her temple was placed near that of Aesculapius, and her statues were even erected in it. She is represented as a youthful maiden with a bowl in her hand, from which she is feeding a snake, the symbol of healing. In 293 BC, her cult was introduced into Rome, where she was known as Valetudo or Salus.

Hyllus *see* **Echemus**; **Nausithous**; **Sthenelus** (1).

Hymen *or* **Hymenaeus** originally the Greek name of the bridal song that was sung by the companions of the bride as she went from her father's house to that of the bridegroom. In Greek mythology, it came to be used for the god of marriage. He is said to be the son of APOLLO and a MUSE, or less often as the son of DIONYSUS and APHRODITE. No marriage took place without his being invoked to sanction it. He is described as a youth with wings having around his brows the flower of the herb marjoram, in his left hand the flame-coloured nuptial veil, in his right the nuptial torch, and on his feet golden sandals. He is a taller and more serious EROS, and is accompanied by song and dance.

Hyperboreans in Greek mythology, the name given in early legends to a people whose land was generally supposed to lie in the extreme northern parts of the world, 'beyond (*hyper*) BOREAS' or the North Wind, and so were not exposed to its blasts. As the favourites of APOLLO, they enjoyed an earthly paradise, a bright sky, a perpetural spring, a fruitful land, unbroken peace, and everlasting youth and health.

Hyperenor *see* **Sparti**.

Hyperion (1) in Greek mythology, a TITAN, son of URANUS and GE, and father of HELIOS, SELENE and EOS. Homer and later writers apply the name to Helios himself.

Hyperion (2) *see* **Megara.**
Hypermnestra *see* **Danaïdes; Danaus.**

Hypnos in Greek mythology, sleep and the god of sleep, called Somnos by the Romans. He was a son of NYX (night) and a brother of THANATOS (death).

Hyppolyte *or* **Hippolyta** in Greek mythology, a queen of the Amazons who was vanquished and killed by HERACLES in pursuit of his ninth labour, to obtain the belt given to her by ARES.

Hypsipyle in Greek mythology, queen of Lemnos who saved her father when the women of LEMNOS vowed to kill all the men. She put her father in either a chest or a boat and set him adrift on the sea. He reached the island of Oenoë. Later she was a nurse to the infant OPHELTES. She was mother of EUNEUS and Deipylus by JASON

Hyrnetho *see* **Deïphontes.**

I

Iacchus in Greek mythology, an obscure deity sometimes described as DEMETER's son, sometimes as her husband. Other legends describe him as being a son of PERSEPHONE identical with Zagreus and some as the son of DIONYSUS, with whom he is sometimes confused. He was honoured at the ELEUSINIAN MYSTERIES with Demeter and Persephone.

Ialmenus in Greek mythology, a son of ARES and Astyoche. He and his brother were joint kings of Minyan ORCHOMENUS (2). They were both Argonauts, and both sought the hand of HELEN. They were the leaders of thirty ships to the TROJAN WAR.

Ianthe *see* **Iphis** (2).

Iapetus in Greek mythology, a TITAN and a son of GE and URANUS. He was the father either by the Oceanid CLYMENE (1) or ASIA of ATLAS, Menoetius, PROMETHEUS and EPIMETHEUS.

Iarbas *or* **Hiarbas** a king of Numidia in North Africa. He is said to have sold the site of CARTHAGE to DIDO and later wooed her. It was his prayer to JUPITER that led to AENEAS's desertion of Dido.

Iasion in Greek mythology, a son of ZEUS and ELECTRA (3), daughter of ATLAS. He left his homeland in Samothrace to go to THEBES to attend the wedding celebrations of CADMUS and HARMONIA, whom some legends claim was the sister of Iasion. The goddess DEMETER fell in love with him and had an affair with him. The result of this union was a son, PLUTUS, who became a minor deity connected with agriculture. In some legends Iasion was killed by Zeus for daring to lie with a goddess. Others say that he was killed by his team of horses and with TRIPTOLEMUS became the constellation GEMINI. According to one legend Iasion and Demeter had another son, PHILOMELUS, who was made into the constellation BOÖTES for his invention of the plough.

Iasus (1) in Greek mythology, a son of PHORONEUS and brother of PELASGUS and AGENOR, or Arestor.

Iasus (2) in Greek mythology, a king of Argos and son of ARGUS PANOPTES and Ismene, daughter of ASOPUS or of TRIOPAS (2). He is said by some to have been the father of Io.

Iasus (3) in Greek mythology, a son of LYCURGUS (2), king of Arcadia. According to some legends he was the father of ATALANTA by CLYMENE (2), daughter of Mynas. Since he wanted only male children he left the child Atalanta to die of exposure. However she was rescued by hunters having been suckled by a bear. When she grew to adulthood she was reunited with her father, who is reputed to have devised the foot race that preserved her virginity.

Icaria an island in the AEGEAN SEA. In Greek mythology, when ICARUS fell to his death in the Icarian Sea his body was washed up on the shores of the island of Doliche. There HERACLES found it, buried it and renamed the island Icaria in memory of Icarus. DIONYSUS was captured by pirates from Icaria.

Icarius (1) in Greek mythology, a son of PERIERES and GORGOPHONE, or of OEBALUS and the nymph Bateia. According to some legends he and his brother TYNDAREUS were expelled from Sparta and were reinstated by HERACLES. According to another legend Icarius helped his brother HIPPOCOÖN expel their brother Tyndareus from Sparta. The nymph Peroboea bore him two daughters, PENELOPE and Ipthime, and also five sons, among whom were Perileus or Perilaus, who may have been the accuser of ORESTES at his trial on the AREOPAGUS. ODYSSEUS arrived in Sparta in order to pay court to Penelope. One legend says that Icarius organized a foot race as a way of deciding which suitor would win Penelope's hand. Other legends say that Tyndareus, brother of Icarius, interceded on behalf of Odysseus with Icarius. In any event Odysseus won Penelope. Icarius was upset at the idea of his daughter leaving and tried to persuade Odysseus to settle in Sparta with Penelope. When Odysseus refused to comply with this request, Icarius followed his chariot pleading with Penelope to stay. Odysseus told Penelope that he wished her to go with him willingly or not at all, that she must choose between him and her father. In response Penelope veiled her face, a gesture by which Icarius deduced that she wished to accompany Odysseus. When his daughter left Icarius erected a statue of Modesty.

Icarius (2) in Greek mythology, an Athenian who was taught the art of vine culture by DIONYSUS because of the hospitality which he and his daughter, ERIGONE (1), had shown to the god. Icarius made some wine and loaded his wagon with wineskins full of wine, taking with him his dog, Maera, and set out. On meeting some shepherds he gave them some wine. They drank this undiluted with water and, not being used to wine drinking, they fell into a drunken stupor. When they recovered from this they deduced that, in view of their stupor, the stranger had tried to poison them. In revenge for this they beat Icarius to death with clubs, threw his body into a well and hurried away. Maera howled by his master's grave and thus led Erigone to it. She had been out anxiously looking for her father. She was so upset at the death of her father that she killed herself by hanging herself from the tree that grew over the well. The dog, Maera, killed himself by jumping into the well. The god Dionysus was furious at the deaths of those who had shown kindness to him. He devised a plan to avenge their deaths by making Athenian girls mad and causing them to hang themselves from trees. Anxious to discover the reason for this, the Athenian leaders consulted the oracle and were told about the murder of Icarius. They apprehended the murderers and punished them. In memory of Icarius and Erigone they established certain rites in their honour to take place at the grape festival. As part of these rites Athenian girls swung from trees in swings in imitation of Erigone. Dionysus honoured Icarius and his daughter and dog by making them all constellations. Icarius became BOÖTES, Erigone VIRGO and Maera is the Dog Star (*see* CANIS MAJOR). When the island of Ceüs suffered from a severe drought that accompanied the intense heat during the rise of the Dog Star APOLLO advised the inhabitants to sacrifice to the ghost o Icarius. It is thought that the murderers of Icarius had fled tc Ceüs.

Icarus in Greek mythology, the son of DAEDALUS, who ignored his father's advice not to fly too near the sun when he was escaping, with his father, from a prison in CRETE by means of wings made of wax and feathers. When he did go too near the sun the wax of his wings melted and he plunged into the sea south of Samos, an area now called the Icarian Sea in his memory. His body was washed up on the island of Doliche. It was buried by HERACLES and the island was renamed ICARIA.

Ida in Greek mythology, a NYMPH of Mount IDA in CRETE. She was a daughter of MELISSEUS and sister of Adrasteia. With her sister she nursed the infant ZEUS. *See also* TITANS.

Ida, Mount (modern Idhi) (1) in ancient geography, a mountain range in Asia Minor, extending from PHRYGIA through MYSIA into the Troad, at the foot of which lay the city of Troy. It is the scene of many ancient Greek legends. The southern part of the range was called Gargarus, and here there was a temple of CYBELE, from which she is known as the Idaean Mother. From Mount Ida flow several streams, as the Granicus, Simois and SCAMANDER.

Ida, Mount (2) in ancient geography, the middle and highest summit of the mountain chain that divides the Island of CRETE from east to west. In Greek mythology, ZEUS was brought up and educated here.

Idaea (1) in Greek mythology, a NYMPH of Mount IDA near Troy. TEUCER (1), king of the region of Troy, was said to have been a son of Idaea and SCAMANDER, a local river-god. Teucer's daughter, BATEIA (1), was one of the ancestors of the royal Trojan line.

Idaea (2) in Greek mythology, the second wife of PHINEUS. By Idaea, Phineus had two sons, Thynius and and Mariandynus. Idaea disliked the sons of Phineus by his first marriage, and she made accusations against them. These were believed by their father, who tortured and imprisoned them. They were rescued by the ARGONAUTS. In disgrace Idaea was sent home to her father, DARDANUS (2), who condemned her to death.

Idaean Mother a name given to CYBELE, who had a temple on Mount IDA (1).

Idaeus in Greek mythology, the herald of the Trojan forces at the time of the TROJAN WAR. It was he who drove the mule cart that carried PRIAM on his secret journey to try to persuade ACHILLES to give him HECTOR's body.

Idas and Lynceus in Greek mythology, sons of APHAREUS, king of MESSENIA. Idas and his younger brother LYNCEUS (2) were inseparable. Idas was strong and bold, but Lynceus was possessed of an unusual gift. He had such sharp powers of vision that he could even see what was hidden in the earth. Both brothers took part in the CALYDONIAN BOAR hunt and were both ARGONAUTS. Idas tended to be rather arrogant and insolent, which got him into trouble on the *Argo*. He also showed this arrogance by abducting Marpessa, daughter of Evenus, despite being well aware of the fact that APOLLO was wooing her. According to some legends, Idas was able to escape with Marpessa at a very rapid pace because he had been lent a winged chariot by POSEIDON. He was, at any rate, too fast for Evenus, who failed to catch up with Idas and his daughter and drowned himself in the river Lycormas, which then became known as the river Evenus. Apollo, however, was swift enough to catch up with Idas and fought with him for Marpessa. ZEUS intervened in the fight, separated the contenders and told them to leave it to Marpessa to decide between them. She, because she felt that Apollo being so powerful would one day desert her, chose Idas. They married, and she bore him a daughter, CLEOPATRA (1), who became the wife of MELEAGER. Idas went on to invade Teuthrania in Mysia while TEUTHRAS was on the throne, but he was driven back by Telephus and Parthenopaeus. Later Idas and Lynceus were involved in a dispute with CASTOR AND POLLUX, who had been with them both on the Calydonian Boar hunt and on the expedition of the Argonauts. The quarrel led to the deaths of all four contenders.

Idmon in Greek mythology, one of the ARGONAUTS and a son of CYRENE (1) and APOLLO, or, according to some legends, ABAS. Idmon was a seer, having been taught the arts of prophecy, augury and the divining of omens. Idmon knew that if he joined the expedition of the Argonauts he would not survive the expedition. A native of ARGOS, he joined the crew of the *Argo* despite this forewarning. When the Argonauts stopped near Mariandynus on the southern shore of the Black Sea, Idmon was killed by a boar. His fellow Argonauts spent three days mourning his passing and planted an olive tree on his grave. Much later Apollo ordered the people who colonized Heracleia to found their city around the olive tree and to honour Idmon who would be their protector.

Idomene *see* **Bias**.

Idomeneus in Greek mythology, a king of Crete and a son of DAEDALUS and grandson of MINOS. During the TROJAN WAR he was the leader of a Cretan force of eighty ships. Despite the fact that he was considerably older than most of the other Greek leaders, he fought boldly and bravely. After the fall of Troy he returned safely to his home in Crete only to discover that his wife, Meda, had had an affair with Leucus, NAUPLIUS (1) having encouraged her in this. Leucus was both ambitious and ruthless, and killed both Meda and her daughter. He seized control of ten Cretan cities and drove out Idomeneus. He and his followers sailed for Italy and settled in the part of the country which forms the 'heel' of Italy, the Sallentine Plain.

Idyia *see* **Eidyia**.

Iliad *see* **Homer**.

Ilione in Greek mythology, the eldest daughter of PRIAM and HECUBA. She was the wife of Polymestor, king of the Thracian Chersonese, and bore him a son. As well as bringing up her own son she was responsible for the rearing of her young brother, Polydorus.

Ilissus *or* Ilisus, River a stream located near ATHENS. In Greek mythology, BOREAS carried off OREITHYIA, daughter of ERECHTHEUS, from the banks of the Illisus.

Ilium *see* **Troy**.

Illyria *or* **Illyricum** a name formerly rather loosely applied to a large tract of country on the east side of the Adriatic, the ancient Illyrians being the ancestors of the modern Albanians. Piracy was carried on by the Illyrians, whose kings were therefore embroiled in quarrels with the Romans, which ended in their subjugation in 228 BC. After the murder of CADMUS's successor, Cadmus, his wife, HARMONIA, and their daughter AGAVE settled in Illyria, as did many of the people of THEBES when they were driven from Thebes by the EPIGONI.

Ilus (1) in Greek mythology, the elder son of DARDANUS, king of DARDANIA, and BATEIA, daughter of TEUCER. Since Ilus died without having fathered any children, his brother succeeded to the throne of Dardania on his death. Ilus is sometimes confused in some legends with ILUS (2), after whom Ilium is called.

Ilus (2) in Greek mythology, a king of TROY who gave his name to Ilium. He was the son of TROS, who gave his name to Troy, and Callirrhoë, daughter of the river-god SCAMANDER. He left Dardania, where his brother Assaracus, was king and went to PHYRGIA. In the Games there Ilus won a wrestling match and was awarded a prize of fifty youths and fifty young women. At the same time he received a dappled cow from the king of Phrygia, who ordered him to found a city where it lay down. The king of Phrygia was acting under instuctions from an ORACLE. Ilus was led by the cow to a hill which was sacred to ATE. There he built a city and called it Ilium after himself, its inhabitants being the young people whom he had won as a prize. As Ilus was praying to ZEUS, the PALLADIUM dropped to the earth from the sky right in front of his tent. Ilus built a temple for it, and a saying came into being that Ilium would be invulnerable as long as the Palladium remained in the city. Ilus married Eurydice (3), daughter of ADRASTUS, and fathered LAOMEDON and Themiste. His daughter, Themiste, married Capys, son o Assaracus, the brother of Ilus. At his death Ilus was succeede as king by his son, Laomedon.

Ilus (3) in Greek mythology, a king of Thesprotian Ephyra wh was descended from Medea. His family were skilled in the a of making poisons and he had inherited the art. He offende Odysseus by refusing to sell arrow poison to him.

Ilva *see* **Elba**.

Inachus the chief river of Argos, in Greek mythology often pe sonified as a god. He was a son of of the Titans Oceanus an Tethys. When Hera and Poseidon were engaged in a disput over possession of Argolis, Zeus asked Inachus and two othe rivers, Cephissus and Asterion, to adjudicate. They decided i favour of Hera. In revenge Poseidon dried up the rivers so th they could flow freely only when it rained. According to som legends, Inachus was not a god but the first king of Argos. He i said to have named the river Inachus after himself and to hav been the first person to worship Hera. His wife was a Melia, a ash-nymph. They had two sons, Phoroneus and Aegialeus (2 and a daughter, Io. Io told her father about some erotic dream that were being sent to her by Zeus. The oracles of Delphi an Dodona told Inachus to exile her. He obeyed their instruction and she was exiled and turned into a heifer. After this Inachu sat down and wept in his cave, the legend being that his tea were the source of the river of the name.

Ino in Greek mythology, a daughter of Cadmus, king of Thebe and Harmonia. She was a sister of Semele and with her sibling Agave and Autonoë, told everyone that Semele was lying whe she claimed that Zeus was the father of the child whom she w expecting. After the death of Semele and after the second bir of the baby, Dionysus, from the thigh of Zeus, Ino was asked b Hermes to rear the child as a girl so that Hera would be d ceived. By this time Ino had married Athamas, king Orchomenus (2). When suffering from divine madness, Ir helped Agave to tear to pieces her son Pentheus, king

Thebes. Athamas had been married before—to NEPHELE by whom he fathered PHRIXUS and HELLE. Ino was very jealous of them and plotted to destroy them. They were saved by flying away on a miraculous ram that could fly and had a GOLDEN FLEECE.

Io in Greek mythology, the daughter of INACHUS, the river god of Argos and its first king. She was beloved by ZEUS, who sent her erotic and seductive dreams. When she told her father, he consulted the oracle, who advised him to exile her or else a thunderbolt from Zeus would destroy his people. Reluctantly he exiled her. There are several versions of the rest of the story. One legend has it that HERA knew about the designs that Zeus had on Io and turned her into a white heifer to protect her and thwart the designs of Zeus. Another legend suggests that Io was fleeing from Zeus when he was spotted by Hera. He changed Io into a white heifer to hide his embarrassment. Hera asked Zeus for the gift of the heifer, and Zeus had to comply with her request in case Hera inquired further. When Zeus sent HERMES to steal the heifer, Hera sent the many-eyed ARGUS PANOPTES to guard her. Io was tied to an olive tree in the grove at MYCENAE, and Argus watched her night and day, at least some of his eyes being always open. Eventually, according to some legends, Hermes disguised himself as a goatherd who lulled Argus to sleep with his stories and tunes on his pipes. Hermes, who was noted for his cunning, then cut off Argus's head as he slept. Hera had to think up another way to keep Zeus from Io and sent a gadfly to sting the heifer and drive her out of Argolis. Io then began her wanderings. Various routes have been ascribed to these wanderings, but she is eventually supposed to have reached the Nile near the Egyptian city of Canobus or Memphis. There Zeus went to her and she conceived a child by the union that took place. Io resumed human shape and gave birth to a son, EPAPHUS. At Hera's request the child was kidnapped by the CURETES, whom Zeus killed in revenge. Epaphus had been taken to Syria where Io found him being nursed by the queen of

Byblus. Io returned with her son to Egypt and married King Telegonus and established the worship of Demeter there.

Iobates in Greek mythology, a king of Lycia who married his daughter, Stheneboea, to Proetus and restored him to power in Argos. He then tried to get rid of Bellerophon but changed his mind and gave him the hand of his daughter Philonoë.

Iolaus in Greek mythology, a son of Iphicles and Automedusa, daughter of Alcathous. He was the nephew of Heracles and his charioteer and frequent companion. Iolaus assisted Heracles in the execution of several of his labours; indeed he played such a major part in the destruction of the Hydra that Eurystheus refused to accept this as one of the labours that Heracles had done alone. Iolaus tried to save the children of Heracles from the persecution of Eurystheus. He is said to have prayed to the gods to make him young again so that he could protect his dead uncle's family. He was temporarily rejuvenated and able to kill Eurystheus and behead him.

Iolcus an ancient city of Magnesia in Thessaly, at the head of the gulf of Pagasae. It was founded by Cretheus, one of the sons of Aeolus (2), and he was also its first ruler. The rightful heir to the throne of Iolcus was the son of Cretheus, Aeson, but he was deprived of the throne by Pelias, his half-brother, who went on to rule the country for many years. Iolcus was captured by the Argonauts under Jason, who was the son of Aeson, after Medea had tricked the daughters of Pelias into killing him. Jason turned over the throne to the son of Pelias, Acastus. Another Argonaut, Peleus, visited Iolcus. The wife of Acastus fell in love with him, but he rejected her advances. To get her revenge she told her husband that Peleus had raped her, and he tried to kill Peleus but he failed. With the help of Jason, Peleus attacked and destroyed Iolcus and gave the throne to Haemones. According to one legend Acastus survived and later either he or his sons banished Peleus from Phthia.

Iole in Greek mythology, a daughter of Eurytus (1), king of Oechalia, promised by her father to anyone who could defeat him in an archery competition. When he was defeated by HERACLES, he refused to honour his promise. Later Eurytus was killed by Heracles who then took Iole as his concubine. On discovering that Heracles had taken a concubine, his wife, DEÏANEIRA, sent him a poisoned robe which caused his death.

Ion in Greek mythology, a son of CREUSA (1), wife of XUTHUS, by either Xuthus or APOLLO. Apollo had visited Creusa in a cave, and when she gave birth to a son she left him to die in the same cave. The god, however, had the child taken to DELPHI and there had him educated by a priestess. When the boy had grown up, Xuthus and Creusa came to consult the oracle about the means of obtaining an heir, the answer was that the first human being whom Xuthus met on leaving the temple would be his son. Xuthus met Ion and recognized him as his son, but Creusa, thinking him to be a son of her husband by a former lover, gave him a cup filled with the poisonous blood of a dragon. Ion, however, before drinking poured out on the ground a libation to the gods, and a pigeon that drank of it died on the spot. Ion was on the point of killing Creusa when a priestess interfered and explained the situation. Mother and son thus became reconciled. Ion later married HELICE, daughter of Seilnus, king of Aegialeia in the northern PELOPONNESUS, and after the king's death succeeded to the throne. Thus the Aegialeans became IONIANS.

Ionia that part of the seaboard of Asia Minor which was inhabited by Ionian Greeks, a beautiful and fertile country opposite the Islands of Samos and Chios, which also belonged to it. According to tradition, the Greek colonists came over from ATTICA after the death of CODRUS, the last king, led by the sons of Codrus, Neleus and Androclus, who were dissatisfied with the abolition of royalty and the appointment of their eldest brother Medon as archon. Here they founded twelve towns, which, though mutually independent, formed a confederacy for common purposes. These included Phocaea, EPHESUS, MILETUS, etc, and afterwards SMYRNA.

Ionian Islands a chain of Greek islands in the Ionian Sea, extending along the western and southern shores of Greece, o which the largest are Corfu, Cephalonia, Zakinthos and Cerigo others being Ithaca and Paxos. All are extremely mountainous The Ionian Islands often figure in the ancient history of Greece but only individually.

Ionian Sea the sea that lies between southern Italy and Sicily o the west and Greece, from Epirus to the Peloponnesus on th east. It may have been named after the Ionians who were said t have once inhabited Peloponnesus.

Ionians a Greek-speaking people called after Ion, son of Xuthu or Apollo who succeeded to the throne of Aegialus in the northern Peloponnesus. At the time of the Dorian invasion th Ionians were driven out of the Peloponnesus and fled to Attica Thereafter many emigrated to the Cyclades or to Asia Minor They founded or conquered several cities in the land later calle Ionia.

Iphianassa (1) in Greek mythology, a daughter of Proetus and Stheneboea and granddaughter of Iobates, who was cured o madness by Melampus and married his brother, Bias as his second wife.

Iphianassa (2) in Greek mythology, a daughter of Agamemnon and Clytemnestra. According to some legends she is identifie with Iphigeneia.

Iphicles *or* **Iphiclus** in Greek mythology, the son of Alemen and Amphitryon, the twin and half brother of Heracles Heracles was the son of Zeus. When the babies were in thei crib, two snakes entered it and were strangled by Heracles Iphicles married Automedusa, daughter of Alcathous, king o Megara, and she bore him a son, Iolaus. Iphicles later marrie the younger daughter of Creon. He took part in the Calydonian Boar hunt and may have died fighting against the sons o Hippocoön.

Iphiclus in Greek mythology, the son of Phylacus, king o Phylace, and Clymene (2), daughter of Minyas (*see* Minyans)

He was a famous runner. JASON was the son of Iphiclus' sister, Alcimede.

Iphigeneia *or* **Iphigenia** in Greek mythology and poetry, daughter of AGAMEMNON and CLYTEMNESTRA. To avert the wrath of ARTEMIS, whom Agamemnon had enraged and who detained at Aulis the Greek fleet that had been prepared for the TROJAN WAR, Iphigeneia was to be sacrificed on the altar, but a stag was miraculously substituted for her, and she was conveyed in a cloud to Tauris (Crimea). She became priestess there to Artemis, and saved her brother ORESTES when on the point of being sacrificed. The story of Iphigeneia is the subject of two plays by EURIPIDES, of one by Racine and another by Goethe.

Iphimedeia in Greek mythology, a daughter of TRIOPAS (1) who married POSEIDON's son ALOEUS, but she fell in love with Poseidon and took to walking by the sea and pouring sea water into her lap. Poseidon came to her, and she bore him two giant sons, OTUS AND EPHIALTES. She also bore a daughter, Pancratis, to her husband. Mother and daughter while taking part as bacchants in a revel were abducted by Thracian pirates to Strongyle (Naxos). Otus and Ephialtes attacked the island and rescued them.

Iphinoë *see* **Megareus**.

Iphis (1) in Greek mythology, a king of ARGOS and a son of ALECTOR, and the person who urged POLYNICES to bribe ERIPHLYE with HARMONIA's necklace. He was the father of ETEOCLUS and of Evadne, who married CAPANEUS. The latter died with Iphis in the war against Thebes (*see* SEVEN AGAINST THEBES) and the kingdom was left to STHENELUS (2), son of CAPANEUS.

Iphis (2) in Greek mythology, the daughter of Ligdus and Telethusa. Ligdus of Phaestus in Crete told his wife when she was already pregnant that she would have to bear him a son and that he would not be able to support a daughter. If one were born to them she would have to be killed. His wife, Telesthusa, was a votary of Isis (the Egyptian name of Io), and the goddess appeared to her before the baby was born wih promises to help her. However, Telethusa went on to give birth to a daughter. I an effort to save her, Telethusa dressed the baby girl in boy' clothes and named her Iphis. Surprisingly she got away with th deception until her daughter was thirteen. At that point her father betrothed his supposed son to Ianthe. Telethusa tried al manner of delaying tactics and, just as it seemed hopeless, th goddess, Isis, transformed Iphis into a boy.

Iphis (3) in Greek mythology, a Cypriot youth who hanged himself from the doorpost of the house of Anaxarete, whom h loved desperately but who had rejected him. During his funera procession Anaxerete was turned to stone.

Iphitus (1) in Greek mythology, a son of Naubolus, king o Phocis, and an ARGONAUT. He was the father of SCHEDIUS (1) an Epistrophus, who is said to have been the leader of the Phocia forces to the TROJAN WAR.

Iphitus (2) in Greek mythology, a son of EURYTUS (1), king o Oechalia. When Eurytus promised his daughter to anyone wh defeated him at archery and then reneged on his promise wher HERACLES won, Iphitus took the side of Heracles. Later, however, he was killed by Heracles, who threw him from the wall of Tiryns, possibly because they had quarrelled over stole mares belonging to Eurytus. For this crime he was smitten wit a terrible disease which could be cured only by selling himsel into slavery.

Ipthime *see* **Icarius** (1).

Iris in Greek mythology, the swift golden-winged messenger o the Olympian gods in the *Iliad*, the office of HERMES in the *Odyssey*. Iris was originally the personification of the rainbow. Sh is represented with wings attached to her shoulders and a herald's staff in her left hand, representative of her office of messenger. She is represented as the daughter of THAUMAS anc ELECTRA (4), and sister of the HARPIES. According to legend sh was the wife of ZEPHYRUS and the mother of EROS.

Iron Race *see* **Races of Man**.

Irus in Greek mythology, a beggar from Ithacus, christened

Arnaeus. It was his practice to beg from the suitors of PENELOPE, and when he saw an aged beggar in his area, Irus threatened him, not knowing that the supposed beggar was ODYSSEUS in disguise. Odysseus felled Irus with one blow, although Irus was much younger than him, in a boxing match that was arranged by the suitors.

Ischys in Greek mythology, a son of ELATUS (2) and lover of CORONIS (1). He was killed by ARTEMIS at APOLLO's request.

Islands of the Blessed *see* **Races of Man**; **White Island**.

Ismene (1) in Greek mythology, a daughter of OEDIPUS, by JOCASTA or Euryganeia. In *Antigone* by Sophocles she is afraid to take part in the illegal burial of POLYNICES but later offers to die with her sister for committing the deed.

Ismene (2) in Greek mythology, a daughter of ASOPUS and Metope and wife of ARGUS by whom she became the mother of IASUS and IO.

Ithaca (modern Ithaki) one of the IONIAN ISLANDS on the west of Greece, a long narrow island lying between the mainland and CEPHALONIA. It is mountainous and the coast is steep and rocky. Ithaca was the royal seat of ODYSSEUS, and is minutely described in the *Odyssey*. It is one of the most famous sites in mythology.

Itoni in Greek mythology, a Lydian tribe who caused much trouble to OMPHALE, queen of Lydia until HERACLES subdued them.

Iulus in mythology, the son of AENEAS and CREUSA (2). He was originally called Ilus and was often called ASCANIUS. With Aeneas he fought against the forces of TURNUS. He founded the city of ALBA LONGA. The Julian line of Roman emperors takes its name from him.

Ixion in Greek mythology, a king of the Lapiths in Thessaly and father of PEIRITHOUS. He married DIA, the daughter of Deioneus, and caused the death of his father-in-law. He prayed for forgiveness to ZEUS, who pardoned him and invited him to his table. Ixion then sought to seduce HERA, and for his wickedness he was chained to a fiery wheel, which rolled for ever in the sky.

J

Jana *see* **Janus**.

Janus in Roman mythology, a god, after whom the first month of the year was named. He was held in great reverence by the Romans, greater even than that of JUPITER, and was represented with two faces, one looking forward, the other backward. All doors, passages and beginnings were under his care. His principal festival was New Year's Day, when people gave each other presents. The temple of Janus, which was open in time of war and closed in time of peace, was shut only three times in the long space of 700 years—once in the reign of NUMA POMPILIUS, again after the first Punic War, and the third time under the reign of Augustus. Vespasian also closed it in AD 71. There was also a goddess, Jana, although she never became prominent in the state religion.

Jason in Greek mythology, the elder son of AESON, a grandson of AEOLUS (2). The half-brother of Aeson, PELIAS, usurped Aeson as heir to the throne of IOLCUS. Aeson was afraid for his life and for the life of the son that was born to him. To preserve the infant's life, he and his wife pretended that the baby had died and sent him to CHIRON the Centaur for protection. The Centaur named the child Jason and reared him in his cave on the mountain of Pelion, east of Iolcus. When Jason was a man, he set out for Iolcus to depose Pelias. Legend has it that Pelias, who did not have the courage to kill Jason, asked Jason what he would do if an oracle said that a certain man would kill him. Jason replied that he would order the person who was supposedly going to kill him to go and bring back the GOLDEN FLEECE. (PHRIXUS had flown to Colchis on the back of a mirculous ram and had nailed to a tree in the grove of ARES the ram's golden fleece where it was guarded by a dragon which never slept). Pelias ordered Jason to do this, making the excuse that the Delphic oracle had revealed to him that the gods of the Underworld had issued a directive that the spirit of Phrixus must be brought back from the foreign land of Colchis to Thessaly and with it the golden fleece. Jason choose the most courageous of the young nobles from the Greek cities and instructed ARGUS to build a ship with the help of ATHENA. The ship was called the *Argo*. During the expedition Jason was under the protection of HERA, whom he had carried over a stream when she was in the guise of an old woman and who hated Pelias. Hera thought that MEDEA would be clever enough to overthrow Pelias, but Medea lived in COLCHIS, a long way from Iolcus. Hera enlisted the help of APHRODITE to cause Medea to fall in love with Jason so that she would return to Iolcus with him and depose Pelias. Jason succeeded in getting the golden fleece, and the ARGONAUTS returned. Meanwhile, Pelias had killed Jason's father and brother. On his return to Iolcus with Medea as his wife, he and Medea avenged the murder of his parents and his brother by putting Pelias to death. He did not take possession of his throne, however, but, according to one legend, went to Corinth, where, he lived with Medea for some time until he married GLAUCE (or Creusa), daughter of the king of Corinth, CREON, and put away Medea and her children. Medea killed his new wife. Different accounts are given of his death. One of these is that he was killed by a wooden beam that fell from the wreckage of the *Argo* as he sat in it. Medea and Jason had two sons, Mermerus and Pheres, and Jason had previously had sons, EUNEUS and either Nebrophonus or Deipylus by HYPSIPYLE, queen of Lemnos.

Jocasta *or* **Epicasta** in Greek mythology, a daughter of MENOECEUS, who married LAIUS when he became king of Thebes. Laius was warned by an oracle that a son born to him would kill him. When Jocasta gave birth to a son they left the baby to die of exposure on Mount Cithaeron, but he was saved by shepherds and brought up by the king of Corinth, Polybus, and his wife, Merope, in Corinth. When he became a young man, Oedipus, as he was called, was warned by the Delphic oracle that he would kill his father and marry his mother. In order to prevent this coming true, he did not return to Corinth. When he left Delphi he met Laius without knowing who he was and killed him in a quarrel. He then went to Thebes, where the people were trying to get rid of the Sphinx who was asking a riddle of passers-by and killing them when they could not answer it. Oedipus solved the riddle that she put to him, and she threw herself from a rock. As a reward he was given the hand of Jocasta by Creon, her brother, and was made king of Thebes. Jocasta and he had two sons, Eteocles and Polynices, and two daughters, Antigone and Ismene (1). Because of this unconsciously incestuous relationship, a plague was sent by the gods to Thebes. When Oedipus was informed by the seer Teiresias that he had murdered his father and married his mother, one legend has it that Jocasta hanged herself and Oedipus gouged out his own eyes.

judgment of Paris *see* **golden apple**.

Juno in Roman mythology, the principal goddess, sister and wife of Jupiter, the equivalent of the Greek Hera. She was the queen of heaven, and under the name of Regina (queen) was worshipped in Italy at an early period. She bore the same relation to women that Jupiter did to men. She was regarded as the special protectress of whatever was connected with marriage and with women. She was also the guardian of the national finances, and a temple, which contained the mint, was erected to her under the name of Juno Moneta on the Capitoline.

Jupiter in Roman mythology, the supreme deity, the same as the Greek Zeus, and the Sanskrit Dyaus ('the sky'), the second part of the word being the same as the Latin *pater*, 'father'. As the supreme deity Jupiter received from the Romans the title of *optimus maximus* (best greatest), and as the deity presiding over the sky he was considered as the originator of all the changes that took place in the sky. From him accordingly proceeded rain, hail and the thunderbolt, and he it was that restored serenity to the sky after it had been obscured by clouds. Hence the epithets of Pluvius ('rainy'), Tonans ('thundering'), etc, were applied to him. The most celebrated of his temples was that on the Capitoline Hill, dedicated to him as Jupiter Optimus Maximus, jointly with JUNO and MINERVA. He was represented with a sceptre as a symbol of his supreme authority. He maintained the sanctity of oaths, he was the guardian of all property, and every Roman was believed to be under his protection, and that of his consort, Juno, the queen of heaven. He was associated with the colour white. White animals were offered up to him in sacrifice, his priests wore white caps, and his chariot was represented as drawn by four white horses.

Juventas in Roman mythology, the goddess of youth, who was identified with the Greek goddess HEBE, whose name also meant truth.

K

Ker in Greek mythology, a spirit associated with death, which is often represented as a woman with talons and fangs. The Keres carried off dead bodies to HADES. They were said to be the daughters of NYX (night) and to be sisters of Moros (doom), THANATOS (death), and HYPNOS (sleep).

Kore in Greek mythology, a name given to PERSEPHONE, a goddess of the Underworld and the daughter of ZEUS and DEMETER. She had been carried off by HADES and had to spend part of the year with him and the rest with her mother. Her annual return from Hades coincided with the sprouting of crops in spring, as though the earth were returning to life again after winter.

Kos *see* **Cos.**

Kronos *see* **Cronos.**

Ktesios in Greek mythology, a spirit who guarded storerooms. Sacred objects representing him were placed in all storehouses to protect them. He is identified with ZEUS.

L

Labdacus in Greek mythology, a son of the Theban king Polydorus and grandson of Cadmus. His father died when Labdacus was young, and he was placed under the guardianship of Nycteus and afterwards under that of Lycus. When he reached manhood Lycus surrendered the government to him, and on the death of Labdacus, which occurred soon after, Lycus again undertook the guardianship of his son Laius.

Labyrinth a structure with numerous intricate winding passages, which render it difficult to find the way through it. The Cretan labyrinth was said to have been constructed by Daedalus for King Minos to contain the Minotaur. There were other labyrinths at Lemnos and Samos.

Lacedaemon in Greek mythology, a son of Zeus by Taÿgete, who was married to Sparte, the daughter of Eurotas, by whom he became the father of Amyclas, Eurydice (4) and Asine. He was king of the country which he called after his own name, Lacedaemon, while he gave to his capital the name of his wife, Sparta.

Lacedaemon the ancient name of Laconia. *See also* Sparta.

Lachesis *see* **Fates**.

Laconia the southernmost part of the Peloponnesus. Its chief city was Sparta or Lacedaemon. It was one of the largest of the ancient Greek regions.

Ladon in Greek mythology, a hundred-headed snake, the offspring of Typhon and Echidna. It was immortal and helped the Hesperides to guard the apples in their garden.

Laelaps in Greek mythology, a hound which some legends say was given by Zeus to to Europa as a watchdog, decreeing that it would catch anything or anyone that it pursued. Artemis, or

Europa's son MINOS, gave the hound to PROCRIS, and she gave it to her husband, CEPHALUS. In turn he lent it to AMPHITRYON, who used it to try to catch the Teumessiam vixen. This proved a real problem since HERA had decreed that the vixen would never be caught. In the face of this dilemma Zeus turned both animals to stone.

Laertes in Greek mythology, king of ITHACA and the only son of Arceisius, or of CEPHALUS and PROCRIS. He is said to have been one of the ARGONAUTS. He conquered the city of Nericus and married Anticleia, who bore him ODYSSEUS. He was too old to protect PENELOPE when she was being pursued by suitors during Odysseus's absence, but she pretended to be weaving a shroud for him to give herself more time. Laertes was still alive when Odysseus returned, and he killed EUPEITHES.

Laestrygonians *or* **Laestrygones** in Greek mythology, cannibal giants who lived in a city called Telepylus. Several ships of ODYSSEUS's fleet, although not his, were crushed with a huge stone by the giants who speared the sailors and ate them.

Laius in Greek mythology, a king of Thebes whose father, LABDACUS, died while he was young. He was placed under the guardianship of LYCUS, and on the death of the latter when the throne was usurped by AMPHION and Zethus, was obliged to take refuge with PELOPS in the Peloponnesus. Laius fell in love with Chryssipus, the king's extremely handsome, illegitimate son, and took him back to Thebes after the death of Amphion and Zethus. Laius married JOCASTA and was advised to have no children because a child of his would kill him. When he had a son, he left him to die of exposure on Mount Cithaeron, but the child, OEDIPUS, was rescued and later killed his father and married his mother without knowing who they were.

Lampetia in Greek mythology, a daughter of HELIOS by the nymph NEAERA. After her birth she and her sister Phaetusa were carried to Sicily in order to watch over the herds of their father.

Laocoön in Greek mythology, a priest of APOLLO among the Trojans, who married against the will of the god, who warned the Trojans against taking the WOODEN HORSE into the city of Troy and threw his spear at it. For one or both of these reasons he was killed, along with his two sons, by two enormous serpents sent by APOLLO, which came up out of the sea. It has been a popular subject for poets, but it is chiefly known as the subject of an ancient sculpture discovered in Rome in 1506.

Laodamas in Greek mythology, a son of ETEOCLES and king of Thebes. It was in his reign that the EPIGONI marched against Thebes. Laodamas led an army against them and slew their leader, AEGIALEUS (1), but he himself was killed by ALCMAEON.

Laodamia in Greek mythology, the daughter of ACASTUS and wife of Protesilaus. Her husband was the first of the Greeks to fall by a Trojan hand, being killed as he leapt on shore from his ship. Laodamia prayed to the gods to give him back to her for only three hours. Her prayer was granted and HERMES led him back to the upper world. When the moment to return came, Laodamia died with him.

Laodice *see* **Elatus** (1).

Laodocus *see* **Dorus** (2); **Echemus**.

Laomedon in Greek mythology, a king of Troy for whom APOLLO and POSEIDON undertook to build a wall round Troy. When he refused to pay them, they punished him by sending a plague and a sea monster to his land. HERACLES saved HESIONE on the understanding that Laomedon would give him his arms but the king reneged on the bargain. Heracles returned after the completion of his labours and killed Laomedon, leaving PRIAM, son of Laomedon, on the throne.

Laphystius, Mount a Boeotian mountain west of Lake Copais. In Greek mythology, It was on this mountain that ATHAMAS was preparing to sacrifice his son PHRIXUS when the miraculous flying lamb wih the GOLDEN FLEECE came to take him and his sister HELLE away to safety.

Lapiths *or* **Lapithae** in Greek mythology, a tribe of northern Thessaly famous for their battle against the CENTAURS.

Larentia *see* **Faustulus**.

lares in Roman mythology, a class of tutelary spirits or deities (domestic and public). All the household lares were headed by the *lar familiaris*, who was revered as the founder of the family. In the mansions of the rich, the images of the lares had their separate apartment. When the family took their meals, some portion was offered to the lares, and on festive occasions they were adorned with wreaths. *See also* LEMURES; MANES; PENATES.

Larissa *see* **Pelasgus**.

larvae *see* **lemures**.

Latins *or* **Latini** the ancient inhabitants of Latium in Italy. In very early times the Latins formed a league of thirty cities, of which ALBA LONGA, said to have been built by ASCANIUS, became the head. ROME was originally a colony of Alba, and thus the language of the Romans is known as the Latin language.

Latinus in Roman mythology, king of Laurentum, after whom the area of Latium was named. He was defeated by AENEAS, who married his daughter LAVINIA and succeeded as king of Laurentum.

Latium the ancient name applied to a district of central Italy on the Tyrrhenian Sea, extending between ETRURIA and Campania, and inhabited by the LATINS, Volsci and Aequi.

Latona the Roman name for LETO.

Laurentum the land ruled by LATINUS, father of LAVINIA, south of ROME.

Lavinia in Roman mythology, the daughter of LATINUS. When AENEAS went to Italy after the burning of TROY with his followers, he overcame the local tribes under the leadership of TURNUS from Ardea or under that of Latinus. Aeneas married Lavinia and became king of the region and named the city which he founded near Laurentum as Lavinium. His followers from Troy agreed to give up the name of Trojans and start speaking the local language. On the death of Aeneas, Lavinia acted as regent until his son, Ascanius, became king. When Lavinium expanded as a city, Ascanius decided to found another city further inland. This he called ALBA LONGA. Acsanius's descendants, thirteen generations on, were Numitor and Amulius. Numitor's daughter, Rea Silva, was the mother by Mars of Romulus and Remus.

Lavinium a city south of Rome, according to tradition built and named by Aeneas after his wife, Lavinia, daughter of Latinus. Thirty years after the city was built, Ascanius founded Alba Longa.

Leander *see* **Hero**.

Leaneira *see* **Elatus** (1).

Leda in Greek mythology, the wife of the Spartan king Tyndareus. By Zeus, who came to her in the form of a swan, she was the mother of Castor and Pollux. In another story she was the mother by Zeus of Pollux and Helen, and by Tyndareus of Castor and Clytemnestra.

Leirope *see* **Narcissus**.

Lelegians *or* **Leleges** a division of the earliest inhabitants of Greece, who lived in the Aegean Islands and were powerful during the Minoan domination. They were driven to Caria in Asia Minor, where they became known as Carians.

Lemnos the most northerly island of the Greek Archipelago, between the Hellespont and Mount Athos. It was sacred to Hephaestus and was said to contain a volcano, Mosychlus, which was regarded as his workshop.

lemures in Roman mythology, the general term for all spirits of the dead, of whom the good were honoured as lares and the bad (larvae) were feared as capable in their night journeys of exerting a malignant influence upon mortals. The festival called Lemuria was held on the 9th, 11th and 13th of May, and was accompanied with ceremonies of washing hands, throwing black beans over the head, etc, and the pronunciation, nine times, of the words 'Begone, you spectres of the house!' which deprived the lemures of their power to harm.

Leonteus *see* **Polypoetes**.

Lepus (The Hare) a constellation. The hare was said to have been put in the sky by Hermes in honour of the fact that the hare was so fleet of foot. The people of Leros introduced hares to the island and became overrun by them because they reproduced so quickly. They finally drove them into the sea.

Lerna *or* **Lerne** *see* **Hydra**.

Lesbos (now Mytilene) a Greek island of the Aegean group. It is mountainous but exceedingly fertile. The island was famous in ancient times as a centre of Greek life and civilization. It formerly contained nine cities, the chief being Mytilene.

Lethe in Greek mythology, the River of Oblivion, one of the streams of the lower regions, whose water had the power of making those who drank of it forget the whole of their former existence. Souls before passing into ELYSIUM drank to forget their earthly sorrows; souls returning to the upper world drank to forget the pleasures of Elysium.

Leto in Greek mythology, daughter of the Titan Coeus and PHOEBE and the mother of APOLLO and ARTEMIS. She was one of the early loves of ZEUS, and HERA was jealous of her. She was worshipped chiefly in Lycia, Delos, Athens and other cities of Greece. The Romans called her Latona.

Leucippus (1) in Greek mythology, a son of PERIERES and GORGOPHONE and brother of APHAREUS, and prince of Messenia. He is mentioned among the hunters of the CALYDONIAN BOAR, and the Boeotian town of Leuctra is said to have derived its name from him.

Leucippus (2) *see* **Oenomaüs**.

Leucus *see* **Idomeneus**.

Liber in Roman mythology, an ancient god of fertiliity. *See* BACCHUS.

Libera in Greek mythology, an ancient fertility goddess.

Libya *see* **Epaphus**.

Licymnius in Greek mythology, a son of ELECTRYON and the Phrygian slave Mideia, and a half-brother of ALCEMENE. He was the father of OEONUS. He was a friend of HERACLES, whose son Tlepolemus slew him, according to some unintentionally and according to others in a fit of anger.

Ligdus *see* **Iphis** (2).

Linus in Greek mythology, the personification of a dirge or lamentation, and described as a son of APOLLO or OEAGRUS and a MUSE, probably CALLIOPE, or of Amphimarus and URANIA.

Locris *or* **Locri** an ancient people of Greece, descended, according to Aristotle, from the LELEGIANS.

Lotis in Greek mythology, a nymph who gave her name to a tree. She was turned into a tree for her protection when she was being pursued by PRIAPUS.

Lotus-eaters *or* **Lotophagi** in Greek mythology, the name of a people inhabiting a portion of Cyrenaica in Northern Africa, who lived on the fruit of the lotus tree, from which they also made wine. According to Homer, they received ODYSSEUS and his followers hospitably, but the sweetness of the fruit induced such a feeling of happy languor that they ceased to desire to return to their native land.

lotus a name applied to a number of different plants, from the lotus famous in Greek legend. One of these is *Zizyphus lotus*, a native of northern Africa and southern Europe. Some think this was the food of the LOTUS-EATERS, although others consider it to have been the date or the berry of the *Rhamnus lotus*.

Lucina in Roman mythology, goddess of light, a title given to DIANA as the goddess who presided over childbirth.

Lucretia in Roman mythology, the wife of Tarquinius Collatinis, who was outraged by Sextus, son of TARQUINIUS SUPERBUS, king of Rome. She summoned her husband and a group of friends and, after making them take a solemn oath to drive out the hated race of Tarquins from the city, stabbed herself. Her death was the signal for the revolution by which the Tarquins were expelled and a republic formed.

Luna in Greek mythology, the goddess of the moon.

Lusi an ancient town of ARCADIA, in the foothills of the Aroanian Mountains. It had a temple of ARTEMIS, which was founded by PROETUS, whose daughters were cured here of their madness by MELAMPUS.

Lycaon (1) in Greek mythology, a son of Pelasgus by Meliboea, the daughter of Oceanus. He was king of Arcadia, a civilized one by some accounts, a barbarian by others. By several wives he became the father of a large number of sons, fifty by some accounts, twenty-two by others.

Lycaon (2) in Greek mythology, a son of Priam and Laothoe, who was taken by Achilles and sold as a slave to Euneus. He was ransomed but on encountering Achilles again was slain by him.

Lycaon (3) *see* **Orchomenus** (1).

Lycia an ancient maritime province in the south of Asia Minor, bounded by Caria on the west, Pamphylia on the east, and Pisidia and Phrygia on the north. It was colonized by the Greeks at a very early period, and its historical inhabitants were Greeks, although with a mixture of aboriginal blood. The Lycians were prominent in the Trojan War.

Lycomedes a king of the Dolopians in the island of Scyros, father of Deidameia (2) and grandfather of Neoptolemus. When Theseus came to Scyros, Lycomedes, dreading the influence of the stranger on his own subjects, thrust him down a rock.

Lycotherses *see* **Agave**.

Lycurgus (1) in Greek mythology, a king of the Edonians of Thrace. When Dionysus came to his country with his maenads, Lycurgus drove them away, and he was later punished. Opinions vary as to what form the punishment took. Some say that he was blinded by Zeus, others that he was driven mad by Dionysus and cut off his own feet, or hacked to death his son, Dryas. A famine was sent to Thrace to punish him, and his people are said to have thrown him to man-eating horses on Mount Pangaeus.

Lycurgus (2) in Greek mythology, a king of Arcadia who ruled the kingdom for his elderly father, Aleus, while his brothers, Cepheus (2) and Amphidamus, went on the Argonauts' expedition.

Lycurgus (3) in Greek mythology, a brother of Admetus and king of Nemea. He was the father of Opheltes.

Lycus (1) in Greek mythology, son of Chthonius, one of the SPARTI, brother of NYCTEUS and king of THEBES.

Lycus (2) in Greek mythology, a king of THEBES who marched against SICYON, the king of which, EPOPEUS, had married ANTIOPE (2), niece of Lycus, when she fled to Sicyon when pregnant by ZEUS. Epopeus was either killed or died of a wound, and Lycus took Antiope back to Thebes.

Lycus (3) a son of PANDION (2) and brother of AEGEUS, NISUS and Pallas. He was expelled by Aegeus and took refuge in the country of the Termili with SARPEDON (1). That country was afterwards called Lycia after him.

Lycus (4) son of DASCLYUS (1) and king of the MARIANDYNIANS was connected with HERACLES and the ARGONAUTS.

Lydia an ancient and powerful kingdom of Asia Minor, which extended eastward from the Aegean and comprised Paphlagonia (BLACK SEA littoral), BITHYNIA, MYSIA (at the HELLESPONT), Lydia Proper, LYCIA, PHRYGIA and part of Cappadocia. Sardis was the capital. Its first mythical dynasty was founded by ATYS (2), who was worshipped there along with CYBELE and the Babylonian gods Tammuz and Istar.

Lyra (The Lyre) a constellation, the lyre in the sky being that used by ORPHEUS.

Lyrnessus a city near Troy, to which AENEAS fled when ACHILLES drove him from Mount IDA. Achilles sacked the city.

Lynceus (1) a son of AEGYPTUS and husband of Hypermnestra, daughter of DANAUS, who, alone among the DANAÏDES, spared her husband's life. Danaus thereupon kept her in strict confinement but was afterwards prevailed upon to give her to Lynceus who succeeded him on the throne of Argos.

Lynceus (2) in Greek mythology, a son of APHAREUS and Arene and brother of IDAS. He was one of the ARGONAUTS and famous for his keen sight. He is also mentioned among the hunters of the CALYDONIAN BOAR and was slain by POLLUX.

Lysinianassa *see* **Busirus**.

M

Maeander *or* **Maeandrus** in Greek mythology, a son of OCEANUS and TETHYS, and the god of the River Maeander in PHRYGIA. The winding course of the river is the origin of the English word meander.

maenads in Greek mythology, female votaries of the god DIONYSUS. The maenads took part in orgiastic rites and encouraged other women to do so also.

Maera in Greek mythology, the dog of ICARIUS (2) who was placed in the constellation CANIS MAJOR by DIONYSUS.

Magnes (1) in Greek mythology, a son of AEOLUS and Enarete, who was the father of POLYDECTES by a NAIAD.

Magnes (2) in Greek mythology, a son of ARGUS (1) and Perimele from whom MAGNESIA derived its name.

Magnesia in ancient Greece, a coastal area of eastern THESSALY which contains Mount PELION and was the home of the CENTAURS.

Maia (1) in Greek mythology, the oldest of the PLEIADES and daughter of ATLAS and Pleïone. In a grotto of Mount Cyllene in ARCADIA she became by ZEUS the mother of HERMES. ARCAS, the son of Zeus by CALLISTO, was given to her to be reared.

Maia (2) *or* **Majesta** in Roman mythology, a divinity mentioned in connection with VULCAN and regarded by some as his wife. She later became identified with MAIA (1), but it is more probable that Maia was an ancient name of BONA DEA.

Malis the southern part of THESSALY. The Malians went to the TROJAN WAR under the leadership of PHILOCTETES, but the Greeks abandoned him at LEMNOS.

manes *or* **di manes** in Roman mythology, the souls or ghosts of the dead, to whom were presented offerings of victims, wine, milk, garlands of flowers, etc. The offerings were made at funerals and at the Parentalia, or Fralia, commemorative ceremonies held by the Romans in February. A similar worship of ghosts or ancestral spirits prevails among many races.

Mantius *see* **Oicles**.

Manto *see* **Epigoni**.

Marathon in Greek mythology, the hero eponymous of the Attic town of Marathon. According to some traditions, he was a son of EPOPEUS and, being driven from PELOPONNESUS by the violence of his father, went to Attica. After his father's death he returned to Peloponnesus, divided his inheritance between his two sons, Sicyon and Corinthus, and then settled in Attica.

Marathon a town of ancient Greece in ATTICA, northeast of ATHENS, said to have been founded by MARATHON. Here XUTHUS, who married the daughter of ERECHTHEUS, is said to have reigned, and here the HERACLEIDAE took refuge when driven out of Peloponnesus, and defeated EURYSTHEUS. It is also celebrated in the legends of THESEUS, who conquered the CRETAN BULL that devastated the plain of Marathon around the town.

Mariandynians *or* **Mariandyni** a tribe inhabiting an area of the BLACK SEA, whose king, DASCYLUS, was assisted by HERACLES in conquering his enemies.

Mariandynus *see* **Idaea**.

Marmara *or* **Marmora, Sea of** (ancient Propontis) the sea separating Asia Minor from Europe. It communicates with the BLACK SEA by the BOSPORUS, and with the AEGEAN and Mediterranean by the Dardanelles (HELLESPONT).

Marpessa *see* **Idas and Lynceus**.

Mars in Roman mythology, the god of war and of husbandry, at an early period identified with the Greek ARES, a deity of similar attributes. Like JUPITER, he was designated *Pater*, 'father', and was regarded in particular as the father of the Roman people, ROMULUS AND REMUS being the fruit of his union with RHEA SYLVIA. Several temples at ROME were dedicated to him, and the Campus Martius, where the Romans practised athletic and military exercises, was named in his honour. The month of March, the first month of the Roman year, was also named in his honour and was sacred to him. His service was celebrated not only by particular *flamines* devoted to him, but by the College of the Salii, or priests of MARS, who danced in complete armour. As the tutelary god of Rome he was called *Mars Quirinus*, and for his special care of Roman citizens he was called *Quirites*. In his character as the god of war he was called *Gradivus* (the striding) and as the rustic god *Silvanus*. The wolf and the woodpecker were sacred to him.

Mecisteus in Greek mythology, one of the SEVEN AGAINST THEBES, who is said to have won the contests at OEDIPUS's funeral games.

Meda *see* **Idomeneus**.

Medea *or* **Medeia** in Greek mythology, daughter of AEËTES, king of COLCHIS, and of the OCEANID Idyia, or of HECATE. When JASON, the leader of the ARGONAUTS, came to Colchis in search of the GOLDEN FLEECE, she fell in love with the young hero, helped him to obtain the fleece, and fled with him. She prevented her father from pursuing by killing her brother ABSYRTUS and strewing the sea with his limbs. She avenged her husband on the aged PELEUS by persuading his daughters to cut him in pieces and boil him in order to make him young again. Medea lived with Jason for ten years, until he discarded her in favour of GLAUCE (or Creusa), daughter of CREON, king of CORINTH. In revenge she sent Glauce a bridal robe which enveloped her in consuming flame, and thereafter she slew her own children by Jason. She fled to Athens in a chariot drawn by dragons, which she obtained from HELIOS. There she was received by AEGEUS, to whom she bore Medos, but afterwards being compelled to flee from Athens, she took Medos to Aria, the inhabitants of which were thenceforth called Medes. She finally became immortal and married ACHILLES in ELYSIUM. The story of Medea was a favourite theme of ancient tragedians, but only Euripides's masterpiece is extant.

Medon *see* **Electra** (1).
Medos *see* **Medea**.
Medusa *see* **Gorgons**.

Megaera in Greek mythology, one of the three FURIES, the others being Alecto and Tisiphone.

Megapenthes (1) in Greek mythology, a son of PROETUS, king of ARGOS. He exchanged his dominion for that of PERSEUS so that the latter received TIRYNS instead of Argos. He is said to have afterwards killed Perseus.

Megapenthes (2) in Greek mythology, son of MENELAUS by an Aetolian slave, Pieris or Teridae. Menelaus brought about a marriage between Megapenthes and a daughter of ALECTOR. According to one tradition, after the death of his father Megapenthes expelled HELEN from ARGOS and she fled to Polyxo at RHODES.

Megara the principal city on the Isthmus of CORINTH, so called because of the *megaras*, or shrines, that Car, son of PHORONEUS and the founder of Megara, built to DEMETER. Twelve generations later, Lelex came from Egypt and gave the inhabitants the name of LELEGIANS. Lelex was succeeded by his son Cleson, and he by his son PYLAS, whose son SCEIRON (2) married the daughter of PANDION (2), king of ATHENS. But NISUS, the son of Pandion, disputing with Sceiron the possession of Megara, AEACUS, who had been called in as arbiter, assigned the kingdom to Nisus and to Sceiron the command in war. Megarian tradition suppresses an account of a capture of the city during the reign of Nisus by MINOS. According to Boeotian tradition, in the reign of Pylas, Pandion being expelled from Athens by the METIONIDAE, fled to Megara, married the daughter of Pylas and succeeded his father-in-law. When the Metionidae were driven out of Athens and the dominions of Pandion were divided among his four sons, Nisus, the youngest, obtained Megara, and the city was called Nisa after him. When Minos attacked Nisus, MEGAREUS, son of POSEIDON, came from ONCHESTUS in BOEOTIA to assist Nisus and was buried in the city, which was called Megara after him. Through the treachery of his daughter SCYLLA, Nisus perished, and Minos obtained possession of the city and demolished its walls. They were subsequently restored by ALCATHOUS, son of PELOPS, who came from ELIS. In this work he was assisted by APOLLO. It was further related that Hyperion (2), the son of AGAMEMNON, was the last king of Megara and that after his death a democratic form of government was established.

Megareus in Greek mythology, a son of Onchestus (1) or of POSEIDON, Hippomenes, APOLLO or AEGEUS by Oenope. He was a brother of Abrote, the wife of NISUS. According to a Boeotian tradition, Megareus with his army went to the assistance of Nisus, king of MEGARA, against MINOS, but he fell in battle and was buried at Megara which was called after him for its previous name had been Nisa. According to a Megarian tradition, which discarded the account of an expedition of Minos against Megara, Megareus was the husband of Iphinoë, the daughter of Nisus, and succeeded his father-in-law. His two sons died before him so he left Megara to ALCATHOUS.

Megaris a small mountainous state of ancient Greece, between ATTICA and the Isthmus of Corinth. Its capital was MEGARA.

Melampus in Greek mythology, one of the great seers. He is said to have been able to understand the language of birds and animals. He was devoted to his brother BIAS. He cured IPHICLUS of impotence in return for a herd of cattle belonging to the young man's father, Phylacus. NELEUS, the father of Pero (1), whom Bias wanted to marry, was demanding the cattle in exchange for his daughter's hand in marriage.

Melanion *see* **Atalanta**.

Melanippus in Greek mythology, a Theban champion in the war against ARGOS. He killed two of the SEVEN AGAINST THEBES.

Melantheus *or* **Melanthius** in Greek mythology, son of DOLIUS and the chief goatherd of ODYSSEUS, who sided with the suitors of PENELOPE even after his master returned. He was mutilated and left to die as a punishment for his treachery.

Meleager the son of OENEUS, king of CALYDON and ALTHAEA. He distinguished himself in the ARGONAUTS' expedition and more particularly at the CALYDONIAN BOAR hunt, where he killed the Boar and gave its skin as the highest token of his regard for ATALANTA. During the hunt he quarrelled with some of his uncles, and as a result his mother brought about his death.

Melia in Greek mythology, a nymph, a daughter of OCEANUS, who became by INACHUS the mother of PHORONEUS and AEGIALEUS (2) or Pegeus. By Seilenus she became the mother of the CENTAUR Pholus and by POSEIDON of Amycus. She was carried off by APOLLO and became by him the mother of Ismenius and of the seer Tenerus.

Meliae in Greek mythology, nymphs of the manna ash trees, who were said to have sprung from the blood of the castrated URANUS.

Melisseus in Greek mythology, an ancient king of CRETE who, by Amalthea, became the father of the NYMPHS Adrasteia and Ida, to whom RHEA entrusted the infant ZEUS to be brought up.

Melpomene in Greek mythology, the MUSE who presides over tragedy, daughter of ZEUS and MNEMOSYNE. She is generally represented as a young woman, with vine leaves surrounding her head and holding in her hand a tragic mask.

Membliarus *see* **Anaphe**.

Memnon in Greek mythology, a hero mentioned in the Homeric poems as the beautiful son of Eos (the morning), and in the post-Homeric accounts as the son of TITHONUS and step-nephew of PRIAM, whom he assisted at the siege of TROY. He slew ANTILOCHUS, but was himself slain by ACHILLES. His mother was filled with grief at his death, which ZEUS endeavoured to soothe by making her son immortal. The name of Memnon was afterwards connected with Egypt, and was attached to a statue still standing at THEBES, being one of the two known from their size as 'the Colossi'. This statue, known as 'the vocal Memnon', was celebrated in antiquity as emitting a sound every morning at the rising of the sun, which was perceived as the voice of

Memnon hailing the newly risen Eos. The sound was perhaps contrived by the priests, although some think it was owing to expansion caused by heat. Both statues seem originally to have been about 70 feet high.

Memphis in Egyptian mythology, daughter of the god Nile who married EPAPHUS who founded the city of Memphis which he named after his wife.

Memphis the ancient city of Egypt, on the left bank of the Nile, at the apex of the Delta, in Greek mythology, said to have been founded by EPAPHUS and named after MEMPHIS.

Menelaus in Greek mythology, a son of ATREUS and Aerope, younger brother of AGAMEMNON and husband of the beautiful HELEN, with whom he received the kingdom of Sparta or Lacedaemon. His wife having been abducted by PARIS, son of PRIAM, king of Troy, he summoned the Greek princes to avenge the affront and himself led sixty ships to the siege of Troy. After its conquest he returned with Helen to his native land in a roundabout voyage which led him to Cypria, Phoenicia, Egypt, and Libya during a period of eight years.

Menestheus in Greek mythology, a king of Athens held to be the first demagogue according to some legends. He roused the people of Athens against the king of the time, THESEUS, who was then detained in HADES. He is said to have encouraged CASTOR AND POLLUX, brothers of HELEN, to invade Athens to take back their sister. This they did and put Menestheus on the throne before going away. He was one of the Greek leaders in the WOODEN HORSE at Troy. There is dispute about his later fate.

Menoeceus (1) in Greek mythology, a Theban grandson of PENTHEUS and father of Hipponome, JOCASTA and CREON.

Menoeceus (2) in Greek mythology, a grandson of MENOECEUS (1) and son of CREON. In the war of the SEVEN AGAINST THEBES, Teiresias declared that the THEBANS would conquer if Menoeceus would sacrifice himself for his country. Menoeceus accordingly killed himself outside the gates of Thebes.

Menoetius in Greek mythology, a son of IAPETUS and CLYMENE (1) or ASIA, and a brother of ATLAS, PROMETHEUS and EPIMETHEUS. He was killed by ZEUS with a flash of lightning in the fight of the TITANS and thrown into TARTARUS.

Mercury in Roman mythology, the name of a god, identified in later times with the Greek HERMES. In representing Hermes he was regarded as the son of JUPITER and MAIA, and was looked upon as the god of eloquence, of commerce, and of robbers. He was also the messenger, herald and ambassador of JUPITER. As a Roman god he was merely the patron of commerce and gain.

Mermerus in Greek mythology, a son of JASON and MEDEA, killed by his mother.

Merope (1) in Greek mythology, a daughter of ATLAS, one of the PLEIADES and the wife of SISYPHUS of CORINTH, by whom she became the mother of GLAUCUS (3). In the constellation of the Pleiades she is the seventh and the least visible star because she is ashamed of having had intercourse with a mortal man.

Merope (2) in Greek mythology, a daughter of OENOPION in Chios. She was loved by ORION, who was in consequence blinded by her father.

Merope (3) *see* **Periboea**.

Messenia an ancient state of Greece located in the southern part of the PELOPONNESUS. Its capital was Messene. Its earliest inhabitants are said to have been LELEGIANS but after five generations Aeolians came there under PERIERES, a son of AEOLUS, who was succeded by his son APHAREUS.

Messina, Strait of the channel separating Italy from Sicily, and connecting the Tyrrhenian with the Ionian Sea. It is deep and the current is strong, and it is almost certain that SCYLLA AND CHARYBDIS were situated here.

Mestor *see* **Electryon**.

metamorphosis any marked change of form, shape, or structure. In ancient mythology the term is applied to the frequent transformations of human beings into beasts, stones, trees, fire, water, etc.

Metaneira in Greek mythology, the wife of CELEUS and mother of TRIPTOLEMUS, who received DEMETER on her arrival in ATTICA.

metempsychosis *or* **reincarnation** the belief that the souls of the dead are reborn in the bodies of other men or animals. In Greek mythology, it was a feature of the worship of DIONYSUS and ORPHEUS. Mentions of it in Roman mythology are all from Greek sources.

Metionidae in Greek mythology, the sons of Metion, a son of ERECHTHEUS and Praxithea and husband of Alcippe. They expelled their cousin PANDION (2) from his kindgom of ATHENS but were themselves afterwards expelled by the sons of Pandion.

Metis in Greek mythology, the personification of prudence, described as a daughter of OCEANUS and THETYS. At the instigation of ZEUS, she gave CHRONOS the emetic that caused him to vomit up his children. She was the first love and wife of Zeus, from whom she had at first endeavoured to withdraw by metamorphosing herself in various ways. She prophesied to him that she would give birth first to a girl and afterwards to a boy, to whom the rule of the world was destined by fate. For this reason Zeus devoured her when she was pregnant with ATHENA and afterwards he himself gave birth to his daughter, who issued from his head.

Metope *see* **Echetus**.

Midas in Greek mythology, the son of GORDIUS and CYBELE, pupil of ORPHEUS and king of PHRYGIA, whose request that whatsoever he touched should turn to gold was granted by DIONYSUS. In this way even his food became gold, and it was not until he had bathed in the Pactolus that the fatal gift was transferred to the river. Another legend is that, in a musical contest between PAN and APOLLO on the flute and the lyre, Midas, who was umpire, decided in favour of the former, whereupon the angry Apollo bestowed upon the presumptuous critic a pair of ass's ears. He hid the deformity under his Phrygian cap, but could not hide it from his barber, who felt the burden of the secret he could not reveal so heavily that he dug a hole in the ground and whispered into it, 'King Midas has ass's ears'. He then filled up the hole and his heart was lightened, but out of the ground sprang a reed which whispered the shameful secret to the breeze.

Midea *see* **Electryon**.

Miletus in Greek mythology, a son of APOLLO and Areia of CRETE. Being loved by MINOS and SARPEDON (1), he attached himself to the latter and fled from Minos to Caria in Asia Minor where he built a town which he called after his own name.

Miletus an ancient city of Caria, Asia Minor, situated near the mouth of the MAEANDER, one of the chief Greek cities of Asia Minor. Its earliest inhabitants were either Carians, or LELEGIANS who were later augmented by Cretan settlers introduced by SARPEDON (1).

Milky Way known to the Greeks as *galaxias kyklos*, 'milky circle'. The name is said to have been derived from a myth in which HERA, furious at being tricked into suckling HERACLES, who was not her child, tore her breast from the infant's mouth and her milk squirted across the sky.

Minerva in Roman mythology, a daughter of JUPITER, and one of the great divinities of ancient Rome. She was looked upon as the patroness of all arts and trades, and her annual festival, called Quinquatrus, lasted from the 19th to the 23rd of March inclusive. This goddess was believed to protect warriors in battle, and to her was ascribed the invention of numbers and of musical instruments, especially wind instruments. At Rome a temple was built for Minerva by Tarquin on the Capital, where she was worshipped along with Jupiter and JUNO; and there was also a temple of the Aventine dedicated to herself alone. This deity is supposed to be of Etruscan origin, and her character has much in common with the Greek goddess ATHENA.

Minos in Greek mythology, a ruler of CRETE, said to have been the son of ZEUS and EUROPA, and a brother of RHADAMANTHUS and SARPEDON (1). He was father by PASIPHAË of DEUCALION, ARIADNE and several others. During his lifetime he was celebrated as a wise lawgiver and a strict lover of justice, and after his death he was made, with AEACUS and Rhadamanthus, one of the judges of the internal world. The story evidently contains reminiscences of Cretan supremacy in the Aegean. This theory is supported by recent discoveries, which tend to prove the existence of a powerful kingdom of CRETE during the Mycenaean Age.

Minotaur in Greek mythology, the offspring of PASIPHAË and the CRETAN BULL, for which she had conceived a passion through the contrivance of POSEIDON. The queen placed herself in an artificial cow made by DAEDALUS, and so became the mother of a monster said to to have had the body of a man with the head of a bull. It fed on human flesh, on which account MINOS, husband of Pasiphaë, shut him up in the labyrinth of Daedalus, and there fed him at first with criminals, but afterwards with youths and maidens yearly sent from Athens as a tribute. The Minotaur was slain by THESEUS with the help of ARIADNE.

Minyans *or* **Minyae** in Greek mythology, an ancient race of heroes at ORCHOMENUS (2), Iolcus and other places. Their ancestral hero, Minyas, is said to have migrated from THESSALY in the northern parts of Boeotia and there to have established the powerful race of Minyans with the capital of Orchomenus. The greater part of the ARGONAUTS were descended from Minyans, and the descendants of the Argonauts founded a colony in LEMNOS which was called Minyae.

Mnemosyne in Greek mythology, daughter of URANUS and GE, and by ZEUS the mother of the nine MUSES.

Moirai the Roman name for the FATES.

moly in Greek mythology, a magical herb given by HERMES to ODYSSEUS, which he used as an antidote to the charms of CIRCE.

moon in classical mythology, the moon is seen as a goddess while the sun is a god. SELENE, LUNA and DIANA are goddesses of the moon.

Mopsus *see* **Calchas.**

Moros *see* **Ker**; **Nyx**.

Morpheus in Roman mythology, the son of sleep and the god of dreams. He is so named because he shapes or moulds the dreams that visit the sleeper. He is represented as an old man with wings, pouring sleep-inducing vapour out of a horn.

Mother Deity *see* **Cybele**.

Mother of the Gods *see* **Rhea**.

Muses in Greek mythology, the daughters of ZEUS and MNEMOSYNE, who were, according to the earliest writers, the inspiring goddesses of song, and according to later ideas divinities presiding over the different kinds of poetry, and over the sciences and arts. Their original number appears to have been three, but afterwards they are always spoken of as nine: CLIO, the muse of history; EUTERPE, the muse of lyric poetry; Thaleia, the muse of comedy and of merry or idyllic poetry; MELPOMENE, the muse of tragedy; Terpsichore, the muse of choral dance and song; ERATO, the muse of erotic poetry and mimicry; Polymnia or Polyhymnia, the muse of the sublime hymn; URANIA, the muse of astronomy; and CALLIOPE, the muse of epic poetry. They were first honoured amongst the Thracians, and as Pieria around OLYMPUS was the original seat of that people, it came to be considered as their native country and they were therefore called Pierides. They are often represented as the companions of APOLLO and as singing while he played on the lyre at the banquets of the Immortals. Various legends ascribed to them victories in musical competitions, particularly over the SIRENS. Among the places sacred to them were the fountains of AGANIPPE and HIPPOCRENE on Mount HELICON, and CASTALIA on Mount PARNASSUS.

Mycenae a very ancient city of ARGOLIS, built on a craggy height in the Peloponnesus. It is said to have been founded by PERSEUS, and before the TROJAN WAR to have been the residence of AGAMEMNON, in whose reign it was regarded as the leading city in Greece. It was destroyed by the inhabitants of Argos about 468 BC and never again rose to its former prosperity. Its ruins are extremely interesting for their antiquity and grandeur. Among them are the Lion Gate, the vaulted beehive tomb called the Treasury of Atreus, the city wall and a great rambling palace.

Mycene in Greek mythology, a daughter of INACHUS and wife of Arestor from whom MYCENAE was believed to have derived its name.

Myrmidons *or* **Myrmidones** an ancient Greek people of THESSALY, who accompanied ACHILLES to the TROJAN WAR. They are said to have emigrated into Thessaly under the leadership of PELEUS and to have colonized the island of AEGINA. ZEUS peopled Thessaly by transforming the ants into men (in Greek, *myrmix* means 'ant'). The term has come to signify the followers of a daring and unscrupulous leader, or the harsh and unfeeling agents of a tyrannical power.

Mysia in ancient geography, a country in the extreme northeasterly corner of Asia Minor, on the modern Aegean, HELLESPONT and Sea of MARMORA. The Mysi were a Thracian people who migrated into Asia. The TROAD was one of the subdivisions of Mysia.

Mysteries certain rites and ceremonies of ancient Greece and Rome, known only to, and practised by, congregations of certain initiated people at appointed times and in strict seclusion. The most important Mysteries were the ELEUSINIAN and Themsophorian, both representing, each from a different point of view, the rape of PERSEPHONE and DEMETER's search for her. In addition there were those of ZEUS of CRETE, of BACCHUS, CYBELE and APHRODITE, the two latter to do with procreation but celebrated in diametrically opposed ways, the former culminating in self-mutilation of the worshippers, the latter in prostitution. There were also the Mysteries of ORPHEUS, who was considered the founder of all Mysteries, and of other gods and goddesses, like HERA, MINERVA, DIANA and HECATE. Towards the end of the classical periods, the mysteries became public orgies and eventually were banned.

N

Naiads in classical mythology, the NYMPHS of fresh water, i.e. lakes, fountains, rivers and streams, as opposed to NEREIDS, nymphs of the sea, and OCEANIDS, nymphs of the ocean, i.e. the boundary round the world.

Nais *or* **Chariclo** *see* **Chiron**.

Narcissus in Greek mythology, the son of the NYMPH Leirope by the river-god CEPHISSUS. The young Narcissus was extremely handsome but was excessively vain and self-centred. ECHO pined away to a mere voice because her love for him went unrequited. NEMESIS determined to punish him for his coldness of heart, and caused him to drink at a certain fountain in which he saw his own image. He was so taken with his own beauty and fell so much in love with himself that he pined away because he was unabe to embrace himself. The gods transformed him into the flower which still bears his name. His name lives on on English in the word 'narcissistic', meaning full of self-love.

Nasamon in Greek mythology, a son of the Cretan Amphithemis and the NYMPH of Lake Tritonis, who gave his name to a Libyan tribe, the Nasamonians.

Naubolis *see* **Iphitus** (2).

Naupactus a port at the entrance to the Gulf of ARGOLIS from which the HERACLIDS embarked on their invasion of the PELOPONNESUS.

Nauplia a seaport near the head of the Gulf of ARGOLIS, home of NAUPLIUS (1), who founded the city. It was the port and arsenal of Argos.

Nauplius (1) in Greek mythology, a son of POSEIDON and Amymone, a native of ARGOS and reputed founder of NAUPLIA. He was a famous navigator who was said to deal in slave trafficking and he was said to have discovered the constellation of URSA MAJOR.

Nauplius (2) in Greek mythology, a son of Clytoneus and a descendant of the navigator NAUPLIUS (1), and an ARGONAUT. Nauplius was an Argivi who offered to steer the *Argo* after the death of TIPHYS. He is liable to be confused with his ancestor.

Nauplius (3) a king of EUBOEA. He was asked by King Aleus of TEGEA either to drown or sell his daughter Auge after she had been seduced by HERACLES. He sold her to TEUTHRAS, king of Teuthrania. He was asked by King Catreus of CRETE to perform a similar function and sell his daughters Aerope and CLYMENE (3) in view of the fact that he had been warned by an ORACLE that he would be killed by one of his children. Although Nauplius carried out his instructions with regard to Aerope and sold her to ATREUS or Pleisthenes, he elected to marry Clymene himself. Clymene bore him three sons, Palamedes, OEAX and Nausimedon. Nauplius was also involved in avenging the death of Palamedes when he was stoned to death by the Greeks at Troy. He sailed to each of the Greek cities and persuaded the wives of the Greek leaders—CLYTEMNESTRA, wife of AGAMEMNON, MEDA, wife of IDOMENEUS, and the wife of DIOMEDES (2)—to commit adultery. He also lit a fire on the Euboean Cape of Caphareus to induce the captains of the Greek ships to make for there when they were caught in a storm. Many of the ships were wrecked, with considerable loss of life. Those Greeks who reached the shore safely were killed by Nauplius.

Nausicaä in Greek mythology, daughter of ALCINOUS and Arete. When ODYSSEUS was shipwrecked he asked her help, and she told him how to get the assistance of her parents. Her father suggested to Odysseus that he marry her but he refused because he was married already.

Nausimedon *see* **Nauplius** (3).

Nausithoüs in Greek mythology, son of POSEIDON and Periboea and king of the Phaecians. His people were lovers of peace and disliked being harassed by their neighbours, the CYCLOPS. So that they could obtain peace Nausithous took them to the faraway island of Scherie or Drepane, usually identified with CORCYRA (Corfu). He helped the son of HERACLES, Hyllus, to found his own city. Nausithous had two sons, ALCINOUS and RHEXENOR, and Alcinous succeeded to the throne on the death of Nausithoüs.

Naxos the largest and most important island of the CYCLADES group, in the Aegean Sea midway between the coasts of Greece and Asia Minor. In ancient times it was also called Strongyle and Dia. The wine of Naxos was famous, and on this account the island was celebrated in the legends of DIONYSUS, and especially in those relating to ARIADNE.

Neaera in Greek mythology, a NYMPH and the mother of LAMPETIA and Phoethusa by HELIOS.

Neleus in Greek mythology, a king of PYLUS. He was the son of TYRO by POSEIDON and had a brother, PELIAS. Tyro wanted rid of the boys as she was about to marry Cretheus, king of IOLCUS. She left them to die of exposure, but they were found by horsemen and brought up by them. When they discovered who they really were, they sought out their stepmother, Sidero, who had treated Tyro badly, and Pelias killed her. Later Neleus and Pelias quarrelled, and Neleus was driven out of Iolcus by his brother. He went to MESSENIA, which was ruled by his cousin APHAREUS, who gave him some of the coastal territory to rule. This territory included the city of Pylus. The founder of the city was still living there, but Neleus banished him and made Pylus his own capital. The city and Neleus prospered, and he became a powerful ruler. He married Chloris, daughter of AMPHION, who bore him a daughter, Pero, and twelve sons, of whom three were NESTOR, Chromius and Periclymenus. Neleus insisted that his daughter marry a man who would bring her the cattle of IPHICLUS from Phylace in Thessaly. The brother of BIAS, the seer MELAMPUS, brought the cattle and thus won Pero (2) for Bias. Neleus had seized the property of Melampus when he was away getting the cattle, and this he now had to return. Meanwhile HERACLES had killed IPHITUS and went to Neleus to be purified of his crime. Because he was a friend of Iphitus's father, Neleus refused. Afterwards Heracles conquered Pylus and killed Neleus, his wife and eleven of his sons. Nestor escaped death because he was away at the time, and he succeeded to the throne.

Nemea a city in northern ARGOLIS. When the forces of the SEVEN AGAINST THEBES were passing through Nemea and accidentally contributed to the death of the infant OPHELTES, they instituted the NEMEAN GAMES in his honour. The NEMEAN LION roamed the area round the city until it was killed by HERACLES.

Nemean Games ancient Greek games held in the valley of NEMEA in Argolis, where HERACLES is said to have killed the NEMEAN LION. They recurred ordinarily every second year, and were similar in character to the other Greek games. They were instituted in honour of the infant OPHELTES by the SEVEN AGAINST THEBES. The victors received crowns of parsley in memory of the bed of parsley that Opheltes had lain on.

Nemean Lion in Greek mythology, a monster which was the offspring of ECHNIDA and TYPHON. Some legends say that it was suckled by SELENE, the moon goddess, and others that it was nursed by HERA. It was killed by HERACLES as the first of his labours, and he then wore its skin. Hera immortalized the lion in a constellation.

Nemesis in Greek mythology, the personification of the righteous anger of the gods, the goddess of retribution for evil deeds or undeserved good fortune. The goddess was said to be a daughter of NYX (night). According to one legend ZEUS fell in love with Nemesis. She rejected his advances and assumed various shapes in order to avoid him. When she became a goose Zeus became a swan and raped her.

Neoptolemus *or* **Pyrrhus** in Greek mythology, a son of ACHILLES by Deidameia. Achilles was brought up at the court of LYCOMEDES, king of the Aegean island of SCYROS, because his mother, THETIS, wanted to keep him away from the TROJAN

WAR. He had an affair with the daughter of Lycomedes, DEÏDAMEIA, who bore him a son named Pyrrhus. After the death of Achilles in the Trojan conflict, the Greeks were informed by the seer HELENUS, whom they had captured at Troy, that the city of Troy would not be taken unless three conditions were fulfilled. These were that the bones of PELOPS must be brought to Troy, that PHILOCTETES, who owned the bow and arrows that had been the property of HERACLES, must fight on the Greek side against Troy, and that the son of Achilles must also fight on the Greek side. ODYSSEUS and PHOENIX came to Scyros to take Pyrrhus to Troy and gave him the armour of Achilles. Pyrrhus fought bravely in the Trojan War and was one of the Greeks who hid in the WOODEN HORSE. He killed PRIAM, king of Troy, and when the ghost of his father asked for the blood of Priam's daughter, he sacrificed her on his father's grave. When the Trojan captives were distributeds, ANDROMACHE, the widow of Hector, was given to Neoptolemus, as by this time Pyrrhus was more commonly called, meaning literally 'young soldier'. By Andromache he became the father of several sons. Legends disagree about what happened to Neoptolemus after the Trojan War. Some indicate that he reached home safely unharmed, others that Thetis saved him from the storms that destroyed many of the Greek ships on their homeward journey, and others that he travelled home by land in response to a warning from Thetis. Some legends say that he did not return to Phthia, his father's homeland, but that he conquered EPIRUS and ruled there.

Nephele in Greek mythology, the first wife of ATHAMAS, king of Boeotian ORCHOMENUS (2), who bore him a son, PHRIXUS, and a daughter, HELLE. Athamas took a second wife who plotted for the downfall of Phrixus. She persuaded Athamas to sacrifice his son, but Nephele took a miraculous ram that had been given to her as a present by HERMES, and the two children flew away on the ram's back, the GOLDEN FLEECE.

Neptune in Roman mythology, the chief sea-god. When the Greek mythology was introduced into Rome, he was completely identified with the Greek POSEIDON, all the traditions relating to whom were transferred by the Romans to their own deity. In art he is usually represented as an old man with copious hair and a beard, and armed with a trident. The horse and the dolphin are his symbols.

Nereides *or* **Nereids** in mythology, sea-NYMPHS, daughters of NEREUS and Doris, daughter of OCEANUS and TETHYS, and constant attendants on POSEIDON or NEPTUNE. Fifty in number, they are represented as riding on sea-horses, sometimes in human form and sometimes with the tail of a fish. They were distinguished on the one hand from the NAIADS, the nymphs of fresh water, and on the other from the OCEANIDES, the nymphs of the ocean.

Nereus in Greek mythology, a sea-god, the father of the NEREIDES. He was the son of PONTUS (Sea) and GE (Earth). In the ancient works of art, and also by the ancient poets, he is represented as an old man, with a wreath of sedge, sitting upon the waves with a sceptre in his hand.

Nessus in Greek mythology, a CENTAUR who was driven from ARCADIA by HERACLES. He set up as a ferryman on the Aetolian River Evenus. DEÏANEIRA, the bride of Heracles, was taken by Nessus in his ferry while he left Heracles to struggle across the water alone. When Nessus tried to rape the girl, Heracles shot him. When he lay dying he cunningly persuaded Deïaneira to make a love potion of his blood and semen. He knew, although she did not, that his blood contained HYDRA venom from the arrow with which Heracles had shot him. It was this potion that later caused the death of Heracles.

Nestor in Greek mythology, one of the Greek heroes at TROY, son of NELEUS, king of Pylos, and Chloris. He escaped destruction when HERACLES slew all his brothers, and married Eurydice (5), by whom he became the father of a numerous family. In his youth he was distinguished for valour, taking part in wars with the Arcadians and the CENTAURS, in the hunting of the CALYDONIAN BOAR and in the ARGONAUTS' expedition, and in his advanced age for wisdom. Although he was an old man when the expedition against Troy was undertaken, he joined it with sixty ships. He is noted as the wisest adviser of the chiefs at Troy, after the fall of which he retired to Pylos, where he lived to a great age.

Nicostratus in Greek mythology, a son of MENELAUS and either HELEN or a slave girl. He and his brother, MEGAPENTHES, in some legends were responsible for banishing Helen from SPARTA after the death of their father. Neither of them inherited their father's throne. Instead ORESTES' claim was recognized.

Nike in Greek mythology, the goddess of victory, the daughter of STYX and PALLAS (1). In Roman mythology she is called VICTORIA. She was rewarded by ZEUS with permission to live in OLYMPUS for the readiness with which she came to his assistance in the war with the TITANS. Her brothers were CRATOS, BIA and ZELUS. There is a temple to her on the Acropolis of Athens. She is represented as resembling ATHENA but has wings and carries a palm or wreath and is engaged in raising a trophy or in inscribing the victory of the conqueror on a shield.

Niobe (1) in Greek mythology, the daughter of TANTALUS (1), king of LYDIA, and wife of AMPHION, king of THEBES. Proud of her numerous progeny, she provoked the anger of APOLLO and ARTEMIS by boasting to their mother LETO, who had no other children but those two. She was punished by having all her children put to death by those two deities. She herself was metamorphosed by ZEUS into a stone (on Mount Sipylus, Asia Minor) which shed tears during the summer. This fable has afforded a subject for art.

Niobe (2) in Greek mythology, a daughter of PHORONEUS and the NYMPH Teledice or Cinna, and the first mortal lover of ZEUS. By Zeus she bore ARGUS and, according to some legends, PELASGUS.

Nisus *or* **Nysus** in Greek mythology, a king of MEGARA and a son of ARES or of Deion or of PANDION (3), the king of ATHENS who became king of Megara. PALLAS (3) and LYCUS (3) were his brothers and AEGEUS his half-brother. All three brothers assisted their half-brother to regain the kingdom of Athens from whic their father had been driven. The right of Nisus to the throne Megara was disputed by Sceiron (2), the son of Pandion's pre ecessor. Aeacus was asked to arbitrate and decided in favour Nisus. Minos of Crete attacked the city of Megara, and Scyll a daughter of Nisus who had fallen in love with him, helpe him. Nisus had been given a warning that his life depended his retaining a single red lock in the middle of his forehea Scylla cut it off while her father slept, but Minos showed her n gratitude. Legends differ as to whether Minos drowned her whether she drowned herself. Nisus on his death was turne into an osprey.

Notus in Greek mythology, the south wind, said to have been son of Eos and Astraeus and a brother of Boreas and Zephyru although, unlike his brothers, he was rarely personified or re ferred to as a god.

Numa Pompilius in the legendary history of Rome, its secon king. He was of Sabine origin and was universally revered fc his wisdom and piety. Unanimously elected king by the Roma people, he soon justified by his conduct the wisdom of thei choice. After dividing the lands that Romulus had conquere he proceeded, with the assistance of the nymph Egeria, wh gave him interviews in a grove near the city, to draw up reli gious institutions for his subjects. His reign lasted for thirty nine years and was a golden age of peace and happiness.

Numitor in the legendary history of Rome, a king of Alb Longa. When he was deposed by his brother, Amulius, he wa restored to the throne with the help of Romulus and Remus.

Nycteïs *see* **Nycteus**; **Polydorus**.

Nycteus in Greek mythology, a king of Thebes, and brother o Lycus. They were the sons of Chthonius, one of the Sparti, o of Hyrieus by the nymph Clonia, or of Poseidon by the Pleia Celaeno. They were brought up in Euboea but had to flee fron there when they killed Phlegyas, king of Orchomenus (1). The were made citizens of Thebes because they were friendly wit

King PENTHEUS. The successor of Pentheus, POLYDORUS, married Nycteis, daughter of Nycteus. She bore him a son, LABDACUS, but Polydorus died before the child grew up, and Nycteus was made regent. Nycteus had another daughter, ANTIOPE (1). ZEUS was attracted by her beauty and seduced her in the guise of a SATYR. Antiope conceived a child by this union, and when her condition became obvious she fled from Thebes and went to SICYON, where she married King EPOPEUS. One legend has it that Nycteus committed suicide out of shame. Another has it that Epopeus seduced and abducted Antiope and that Nycteus marched against him, was wounded and went back home to die.

Nyctimene in Greek mythology, a daughter of Epopeus, king of LESBOS. She was raped by her father and hid in the woods becaused she was so ashamed. ATHENA felt sorry for her and turned her into an owl, which does not come out in daylight.

Nyctimus in Greek mythology, a king of ARCADIA. His forty-nine brothers were destroyed by ZEUS but he was saved by GE. He is assumed to have been killed in the flood sent by Zeus.

nymph in Greek mythology female divinities of inferior rank, inhabiting the sea, streams, groves, meadows and pastures, grottoes, fountains, hills, valleys and trees. Among them different classes were distinguished, particularly the Oceanids, daughters of OCEANUS (nymphs of the great ocean which flows around the earth), the Nereids, daughters of NEREUS (nymphs of the inner depths of the sea, or of the Inner Sea, i.e. the Mediterranean), Potameides (river nymphs), Naiads (nymphs of fountains, lakes, brooks and wells), Oreads (mountain nymphs), Napoeoe (nymphs of valleys) and Dryads or Hamadryad (forest nymphs, who were believed to die with the trees in which they dwelt). They were imagined as beautiful maidens, not immortal, but always young, who were considered as tutelary spirits not only of certain localities, but also of certain races and families. They occur generally in connection with some other divinity of higher rank, and they were believed to be possessed of the gift of prophecy and of poetical inspiration.

Nysa the mountain on which DIONYSUS was reared by NYMPHS, of uncertain location.

Nysus *see* **Nisus**.

Nyx in Greek mythology, night and the goddess of night, called Nox by the Romans. She was born out of CHAOS together with EREBUS (darkness), GE (earth), TARTARUS, and EROS (love). By Erebus she is the mother of Aether (upper air) and HEMERA (day). Without a mate she spawned Moros (doom), THANATOS (death), HYPNOS (sleep), the FATES and NEMESIS. She saved her son Hypnos when ZEUS was going to expel him from OLYMPUS.

O

Oceanids *or* **Oceanides** *see* **nymphs**; **Oceanus**.

Oceanus in Greek mythology, the eldest of the TITANS, regarded as the god of the ocean. The god Oceanus married his sister TETHYS and by her became father of all river-gods and of the three thousand Oceanids or ocean NYMPHS. He and Tethys also reared the goddess HERA, the daughter of their sister RHEA. Oceanus did not join his brother Titans in opposing ZEUS when he usurped URANUS. Oceanus was also the river that issued from the Underworld and flowed in a circular stream around the earth. The Greeks considered the earth as a flat circle surrounded by a river (Oceanus). The term 'ocean' was thus applied specially to the Atlantic, in contradistinction to the Mediterranean Sea.

Ocnus in Greek mythology, one of the damned in HADES. His punishment was continually to plait a rope of straw that was eaten by a she-ass as rapidly as Ocnus could plait it.

Ocypete *or* **Okypete** *see* **Harpies**.

Odius in Greek mythology, a Greek herald at the TROJAN WAR. He was part of the embassy that AGAMEMNON sent to placate ACHILLES.

Odysseus in Greek mythology, king of the island of ITHACA and one of the Greek heroes who engaged in the war against TROY. In Roman mythology he is called ULYSSES. In returning to his own country after the siege he had many adventures. He visited the country of the LOTUS-EATERS in North Africa, the CYCLOPS in Sicily (*see also* POLYPHEMUS), and the island of Aeolus, king of the winds. He also reached the island of AEAEA, where CIRCE changed (temporarily) his companions into swine; and visited the infernal regions, where he consulted the soothsayer TEIRE-

SIAS on how to return to his country. He succeeded in passing in safety the coast of the SIRENS, and successfully negotiated the joint dangers of SCYLLA AND CHARYBDIS. He remained for seven years on OGYGIA with the nymph CALYPSO after losing all his men and at last, after an absence of twenty years, returned to Ithaca. Here he found his palace occupied and his property wasted by suitors for the hand of his wife PENELOPE, people having assumed that he, Odysseus, was dead. With the aid of his son, TELEMACHUS, he put them to death. He lived about sixteen years after his return. These adventures of Odysseus are the subject of Homer's *Odyssey*.

Odyssey *see* **Homer**.

Oeagrus in Greek mythology, a king of THRACE, the father of ORPHEUS and Linus by the Muse CALLIOPE.

Oeax in Greek mythology, son of NAUPLIUS (1) and Clymene, who hated the ARGIVES for their unjust execution of his brother Palamedes at Troy by stoning him. He may have been the cause of CLYTEMNESTRA plotting AGAMEMNON's death since he told her that Agamemnon was bringing home a Trojan concubine. Later he tried to persuade the Argives to banish ORESTES after he murdered his mother.

Oebalus in Greek mythology, a king of Sparta who was a son of Cynortas or of his son PERIERES. He married GORGOPHONE, widow of the Aeolid Perieres, and the daughter of PERSEUS. Either she or the Naiad bore him TYNDAREUS, HIPPOCOÖN and ICARIUS (1).

Oechalia an ancient Greek city whose location is uncertain.

Oedipus *or* **Oedipodes** in ancient Greek mythology, son of the Theban King LAIUS and his queen JOCASTA. He was left to die of exposure on Mount Cithaeron as an infant with his feet pierced through—on account of an oracle saying that Laius would be killed by his son—but he was saved by a shepherd, who named him Oedipus because of his swollen feet, and was brought up at the court of CORINTH by Periboea (2), wife of Polybus, king of Corinth. Believing Corinth to be his native land, he left his foster-parents because the Delphic ORACLE had advised him that he was destined to slay his father and commit incest with his mother. On his way to THEBES to escape his fate, he met on a narrow road in Phocis the chariot of King Laius. The charioteer ordered him out of the way, and a quarrel ensued in which he unknowingly killed Laius. In the meantime, the SPHINX had appeared near Thebes and was asking a riddle of everyone who passed by, putting to death all who failed to solve it. In despair, the Thebans offered the kingdom, together with the hand of the queen, to whoever should deliver them from the monster. Oedipus offered himself, whereupon the Sphinx asked, 'What being has four feet, two feet, and three feet; only one voice; but whose feet vary, and when it has most, is weakest?' Oedipus replied that it was man, at which the Sphinx threw herself headlong from the rock on which she sat. Having solved the riddle, Oedipus became king of Thebes and married his mother, Jocasta. She bore him two sons, ETEOCLES AND POLYNICES, and two daughters, ANTIGONE and ISMENE. According to legend a plague was sent to Thebes, and CREON, brother of Jocasta, was sent to the Delphic oracle to inquire its cause. He was told by the oracle that the plague had been sent because the murderer of Laius was living unpunished in the city. An enquiry was launched by Oedipus, and the shepherd who had saved Oedipus when he was left to die as an infant gave evidence, as did the person who was with Laius when he died. On realizing the truth and what he had done, Oedipus gouged out his own eyes, and Jocasta killed herself. The details of Oedipus's later life are uncertain. One legend has it that he was exiled and wandered for many years as an outcast, accompanied only by his daughter Antigone. Before leaving Thebes he is supposed to have cursed his sons.

Oeneus in Greek mythology, a king of CALYDON and a son of Porthaon (or Portheus) and Euryte. He married ALTHAEA, daughter of Thestius, by whom he had MELEAGER, GORGE, and other sons and daughters. Oeneus was a very generous ruler and welcomed guests, being noted for his hospitality. When DIONYSUS visited his court and Oeneus suspected that the god had designs on his wife, Althaea, he left the country for a time, supposedly to attend to some religious rituals and left Althaea alone with the god by whom she conceived DEÏANEIRA. Dionysus gave his host the gift of vine culture in recognition of his somewhat unusual hospitality. Oeneus gave HERACLES Deïaneira's hand in marriage, despite the fact that, while a guest of Oeneus, he had killed Cyathus or Eunomus, the young cup-bearer to the king, for some minor misdemeanour. Oeneus incurred the wrath of ARTEMIS by forgetting to ask her to a harvest festival. The goddess took revenge for this accidental insult by sending a giant boar which caused destruction to the crops and people of Calydon. Oeneus appealed to the bravest men from other cities to come and help him get rid of the boar. The CALYDONIAN BOAR hunt was organized under the leadership of Meleager and they succeeded in killing the boar. However, a quarrel arose which resulted in Meleager's death. After her son's death, Althaea killed herself, and Oeneus later married PERIBOEA (1), having conquered OLENUS, where her father, Hipponous, was king. Periboea bore him two sons, Olenias and TYDEUS, although some legends indicate that it was Gorge, his own daughter, who bore Tydeus by Oeneus. Tydeus was exiled from Calydon after he killed someone, and the sons of Agrius deposed Oeneus and threw him in prison. Tydeus returned and rescued his father, killed his enemies and took Oeneus back to Argos with him. The name Oeneus may be derived from the Greek word for wine (*oinos*) since Oeneus is said to have introduced vine-growing in Calydon.

Oenoë in Greek mythology, a water NYMPH who gave her name to the island of Oenoe. She bore Sicinus, after whom the island of that name (Zykinthos) was called.

Oenomaus in Greek mythology, a king of Pisa in ELIS and son of Alxior or Areas and Harpius or the Pleiad Asterope. He was the father of HIPPODAMIA and LEUCIPPUS (2). Legends differ as to the identity of his wife. Some say that he was married to Evarete, but others say that Asterope was his wife rather than his mother, as some legends claim. Oenomaus killed all of the suitors of Hippodamia until he himself was killed by PELOPS.

Oenone (1) in Greek mythology, NYMPH of Mount IDA and a daughter of the river-god of the River Cebren. She was skilled in the art of healing and learned the art of prophecy from RHEA. She was the wife of PARIS until he went to win the hand of HELEN. When Paris was severely wounded by PHILOCTETES, he went to Mount Ida to get Oenone to heal his wounds, but in view of his rejection of her for Helen she refused. She reversed her decision, but it was too late to save his life. She was extremely remorseful when he died and hanged herself.

Oenone (2) *or* **Oenopia** *see* **Aegina** (1).

Oenopion in Greek mythology, a son of DIONYSUS and ARIADNE and king of the island of CHIOS which was a wine-growing area. The island was colonized by Oenopion, who originally came from Crete. ORION, the giant, wanted to marry MEROPE (2), daughter of Oenopion, but her father kept putting off the wedding, and Orion raped her. In revenge, Oenopion blinded Orion and banished him. Later Orion's sight was restored, and he returned to the island. Anxious for Oenopon's safety, the people of Chios hid him in an underground chamber until Orion left the island,.

Oeonus in Greek mythology, a son of LICYMNIUS. When he was attacked by a dog belonging to the sons of HIPPOCOÖN, he threw a stone at it. In revenge they killed him. In turn his death was avenged by HERACLES, his cousin, who killed Hippocoön and all his sons.

Oeta, Mount a mountain range northeast of AETOLIA which HERACLES climbed to get to his funeral pyre when he was dying.

Ogyges *see* **Ogygus**.

Ogygia in Greek mythology, the name given by Homer in the *Odyssey* to the island inhabited by the nymph CALYPSO. He describes it as the central point or navel of the sea, far from all other lands. ODYSSEUS reached it after being borne at sea for eight days and nights after he had escaped from Charybdis (*see* SCYLLA AND CHARYBDIS), and that when he left it again he sailed for seventeen days and nights in an easterly direction until he came to the land of the PHAEACIANS.

Ogygus *or* **Ogyges** in Greek mythology, one of the kings of BOEOTIA and the ruler of the ECTENES, who inhabited the region of THEBES. His people are said to have died of the plague, and some legends indicate that he did also. Thebes was sometimes known as Ogygia.

Oicles in Greek mythology, king of ARCADIA, son of either Mantius or Agrianome and father of AMPHIARAUS.

Oileus in Greek mythology, son of Hodoedocus and Agrianome and one of the ARGONAUTS. He was loved by APOLLO. He was the father of AJAX THE LESS by Eriopis.

Okypete *or* **Ocypete** *see* **Harpies**.

Olenias *see* **Oeneus**.

Olenus a city on the Gulf of Patra of which DEXAMES was one of the kings. Olenus was conquered by OENEUS, king of CALYDON, when Hipponous (2) was king. Oeneus married PERIBOEA(1), daughter of Hipponous.

Olympia a locality in Greece, the scene of the OLYMPIC GAMES, a valley of the River ALPHEUS, lying in the middle portion of the ancient district of ELIS, in the western part of the PELOPONNESUS. As a national sanctuary of the Greeks, collected here were thousands of statues of the gods and of victors in the games, treasure-houses, temples, tombs, and treasures of Greek art.

Olympians in Greek mythology, the gods and goddesses who occupied OLYMPUS.

Olympic Games the great national athletic festivals of the ancient Greeks, so called from being held at OLYMPIA. In legend, they were founded by HERACLES in a celebration of a victory, but their existence is only clearly recorded from 776 BC, when they were established as a national festival, but their origin goes far back beyond that date. They were held every fifth year, or rather in the first month after the lapse of four years from the previous celebration, and lasted five days. In its early days the festival was one of local interest only, organized and taken part in by the Peloponnesians. Later other Greek states were attracted to the games, and the assembly became pan-Hellenic. Women were excluded even from being present, upon pain of death, although it is clear that this rule was not always strictly observed, for women are known to have taken part on some occasions, and to have received the victor's crown. Previous to the games all intending competitors had to spend ten months of severe training. The first day of the festival appears to have been devoted to the offering of sacrifices, and to the classing and arranging of the competitors by the judges, previously sworn to strict impartiality and to the rejection of bribes. On this day there were also contests for the trumpeters. The second day was allotted to boys, who contested in wrestling, boxing, and foot- and horse-racing. Their place was taken on the third day by men, who engaged in similar events. On the fourth day took place the pentathlon, or five-fold contest, the events of which included running, leaping, wrestling, throwing the discus, and throwing the spear. These were followed by horse- and chariot-races, with contests for the heralds. The proceedings terminated on the fifth day with further sacrifices, processions, banquets to the victors, and the presentation of the crowns. These last, the sole rewards, were of no intrinsic value, being merely wreaths of twigs gathered from a sacred olive tree believed to have been planted by HERACLES—which grew in the Altis, but these simple prizes were greatly coveted, and winning them brought much honour.

Olympus the ancient name of several mountains or chains of mountains. The most famous of them was situated between and Macedonia, and was the highest mountain in ancient Greece, its eastern side fronting the sea. It was regarded as the chief abode of the gods, and the palace of ZEUS was supposed to stand on its broad summit. According to legend, it was formerly connected with OSSA but was separated from it by an earthquake, allowing a passage for the River Peneus through the narrow vale of TEMPE to the sea. The abode of the gods was later transferred to heaven.

Omphale in Greek mythology, a queen of LYDIA, a daughter of Iardanus. and mother of Lamus. She became queen of Lydia on marrying Tmolus, king of Lydia, and became queen in her own right on his death. Omphale bought HERACLES when he was sold into slavery. He was involved in many adventures while in her service. He destroyed a huge snake that was wreaking destruction in part of Lydia, he killed the outlaw Syleus and his daughter, and razed the city of the ITONI to the ground. Some legends indicate that Omphale forced him to wear womanish clothes during his servitude. After three years in slavery Heracles was freed by Omphale. According to some legends she married him.

omphalos a sacred stone at DELPHI supposed to mark the centre of the world.

Onca *or* **Onga** in mythology, a Phoenician goddess who was equated with the Greek goddess ATHENA. There was a shrine to Onca at THEBES, the worship of the Phoenician goddess having been brought to Greece by CADMUS.

Onchestus in Greek mythology, a son of POSEIDON and founder of the city of ONCHESTUS.

Onchestus a Boeotian city on Lake Copais. It was celebrated for its grove dedicated to POSEIDON. In this grove there was a fight which led to a long-drawn-out feud between Onchestus and THEBES, a feud which eventually led to the rise of Thebes and the decline of Onchestus. According to one legend, Hippomenes, son of MAGAREUS, a king of Onchestus, won the hand of ATALANTA.

Oncius *or* **Oncus** in Greek mythology, a son of APOLLO and a king of Thelpusa. He gave his horse, ARION, to HERACLES.

Opheltes in Greek mythology, a son of LYCURGUS (3), king of Nemea, and Amphithea or Eurydice (6). His father had been warned by an ORACLE not to put Opheltes on the ground before the child could walk. The child's nurse, HYPSIPYLE, was asked for directions by the SEVEN AGAINST THEBES, and when she was showing them the way to a spring she had to put Opheltes down. She did not lay him on the ground but on a thick bed of parsley. Nevertheless, harm came to the child. He was killed by the snake that guarded the spring. The Seven against Thebes buried Opheltes under the name of Archemorus, a name meaning 'beginning of doom', having been told by a seer, AMPHIARAUS, that the death of the child was the beginning of the path to their destruction. The NEMEAN GAMES were founded in honour of Opheltes by ADRASTUS.

Ophion in Greek mythology, an ancient god whom some legends indicate ruled OLYMPUS with the Oceanid EURYNOME before being defeated by CRONOS and falling into OCEANUS.

Ophiuchus (The Serpent-bearer) one of the ancient northern constellations, representing a man holding a serpent which is twined about him. Legends differ as to the origin of Ophiuchus. Some say it is HERACLES killing a Lydian snake for OMPHALE when he was her slave, others that it is AESCULAPIUS, who was usually depicted with a snake.

Opis *or* **Upis** in Greek mythology, perhaps a name given to ARTEMIS. Opis is said to have been a HYPERBOREAN maiden who went to DELOS with her friend, Arge, at the same time as Artemis and APOLLO. According to some legends, Opis was raped by ORION, who was then killed by Artemis in revenge.

Ops in Roman mythology, a goddess of plenty, equated with the Greek goddess RHEA and with CYBELE.

Opus an ancient city whose inhabitants claimed that DEUCALION (1) and PYRRHA settled there after being saved from the flood.

oracle the response delivered by a deity or supernatural being to a worshipper or inquirer, and also the place where the response was delivered. These responses took the form of divine inspiration, either on a person, as in the dreams of the worshipper in the temples, or by its effect on certain objects, as the tinkling of the cauldrons at DODONA, the rustling of the sacred laurel, the murmuring of streams, or by the actions of sacred animals. Oracles were limited to a particular place and could not be moved. The most renowned of the Greek oracles was the Delphic oracle (*see* DELPHI). Sacrifices were offered by the inquirers, who walked with laurel crowns on their heads and delivered in questions inscribed on lead tablets. The response was deemed infallible and was usually dictated by justice, sound sense, and reason. Other oracles of APOLLO were at Abae in Phocis and in DELOS. Zeus had oracles at OLYMPIA and Dodona, and those of other deities existed elsewhere. There was also a secondary class of oracles of heroic or prophetic persons, the two most celebrated of which were those of the seers AMPHIARAUS and Trophonius. The oracle of Amphiaraus was situated at Oropus in Attica. Those who consulted it fasted a whole day, abstained from wine, sacrificed a ram to Amphiaraus and slept on the skin in the temple, where their destiny was revealed by dreams. The oracle of Trophonius was at Lebadea in BOEOTIA and was given in a cave into which the votary descended, bathed and anointed, holding a honeyed cake.

Orchomenus (1) in Greek mythology, a son of Lycaon, said to have founded the Arcadian towns of ORCHOMENUS (1) and Methydrium.

Orchomenus (2) in Greek mythology, a king of ORCHOMENUS (2). He is in some legends a son of Minyas (*see* MINYANS) and in some is the father of Minyas and son of ZEUS.

Orchomenus (1) an Arcadian city, whose founder is said to have been called after its founder, one of the sons of Lycaon (3).

Orchomenus (2) the principal city of northern BOEOTIA, situated at the northwestern corner of Lake Copais where it was joined by the CEPHISSUS. It was an extremely wealthy city and the centre of MINYAN power. It sent thirty ships to the TROJAN WAR. Its government was thoroughly aristocratic, and was involved in several wars with the democratic THEBES. The rise of Thebes probably contributed to its decline.

Orcus in Roman mythology, a name for PLUTO and for his kingdom.

oread *see* **nymphs**.

Oreithyia in Greek mythology, a daughter of ERECHTHEUS and Praxithea. She was abducted by BOREAS, the north wind, as she danced by the River ILISSUS. He took her to Sarpedon's Rock in THRACE and raped her. She bore him two daughters, Chione and Cleopatra (2), and two sons, ZETES AND CALAÏS.

Orestes in Greek mythology, the son of AGAMEMNON and of CLYTEMNESTRA. When his father was murdered, he was saved from a similar fate by his sister ELECTRA (1). He was sent to Phocis, where he formed an intimate friendship with PYLADES, the son of King Strophius. He was then called upon by the ORACLE at DELPHI to avenge his father, and hastened to MYCENAE, where he slew Clytemnestra and AEGISTHUS. For this murder he was relentlessly pursued by FURIES, and only succeeded in appeasing those terrible goddesses by carrying out the instructions of the Delphic oracle to bring back the statue of ARTEMIS from Tauris to ARGOS. He recovered his father's kingdom at Mycenae, slew NEOPTOLEMUS and married his wife HERMIONE, daughter of MENELAUS, who had been formerly promised to himself. Orestes also ruled over Argos on the death of its king. Orestes is the hero of several Greek tragedies.

orgies secret rites or customs connected with the worship of some gods, such as the secret worship of DEMETER and the festival of DIONYSUS, which was accompanied with many customs of mystic symbolism and much licence. From this comes the modern sense of drunkenness and debauchery.

Orion in Greek mythology, a giant who was a hunter and is said to have been extremely handsome. Legends differ as to his origins but he is held to have been the son of Euryale, daughter of MINOS, and of POSEIDON. He married Side but she boasted that she was more beautiful than HERA and was punished for her arrogance by being sent to HADES. He then went to the island of Chios and asked for MEROPE'S (2) hand in marriage. She was the daughter of the king of Chios, Oenopion. It is said that the king kept postponing the date of the wedding, and Orion raped Merope. In revenge Oenopion blinded him while he slept and banished him from the island. Since his father, Poseidon, had given Orion the power to walk on the sea he was able to go northwards to Lemnos. There Hephaestus had a smithy, and he gave Orion his servant, Cedalon, to be his guide. Orion carried the boy on his shoulders and asked to be directed east to where the sun rose. There Helios, the sun god, cured his blindness. When he was cured he returned to Chios to exact vengeance on Oenopion, but his people hid him in an underground chamber. Failing to find his enemy, Orion went off to Crete to hunt with Artemis. There are various and differing legends about the relationship between Orion and Artemis. According to one she fell in love with him. Apollo, brother of Artemis, resented this and tricked Artemis into shooting with an arrow what seemed to be a black object floating on the surface of the sea. It was in fact the head of Orion swimming in the sea, and she killed him accidentally. Artemis is then said to have placed Orion in the sky as a constellation in recognition of their friendship. According to other legends, Artemis shot Orion for challenging her to a game of quoits or for trying to rape either her or the Hypo-borean maiden Opis. In another legendary explanation of his death, Orion is stung to death by a giant scorpion that Ge sent to punish him for boasting that he could kill all animals on the earth. After his death Artemis asked Zeus to place him in the sky as the constellation which bears his name. The constellation is considered to represent the figure of a man with a sword hanging from his belt. The principal stars are four, forming a large quadrilateral representing the right and left shoulders, right knee and left foot, and three in a slanting line representing the belt. The middle star in the sword is a mutiple star, surrounded by the Great Nebula. Being a hunter, Orion is accompanied by a dog, the constellation Canis Major.

Ornytion *see* **Corinth**.

Orpheus in Greek mythology, a hero and legendary singer, the chief representative of the art of song. He is also represented as the founder of a religious sect. Orpheus was the son of OEAGRUS, king of THRACE, or of APOLLO, and the Muse CALLIOPE. He is credited with the application of music to the worship of the gods. Some legends indicate that Apollo taught him to play the lyre and others that it was the MUSES. In either event he played it so well so that he moved not only people and the beasts, but the woods and rocks with its melody. Orpheus is at the centre of a number of legends. In one, having lost his wife Eurydice (1) by the bite of a serpent, he descended to HADES to try and get her back. His music so moved the infernal deities Hades and PERSEPHONE that they allowed her to return to earth, on condition that her husband, whom she was to follow, would not look back until they had reached the upper world. Love or doubt, however, drew his eyes towards her, and she was lost to him for ever. His death is sudden and violent. According to some accounts, it was the thunderbolt of ZEUS that killed him because he revealed the divine MYSTERIES. According to others, it was DIONYSUS, who, angry at Orpheus refusing to worship him, caused the MAENADS to tear him to pieces, which pieces were collected and buried by the Muses at the foot of OLYMPUS. Others again said he met his death at the hands of a band of furious Thracian women who divided his limbs between them, either from excessive madness of unrequited love or from anger at his drawing their husbands away from them. In another legend he is represented as one of the ARGONAUTS. He is said to have kept the rest of the Argonauts from being too unruly by his playing, He introduced the Argonauts to the Samothracian mysteries on the outward journey and on the return journey drowned out with the playing of his lyre the singing of the SIRENS guaranteed to seduce all sailors.

Orseis *see* **Dorus**; **Xuthus**.

Orthus *or* **Orthrus** in Greek mythology, a two-headed dog and an offspring of TYPHON and ECHIDNA. In company with his master, Eurytion (3), he guarded the cattle of GERYON in Erytheia. HERACLES killed both Orthus and Eurytion and stole the cattle.

Ortygia the original name of the island of DELOS or the name of an island nearby it.

Ossa, Mount the ancient name of a mountain in MAGNESIA on the east side of THESSALY, near PELION and separated from OLYMPUS by the vale of TEMPE. In Greek mythology, Ossa was the seat of the CENTAURS and GIANTS and was one of the three mountains that OTUS AND EPHIALTES piled up to form a structure that would enable them to storm heaven.

Otreus in Greek mythology, a king of PHRYGIA who fought with PRIAM of Troy against the AMAZONS.

Otus and Ephialtes in Greek mythology, twin giants, sons of IPHIMEDEIA, daughter of TRIOPAS (1), and wife of ALOEUS. She fell in love with his father, POSEIDON, and poured water into her lap until she conceived her two sons. The twins were not only very large and very strong but they were very arrogant and unruly. They tried to storm heaven by heaping Mount OSSA on Mount OLYMPUS and Mount PELION on Mount Ossa, They also captured ARES, the god of war, and kept him in a brass jar. He was eventually rescued by HERMES. As punishment for their behaviour one legend indicates that APOLLO shot them. Another indicates that Apollo sent a deer between them and that while trying to pierce the deer with their spears, they killed each other instead. They founded the city of Ascra at the base of Mount HELICON and may have been the first to worship the MUSES, although these were then three in number, not nine. In HADES the twins continued to be punished for their misdeeds and were bound back to back with snakes to a pillar on which a screech owl sat.

Ourea *see* **Ge.**

Ovid (Publius Ovidius Naso), Roman poet, born 43 BC, died AD 17. His best-known work is the *Metamorphoses*, a long poem that relates all the mythological tales which have to do with TRANSFORMATIONS. It begins with the transformation of CHAOS into

Cosmos, and ends with the metamorphosis of Julius Caesar into a star.

Oxylus in Greek mythology, a king of ELIS and son of Andraemon or of HAEMON. He was a native of Aetolia but was banished from his native land for killing his brother Thermius or else a man named Allcidocus. During the invasion of Pelopennsus the leaders of the HERACLID, the sons of Aristomachus, engaged him as a guide on condition that he was rewarded with the kingship of Elis. There was already a king of Elis, DIUS, but he agreed to let the rights to the throne be decided by the outcome of a single combat between an Aetolian slinger, Pyrchaechmes, on the side of Oxylus and an Eleian archer, Degmenus, on the side of Dius. Pyrchaemes won and so Oxylus was declared king of Elis. On the advice of an oracle, he asked Agorius, great-grandson of ORESTES, a descendant of the famous Elian king PELOPS, to share the throne of Elis, and the city prospered.

P

paean in Greek, a hymn to Apollo or to other gods, or a song in praise of heroes. A paean was sung before a battle in honour of Ares (Mars), and after a victory, in praise of Apollo. The word is derived from Paean, an ancient Greek god of healing, afterwards identified with Apollo. In the hymns to Apollo the phrase *Io paean* was frequently repeated, and hence these hymns were also called *paeans*.

Palamedes *see* **Nauplius** (3); **Oeax**.

Palladium in Greek mythology, a wooden image of Pallas (4) Athene which is said to have fallen from heaven and to have been preserved in Troy. The Trojans believed that their city would be invincible so long as it contained the Palladium. Odysseus and Diomedes (2) stole it and so helped to secure victory for the Greeks. The Romans pretended that it was brought to Italy by Aeneas, and preserved in the temple of Vesta at Rome, but several Greek cities claimed to possess it.

Pallas (1) in Greek mythology, one of the Titans, a son of Crius and Eurybia and brother of Astraeus and Perses (1). He was married to Styx by whom he became the father of Zelus, Cratos, Bia and Nike.

Pallas (2) in Greek mythology, a giant who in a fight with the gods was slain by Athena and flayed by her.

Pallas (3) in Greek mythology, a son of the Athenian king Pandion (2) and a brother of Aegeus, Nisus and Lycus. He was slain by his nephew Theseus.

Pallas (4) in Greek mythology, the epithet most commonly applied to Athena, as Pallas Athene. The word may be an early Greek word for a girl.

Pan in Greek mythology, a rural divinity, the god of shepherds, represented as old, with two horns, pointed ears, a goat's beard, goat's tail, and goat's feet. Sometimes he appeared to travellers, startling them with sudden fear, from which has come the word 'panic'. During the heat of the day he would sleep in shady woods and was very angry if his slumber was disturbed by hunters. He was patron of all occupied in the care of cattle and bees, and in hunting and fishing. The worship of Pan originally existed in ARCADIA, and was first introduced into ATHENS after the battle of MARATHON, in which it was asserted that he had assisted the Athenians. His festivals were called by the Greeks Lycoea. He was identified by the Romans with FAUNUS, and his festivals there were known as the Lupercalia. He was afterwards regarded by some philosophers as the all-supporting god of nature, and personified the universe. He is also represented as fond of music and of dancing with the forest NYMPHS and invented the syrinx, or pandean pipes.

Pancratis *see* **Iphimedeia**.

Pandarus in Greek mythology, the leader of the forces of Zeleia in Lycia at the TROJAN WAR. He went to the war on foot as a bowman, being, next to PARIS, the best of the Greek archers.

Pandion *see* **Butes** (3); **Nisus**.

Pandion (1) in Greek mythology, a son of Erichthonius, the king of Athens by the NAIAD Pasithea. He was married to ZEUXIPPE by whom he became the father of PROCNE and PHILOMELA and of the twins ERECHTHEUS and BUTES (3). In a war against LABDACUS, king of Thebes, he called upon TEREUS of Daulis in Phocis for assistance and afterwards rewarded him by giving him his daughter Procne in marriage. It was in his reign that DIONYSUS and DEMETER were said to have come to Attica.

Pandion (2) in Greek mythology, a son of CECROPS and Metiadusa and a king of Athens. Being expelled from Athens by the METIONIDAE, he fled to MEGARA and there married Pylia, the daughter of king PYLAS. When the latter, following a murder, emigrated to PELOPONNESUS, Pandion obtained the government of Megara. He became the father of AEGEUS, PALLAS (3),

NISUS, LYCUS and a natural son, OENEUS, and also of a daughter who was married to SCIRON (2).

Pandora in Greek mythology, the first woman on earth, .made from clay by HEPHAESTUS, and sent by ZEUS to mankind in vengeance for PROMETHEUS's theft of heavenly fire. Each of the gods gave her some gift fatal to man. According to later accounts, the gods gave her a box full of blessings for mankind, but on her opening the box they all flew away, except hope. EPIMETHEUS, brother of Prometheus, married her.

Pangaeus, Mount a mountain in western THRACE where in Greek mythology LYCURGUS (1) was torn to pieces by horses when his treatment of the MAENADS brought famine to the land.

Paphos two ancient cities in Cyprus—Old Paphos, on a hill near the southwestern coast, and New Paphos (modern Baffa), to the northwest and on the shore. APHRODITE was said to have risen from the sea at Old Paphos.

Parcae the Greek name for the FATES.

Paris also called Alexander, in Greek mythology the second son of PRIAM, king of Troy, by HECUBA. His mother dreamed before his birth that she had brought forth a firebrand, which was interpreted to mean that he would cause the destruction of Troy. To prevent this, the child was exposed on Mount IDA, where he was discovered by a shepherd, who brought him up a his own son. Here his grace and courage commended him to the favour of OENONE, a NYMPH of Ida, whom he married. An accident having revealed his parentage, Priam became reconciled to his son. At the marriage of PELEUS and THETIS, a dispute arose whether HERA, ATHENA or APHRODITE was the most beautiful, and as such entitled to the GOLDEN APPLE, Paris was chosen as judge. Hera promised him wealth if she won and Athena promised him military renown and wisdom, but he decided in favour of Aphrodite, who had promised him the fairest woman in the world for this wife—hence the animosity which the other two goddesses later displayed against the Trojans. Subsequently he visited SPARTA, the residence of MENELAUS, who had married

HELEN, the fairest woman of the age, whom Paris persuaded to elope with him. This led to the siege of Troy, at the capture of which he was wounded by a poisoned arrow. He went to Mount Ida to be cured by Oenone, but she avenged herself for his unfailthfulness to her by refusing to help him, and he returned to Troy to die. An arrow from his bow caused the death of ACHILLES. *See also* WOODEN HORSE.

Parmesses *or* **Termessos** in Greek mythology, a river-god, father of AGANIPPE.

Parnassus, Mount a mountain of Greece, situated in Phocis, northwest of Athens. It has two prominent peaks, the higher of which was dedicated to the worship of DIONYSUS. All the rest of the mountain was sacred to APOLLO and the MUSES, while on its southern slope was situated DELPHI and the fountain of CASTALIA.

Parthenon the temple of ATHENA at Athens, situated on the Acropolis and probably the most perfect specimen of Greek architecture.

Parthenopaeus *see* **Idas and Lynceus**.

Parthenos *see* **Virgo**.

Pasiphaë in Greek mythology, the wife of MINOS and mother by the CRETAN BULL of the MINOTAUR.

Patrae the ancient name of Patras, a seaport of Greece, in the northwest of the Morea, on the gulf of the same name. It was one of the twelve cities of the ACHAEAN Confederacy of ancient Greece and is the only survivor. The Gulf of Patras lies between the northwest part of the Morea and northern Greece, and communicates on the east with the Gulf of LEPANTO.

Patroclus in Greek mythology, the friend of ACHILLES, whom he accompanied to the TROJAN WAR. His success was at first brilliant, but, APOLLO having stunned him and rendered him defenceless, he was slain by Euphorbus and HECTOR.

Pegasus in Greek mythology, a winged horse, said to have sprung from the trunk of Medusa when she was slain by PERSEUS. He is said to have received his name because he first appeared beside the springs (*pegai*) of OCEANUS. He afterwards ascended to heaven to carry the thunder and lightning of ZEUS. BELLEROPHON had sought in vain to catch Pegasus for his combat with the CHIMAERA, and at length was advised by the seer Polyidus (2) of Corinth to sleep in the temple of MINERVA. The goddess appeared to him in his sleep and gave him a golden bridle with which he caught him and with his help overcame the Chimaera. Later writers made Pegasus the horse of the MUSES, as he had created the sacred well HIPPOCRENE, on Mount HELICON, with a single kick of his hoof.

Peiras *see* **Echidna**.

Peirene *see* **Gorgophone**.

Peirithous in Greek mythology, a king of the LAPITHS and a son of IXION by DIA. He waged a war against the CENTAURS and helped THESEUS carry off the AMAZON Antiope and later HELEN. He tried to carry off PERSEPHONE, queen of the underworld, and was bound with chains to a stone seat by her husband HADES. He remained a prisoner in the underworld.

Pelasgians the earliest inhabitants of Greece and the islands. They were succeeded by the HELLENES.

Pelasgus in Greek mythology, the mythical ancestor of the PELASGIANS, different origins being accorded to him in different parts of the country occupied by the Pelasgians. To the Arcadians he was either an autochthon or a son of ZEUS by NIOBE (2) and became the father of LYCAON (1) by the OCEANID Meliboea, the NYMPH Cyllene or DEÏANEIRA. In ARGOS he was believed to have been a son of TRIOPAS (1) and Sois and a brother of Iasus, Agenor and Xanthus, or a son of PHORONEUS. The ARGIVES also believed that he taught the people agriculture and that he received DEMETER at Argos on her wanderings. In THESSALY Pelasgus was described as the father of Chlorus or as the father or grandfather of HAEMON or again as a son of POSEIDON and Larissa.

Peleus in Greek mythology, a king of Phthia in THESSALY. He was a son of AEACUS, king of AEGINA and Endeis. He and his brother

TELAMON killed their half-brother and were banished by their father when he discovered the crime. He went to Phthia, where he was purified of his crime and married ANTIGONE (2), daughter of the king, EURYTION (1). He joined the CALYDONIAN BOAR hunt with his father-in-law and accidentally killed him. He did not go back to Phthia for fear of what would happen. Instead he went to IOLCUS and was purified by King ACASTUS. He repelled the advances of the wife of ACASTUS, and she sent word to Antigone that Peleus was going to marry Acastus's daughter, Sterope. Antigone killed herself. Acastus was told by his wife that Peleus had tried to rape her, and Acastus plotted to get rid of him. He contrived to leave him unarmed on Mount PELION, where the CENTAURS would get him, but CHIRON, king of the Centaurs, spared his life. He later killed Astydamia, wife of Acastus, and returned to Phthia where he became king.

Pelion, Mount a mountain of ancient Greece, in THESSALY, near the sea. In Greek mythology, in the war of the TITANS with the gods the former piled Pelion upon OSSA to aid them in climbing to OLYMPUS.

Pelias in Greek mythology, a king of IOLCUS who became one of the most powerful Greek kings of his time and had rather a violent nature. He killed his half-brother, AESON, and banished his brother NELEUS to get the throne. He was killed by JASON, son of Neleus, after he had tricked him into going on the quest for the GOLDEN FLEECE.

Pellonia in Roman mythology, a goddess who was believed to assist mortals in warding off their enemies.

Pelopia *see* **Atreus**.

Peloponnesus the peninsula which formed the southern part of ancient Greece, HELLAS proper being north of the isthmus of Corinth. Among its most important cities were SPARTA and ARGOS. After war with MESSENIA, Sparta acquired supremacy over the others states and disputed the supremacy with ATHENS in the Peloponnesian War.

Pelops in Greek mythology, son of TANTALUS, king of LYDIA. He married HIPPODAMIA, a daughter of King OENOMAUS of Elis, and succeeded his father-in-law in that kingdom by conquering him in a chariot race, establishing the house of AGAMEMNON. PELOPONNESUS received its name from him. Of his sons by Hippodamia, ATREUS and THYESTES are the most famous.

Pelor *see* **Sparti**.

penates *or* **di penates** in Roman mythology, gods of the storeroom and kitchen. The images of these gods were kept in the *penetralia*, or central part of every house, each family having its own penates and the state its public penates. The LARES were included among the penates but were not the only penates, for each family had generally only one lar whereas the penates are usually spoken of in the plural. Their worship was closely connected with that of VESTA.

Penelope in Greek mythology, the wife of ODYSSEUS and mother of TELEMACHUS. During the protracted absence of Odysseus, he was generally regarded as dead, and Penelope was surrounded by a host of suitors, whom she put off on the pretext that before she could make up her mind she must first finish a shroud that she was weaving for her aged father-in-law, LAERTES. To gain time, she undid by night the work she had done by day. When the suitors had discovered this device, her position became more difficult than before, but fortunately Odysseus returned in time to rescue her and slay the importunate wooers who had been living riotously and wasting his property.

Penthesilea *see* **Amazons**.

Pentheus in Greek mythology, a son of ECHION (1) and AGAVE, and successor of CADMUS as king of Thebes, formerly Cadmeia. He refused to do homage to DIONYSUS and refused to allow the women of the country to join in the revels of the bacchants. He was pulled to pieces by his mother and her sisters, who in a fit of madness thought he was a wild boar.

Penthilus in Greek mythology, a son of ORESTES and ERIGONE (2), who is said to have led a colony of AEOLIANS to THRACE.

Pereus *see* **Elatus**.

Periboea (1) in Greek mythology, a daughter of Hipponous, king of Olenus, and wife of OENEUS. She was the mother of Olenias and possibly of TYDEUS.

Periboea (2) *or* **Merope** in Greek mythology, wife of POLYBUS and the foster-mother of OEDIPUS.

Periclymenus *see* **Neleus**.

Perieres a king of MESSENIA and husband of GORGOPHONE, daughter of PERSEUS, by whom he had two sons, APHAREUS and LEUCIPPUS (1). He was also the father of BORUS and Pisus. Some legends make him the father of TYNDAREUS and ICARIUS (1), but others indicate that these were the offspring of Gorgophone by her second husband, OEBALUS.

Perileus *or* **Perilaus** *see* **Icarius** (1).

Pero (1) in Greek mythology, the mother of the river-god ASOPUS by POSEIDON.

Pero (2) in Greek mythology, a daughter of NELEUS and Chloris, who was married to BIAS and celebrated for her beauty.

Peroboea *see* **Icarius** (1).

Perse in Greek mythology, a daughter of OCEANUS and wife of HELIOS, by whom she became the father of AEËTES and CIRCE. She is sometimes called the mother of PASIPHAË.

Persephone in Greek mythology, a goddess of the underworld, the only child of ZEUS and DEMETER. She was abducted by HADES and was found by Demeter after an unceasing quest, but she had to remain a third of the year with Hades and the rest of the year with her mother. In Roman mythology she is called PROSERPINE.

Perses (1) in Greek mythology, a son of the TITAN Crius and Erybia, and husband of Asteria by whom he became the father of HECATE.

Perses (2) in Greek mythology, a son of PERSEUS and ANDROMEDA who is described as the founder of the Persian nation.

Perses (3) in Greek mythology, a son of HELIOS and PERSE and brother of AEËTES and CIRCE.

Perseus in Greek mythology, king of MYCENAE and TIRYNS and son of ZEUS and DANAË. Perseus promised to bring the head of the GORGON Medusa to King POLYDECTES. It was a virtually impossible task because escape after an attack was impossible since her sisters could fly. With the help of NYMPHS who gave him a pair of winged sandals and a cap of darkness which made him invisible. He received a sword of adamant from HERMES. Polydectes and his court were turned to stone when he brought the head back.

Phaea *see* **Crommyonian Sow**.

Phaeacians in Greek mythology, a seafaring people who lived on the island of Scherie or DREPANE. They were led there by their king, NAUSITHOUS, a son of POSEIDON, after being driven out of Hypereia by the CYCLOPS.

Phaedra in Greek mythology, a daughter of MINOS, king of Crete, and Pasiphaë. Her unrequited love for HIPPOLYTUS, son of THESEUS, led to his death and her suicide.

Phaethon (1) a frequent title of HELIOS and subsequently used as his name.

Phaethon (2) in Greek mythology, a son of HELIOS, famous for his unfortunate attempt to drive his father's chariot. Scarcely had he seized the reins than the horses, perceiving his weakness, ran off and, approaching too near Earth, almost set it on fire. Earth cried to ZEUS for help, and he struck down Phaethon with a thunderbolt into the ERIDANUS or Po. His sisters, the Heliades, who had harnessed the horses of the Sun, were changed into poplars and their tears into amber.

Phalces *see* **Deïphontes**.

Pherae an ancient city of THESSALY, near Mount PELION. In Greek mythology, it was the royal seat of ADMETUS and ALCESTIS, and afterwards, under the rule of tyrants, became a controlling power of the whole of Thessaly, and for long made its influence felt in the affairs of Greece.

Pheres *see* **Jason**.

Philoctetes in Greek mythology, a famous archer, the friend and armour-bearer of HERACLES, who bequeathed him his bow and poisoned arrows. As one of the suitors of HELEN, he led seven ships against TROY, but being bitten in the foot by a snake (or, according to one story, wounded by his own arrows), he fell ill. As his wound gave forth an unendurable stench, the Greeks left him on the island of LEMNOS, where for ten years he spent a miserable life. But an oracle declared that Troy could not be taken without the arrows of Heracles, so ODYSSEUS and NEOPTOLEMUS were despatched to bring Philoctetes to the Greek camp where, healed by AESCULAPIUS or his sons, the restored hero slew PARIS and helped powerfully in the taking of Troy. After the war he settled in Italy.

Philomela or **Philomena** in Greek mythology, a daughter of PANDION and ZEUXIPPE who, after being raped by her brother-in-law TEREUS was metamorphosed into a nightingale or swallow.

Philomelus in Greek mythology, a son of IASION and DEMETER and brother of PLUTUS. He is said to have invented the wagon. As a reward for his ingenuity his mother, on his death, placed him in the sky as the constellation BOÖTES.

Philonoë in Greek mythology, a daughter of IOBATE, king of Lycia, and wife of BELLEROPHON.

Philyra in Greek mythology, a daughter of OCEANUS and TETHYS, who bore a child by CRONOS. Her son was CHIRON, who had the body of a horse from the waist down. He became king of the CENTAURS. Philyra was so ashamed at the sight of her son that she asked ZEUS to turn her into a tree, and she became a linden tree.

Phineus in Greek mythology, king of Salmydessus and husband of CLEOPATRA (2), daughter of BOREAS. His second wife, IDAEA, made him torture or blind his sons by Cleopatra, and they were rescued by the ARGONAUTS. Phineus may have been blinded as a punishment by them, but he may already have been blind. He is noted for having his food snatched away by the HARPIES every time that he tried to eat.

Phlegyas in Greek mythology, a son of ARES and a very warlike leader. He became king of Andreis, later ORCHOMENUS (2), and called the region Phlegyantis. He was killed by NYCTEUS.

Phocis one of the original states of ancient Greece, west of BOEOTIA in northern Greece. The greater part of it consisted of the mountain range of PARNASSUS and it possessed the famous oracle of DELPHI. The Phocians waged the Sacred or Phocian War over the use of a piece of land belonging to the temple of Delphi, but it ended disastrously for them. Twenty-one of their twenty-two cities were destroyed and the inhabitants parcelled out among the hamlets.

Phoebe (1) an epithet of ARTEMIS.

Phoebe (2) in Greek mythology, a female TITAN, a daughter of URANUS and GE. She was the mother of LETO and ASTERIA by her brother Coeus.

Phoebus an epithet, and subsequently a name, of APOLLO. It referred both to the youthful beauty of the god and to the radiance of the sun when latterly Apollo became identified with HELIOS.

Phoenix in Greek mythology, a king of the Dolopians. As a young man he took part in the CALYDONIAN BOAR hunt and was in charge of the young ACHILLES. As an old man, he accompanied Achilles to the TROJAN WAR, having persuaded him to join the battle, and tried to persuade him to rejoin the war after he quarrelled with AGAMEMNON and withdrew. He remained with Achilles, and at the end of the war set out for home with NEOPTOLEMUS, son of Achilles.

Phoetusa in Greek mythology, daughter of HELIOS and NEAERA.

Phorbas (1) in Greek mythology, a king of THESSALY, According to some legends he was immortalized as the constellation OPIUCHUS, the Serpent-bearer.

Phorbas (2) *see* **Augeas**.

Phorcys in Greek mythology, a sea-god, a son of Pontus and GE. By his sister CETO, a sea monster, he fathered a series of monsters, such as the Gorgon ECHIDNA, and LADON, the snake. He may have fathered SCYLLA (2).

Phoroneus in Greek mythology, a son of INACHUS, a river-god. The city of ARGOS was originally called Phoronea after him. He was the father of NIOBE (2) and Car, the founder of MEGARA.

The ARGIVES claimed that he, and not PROMETHEUS, discovered fire.

Phrixus in Greek mythology, a son of ATHAMAS and NEPHELE. His father's second wife, INO, forced her husband to sacrifice his son, but just as the boy was about to die, a ram with a GOLDEN FLEECE appeared and carried off him and his sister, HELLE. Phrixus reached Aea, capital of Colchis, and the ram told him to sacrifice it and hang its golden fleece on an oak tree in a grove sacred to ARES. This fleece was the object of JASON's quest for the golden fleece. *See* HELLESPONT.

Phrygia in ancient geography, a country in Asia Minor, stretching along the shores of the HELLESPONT and Troad. Its early history is mythological, with GORDIUS and MIDAS as its kings. On the death of ADRASTUS, the royal family became extinct, and it became a province of LYDIA.

Phthia the principal city of PHTHIOTIS or ACHEA in southern Thessaly and the adopted home of PELEUS.

Phthiotis the southeast corner of Thessaly and the home of ACHILLES.

Phylacus in Greek mythology, a king of Phylace and father of IPHICLUS and ALCIMEDE, mother of JASON. *See also* MELAMPUS.

Phyleus in Greek mythology, king of Dulichium, who was exiled from his native Elis by his father. He was later given the throne of Elis by HERACLES because of his help in protesting against the treatment of Heracles by AUGEAS, the father of Phyleus. Timandra is said to have deserted ECHEMUS for him.

Phyllis in Greek mythology, a daughter of the Thracian king, Sithon. See DEMOPHON.

Picus an old sylvan deity in Italy, who was represented with the head of a woodpecker and presided over divination.

Pierus in Greek mythology, a king of Pella in Macedonia. The region of Pieria round OLYMPUS is named after him. He was closely associated with the MUSES and introduced worship of them to Thespiae in BOEOTIA. He was the father of HYACINTH by the Muse CLIO.

Pisces (The Fishes) a constellation. The two fish are APHRODITE and EROS, who leapt into the River Euphrates and became fish to escape the monster TYPHON.

Pisus *see* **Perieres.**

Planctae *see* **Wandering Rocks.**

Pleiades the so-called 'seven stars' in the neck of the constellation TAURUS (2). Ancient Greek legends associate the Pleiades with the seven daughters of ATLAS and the NYMPH Pleione, fabled to have been placed as stars in the sky, possibly to save them from pursuit by Orion. Their names are ELECTRA (3), Maia, Taÿgete, Alcyone, Celaeno, Sterope (the invisible star) and MEROPE (1).

Pleïone *see* **Pleiades.**

Pleisthenes *see* **Atreus; Nauplius** (3).

Pleuron in Greek mythology, a son of AETOLUS and Pronoe, and brother of CALYDON, was married to Xanthippe, by whom he became the father of Agenor, Sterope, Stratonice, and Laophonte. He is said to have founded the town of Pleuron in Aetolia.

Pluto in Greek mythology, originally only a surname of HADES, as the giver or possessor of riches, the third son of CRONOS and RHEA, and the brother of ZEUS and RHEA. He obtained the sovereignty of the underworld and ruled the spirits of the dead. He married PERSEPHONE, daughter of DEMETER, after carrying her off from the plains of Enna. He assisted his brothers in their wars against the TITANS, and received from the CYCLOPS, as a reward for delivering them from TARTARUS, the helmet that made him invisible, which he lent to HERMES in the wars against the Titans and to PERSEUS in his fight with the GORGON.

Plutus in Greek mythology, a god of wealth, the son of DEMETER and IASION. He was commonly represented as a boy bearing a cornucopia.

Podarge in Greek mythology, one of the HARPIES and mother of XANTHUS AND BALIUS by ZEPHYRUS.

Podes *see* **Eëtion.**

Pollux *or* **Polydeuces** *see* **Castor and Pollux.**

Polybus in Greek mythology, a king of CORINTH and husband of Merope (3). He was the foster-father of OEDIPUS. *See also* JOCASTA.

Polydectes in Greek mythology, a king of SERIPHOS, son of Magnes (1) and brother of DICTYS. He was turned to stone by PERSEUS.

Polydeuces *see* **Pollux**.

Polydora in Greek mythology, a daughter of PELEUS and ANTIGONE (1) and wife of BORUS. She was the mother of MENESTHEUS by the river-god SPERCHEIUS.

Polydorus in Greek mythology, a son of CADMUS and HARMONIA. He was king of THEBES and husband of Nycteïs by whom he became the father of LABDACUS.

Polyidus (1) *or* **Polyeidus** in Greek mythology, a seer of ARGOS. *See* GLAUCUS (1).

Polyidus (2) in Greek mythology, a seer of CORINTH. *See* PEGASUS.

Polymester *see* **Bistonians**; **Ilione**.

Polynices *or* **Polyneices** in Greek mythology, brother of ANTIGONE (2) and son of OEDIPUS and cursed by him. He and his brother, ETEOCLES, were meant to rule THEBES in alternate years, but Eteocles refused to relinquish the throne, and Polynices sought the help of ADASTRUS, king of Thebes, whose daughter, Argeia, Polynices married. This led to the expedition by the SEVEN AGAINST THEBES. Polynices and Eteocles killed one another in single combat.

Polypemon *see* **Procrustes**.

Polyphemus (1) in Greek mythology, the most famous of the CYCLOPS, who is described as a cannibal giant with one eye in his forehead, living alone in a cave of Mount ETNA and feeding his flocks on that mountain. ODYSSEUS and his companions, having been driven upon the shore by a storm, unwarily took refuge in his cave, and Polyphemus killed and ate four of the strangers. Odysseus, however, intoxicated the monster with wine, and as so on as he fell asleep, forced out his one eye with the blazing end of a stake. He then escaped from the cave with his companions. Polyphemus was the despised lover of the nymph GALATEA.

Polyphemus (2) in Greek mythology, a son of ELATUS (2) and an ARGONAUT. He was abandoned by the Argonauts with HERACLES in Mysia and founded the city of Cius. In his youth he fought against the CENTAURS.

Polypoetes in Greek mythology, brother of DORUS and son of PEIRITHOUS. He was a great warrior, and with Leonteus he led forty ships to the TROJAN WAR.

Polyxo *see* **Helen**.

Pomona in Roman mythology, the goddess of fruit and the wife of VERTUMNUS. She was usually represented with a basket of fruit, or with fruit in her bosom.

Pontus in Greek mythology, a personification of the sea and described as a son of GE and as the father of NEREUS, Thaumas, PHORCYS, CETO and Erybia by his own mother.

Porthaon *or* **Portheus** *see* **Oeneus**.

Poseidon in Greek mythology, son of CRONOS and brother of ZEUS and PLUTO. He was god of the sea, of earthquakes and of horses. The Roman equivalent was NEPTUNE.

Ppeiras *see* **Echidna**.

Praxithea *see* **Oreithyia**.

Priam in Greek mythology, son of LAOMEDON and king of TROY at the time of the TROJAN WAR. His name means 'the ransomed' and was given to him on account of his having been ransomed by his sister HESIONE from HERACLES, into whose hands he had fallen. His second wife was HECUBA, by whom he had many children. The best known of these are HECTOR, PARIS, HELENUS, TROILUS, CREUSA (2) and CASSANDRA. He was too old to take an active part in the war. After Hector's death he went to the tent of ACHILLES to beg the body for burial.

Priapus in Greek mythology, a Phrygian god. of fertility, son of DIONYSUS and APHRODITE. He was represented as being very ugly and SATYR-like with huge genitals.

Procne in Greek mythology, a daughter of King PANDION of Athens and ZEUXIPPE. She was the wife of TEREUS and was changed into a swallow.

Procris in Greek mythology, a daughter of Erechtheus and wife of CEPHALUS. MINOS or ARTEMIS gave her the hound LAELAPS. Because of the anger of PASIPHAË, wife of Minos, she returned to Athens and gave the dog to her husband, Cephalus.

Procrustes ('the Stretcher') in Greek mythology, the surname of a robber of ancient times, named Polypemon or Damastes. He had two beds, one short and the other long, and boasted that they would fit everybody. If his victims were too short for the bed, he stretched them to death, while if they were too tall, he cut off their feet or legs. THESEUS served him in the same way.

Proetus in Greek mythology, a son of Abas and twin brother of Acrisius (*see* DANAË). In a dispute between the two brothers for the kingdom of ARGOS, Proetus was defeated and expelled. He fled to IOBATES in Lycia and married his daughter STHENEBOEA by whom he had three daughters and a son, MEGAPENTHES. Iobates restored Proetus to his kingdom by armed force, and Acrisius then agreed to share it, surrendering TIRYNS to him. When BELLEROPHON came to Proteus to be purified for a murder that he had committed, Stheneboea fell in love with him. As Bellerophon refused to comply with her desire, she charged him before Proetus with having made improper proposals to her. Proetus then sent Bellerophon to Iobates with a letter in which Iobates was asked to murder Bellerophon.

Promachus *see* **Epigoni**.

Prometheus in Greek mythology, one of the TITANS, brother of ATLAS and of EPIMETHEUS, and the father of DEUCALION. His name means 'forethought', as that of his brother Epimetheus signifies 'afterthought'. He gained the enmity of ZEUS by bringing fire from heaven to men, and by conferring other benefits on them. To punish this offence, Zeus caused Prometheus to be chained by HEPHAESTUS on a rock of the Caucasus (the eastern extremity of the world, according to the notions of the earlier

Greeks), where his liver, which was renewed every night, was torn by a vulture or an eagle. He was ultimately saved by HERACLES.

Pronoe *see* **Pleuron.**

Propontis the ancient name of the Sea of Marmara, from being before or in advance of the Pontus Euxinus or BLACK SEA.

Proserpina the Roman name of PERSEPHONE.

Protesilaus *see* **Laodamia.**

Proteus (1) in Greek mythology, king of Egypt who succeeded Pharos. HERMES brought HELEN to him for her protection during the TROJAN WAR. There is some confusion between him and PROTEUS (2), 'the old man of the sea'.

Proteus (2) in Greek mythology, a minor sea-god, sometimes called the 'old man of the sea', who was in charge of POSEIDON's herd of seals. In an effort to persuade Proteus to tell him how to get back to Sparta when he became stranded on the Egyptian island of Pharos after the TROJAN WAR, MENELAUS disguised himself and three of his followers as seals and bound the old man up when he was asleep. Despite changing himself into various shapes, such as a lion, a leopard and a snake, Proteus failed to free himself and was forced to give Menelaus directions. There is some confusion between him and PROTEUS (1).

Psyche in Greek mythology, a beautiful daughter of an unknown king. APHRODITE was jealous of her and asked EROS to make Psyche fall in love with a lowly person. APOLLO's oracle told Psyche's father that she must marry an evil spirit on a lonely mountain top. When she was on the mountain she was wafted by the west wind to a beautiful palace and an unknown lover or husband who always left at dawn. She was not to try to find out his identity. She must not look at his face, Her two older sisters persuaded her that he was a serpent and gave her a light to see him and a knife to kill him. When she looked at Eros he fled, leaving her inconsolable. To punish her, Aphrodite gave her a variety of difficult tasks. Eventually she was overcome by a death-like sleep and ZEUS made her immortal and married her to Eros.

Pterelaus *see* **Electryon**.

Pygmalion in Greek mythology, a king of CYPRUS, who, disgusted with the debaucheries of his countrywomen, took an aversion to the sex. According to Ovid, he made an ivory image of a maiden, fell in love with his own work, and entreated APHRODITE to endow it with life. His prayer was granted, and the maiden became his wife. W.S. Gilbert's drama of *Pygmalion and Galatea* is founded on this story.

Pylades in Greek mythology, son of Strophius (1), king of Phocis, and Anaxabia, the sister of AGAMEMNON, after whose murder by CLYTEMNESTRA, their son ORESTES, being carried secretly to the court of Strophius, formed the friendship with Pylades which has become proverbial. He assisted Orestes in murdering Clytemnestra, and eventually married his sister ELECTRA (1).

Pylas in Greek mythology, a king of MEGARA, who, after having slain his uncle, founded the town of Pylos in PELOPONNESUS and gave Megara to PANDION (2), who had married his daughter Pylia.

Pyramus and Thisbe according to Ovid, young Assyrian lovers who lived next to each other and fell in love. Their parents would not allow them to see each other, and they spoke to each other through a chink in the adjoining wall. One night they decided to disobey their parents and meet at the tomb of King Ninus. Thisbe arrived first but was frightened away by a lioness, which then tore her cloak up with his bloody jaws as she had dropped it while running. Pyramus thought that she had been killed when he arrived and killed himself with his sword. Thisbe returned and also killed herself with his sword.

Pyrchaechmes *see* **Oxylus**.

Pyrrha in Greek mythology, a daughter of EPIMETHEUS and PANDORA, the first mortal-born woman. *See* DEUCALION.

Pyrrhus *see* **Neoptolemus**.

Python in Greek mythology, a dragon that guarded the oracle of DELPHI, a son of GE. He lived in the caves of Mount PARNASSUS but was killed by the infant APOLLO who then took possession of the oracle.

Q

Quirinus in Roman theology, a surname of ROMULUS after he had been raised to the rank of a divinity. Hence Quirinalia, a festival in honour of Romulus, held annually on the thirteenth day before the calends of March, that is, 17th February. Quirinus is the third great god, ranking next to JUPITER and MARS.

R

Races of Man in Greek mythology, the gods created five races of man, the ages in which they lived being called the five ages of man. The first race was a Golden Race living in a GOLDEN AGE under the rule of CRONOS. Members of this race led happy lives and died in peace, becoming on their death guardian spirits of mortals. The next race was a Silver Race living in a Silver Age. Members of this race did not lead such good or contented lives as those of the Golden Age and were so unappreciative of the work of the gods that the OLYMPIANS destroyed them. The next race was a Brazen or Brass Race. This race did not last very long because they were so warlike that they were soon all killed. Next came a race of demigods, who lived in what is called the Heroic Age. It is this age that is most usually celebrated in Greek mythology. The war of the SEVEN AGAINST THEBES and the TROJAN WAR claimed the lives of many of these, and the rest went to live a happy existence in the Islands of the Blessed ruled over by Cronos, who by then had been deposed from OLYMPUS. The fifth race is the present one, the Iron Race, and the worst one, with members of it leading wicked lives. Legend has it that the Iron Race will be destroyed by ZEUS when babies emerge from their mothers' wombs already old. Legend does not indicate whether the end of the iron race would be the end of mankind, the gods having given up on mortals.

Rea Silvia in Roman mythology, the daughter of NUMITOR, king of ALBA Longa and the mother of twin boys, ROMULUS AND REMUS.Their father was MARS, who seduced her although she was a Vestal Virgin (*see* VESTA). She had been appointed a Vestal Virgin because her uncle, AMULIUS, who had deposed her father from the throne, did not wish her to bear any children who would be heirs to the throne and thus prevent his claim to it. When her sons were born, he threw her in prison and put the babies in a basket which was put in the River Tiber in the hope that they would die of exposure. They were saved and suckled by a wolf and reared by the wife of FAUSTULUS, the shepherd who found them by the river.

Regina *see* **Juna**.

reincarnation *see* **metempsychosis**.

Remus *see* **Romulus and Remus**.

Returns, The a name given to the homeward or return journey of the Greek leaders at the end of the TROJAN WAR. The Greek word was *Nostoi*.

Rhadamanthus *or* **Rhadamanthys** in Greek mythology, the son of ZEUS and EUROPA, and brother of MINOS, king of CRETE, whom he assisted in his kingly duties and whose jealousy he aroused by his inflexible integrity, which earned for him the admiration of the Cretans. Because of this jealousy, Rhadamanthus subsequently fled to BOEOTIA, where he married ALCMENE. After his death he became, on account of his supreme love of integrity and justice, one of the three judges of the lower world with Minos and AEACUS.

Rhamnusia in Greek mythology, a name given to the goddess NEMESIS. The name is derived from the town of Rhamnus, a town in ATTICA which was the chief centre of her worship.

Rhea *or* **Rheia** in Greek mythology, one of the female TITANS, the equivalent of the Roman goddess, OPS, the daughter of URANUS and GE, sister and wife of CRONOS, and mother of HESTIA, DEMETER, HERA, HADES, POSEIDON and ZEUS. She received the title of 'Mother of the Gods', and 'Great Mother', being subsequently identified with CYBELE.

Rhesus in Greek mythology, a son of of Strymon, the river-god, and one of the MUSES. He was king of THRACE and an ally of the Trojans against the Greeks. DOLON, the Trojan spy, having been caught by the Greeks, tried to gain favour by taking them to Rhesus's camp, where they killed him and drove off his valuable horses. Dolon's attempts at ingratiating himself were in vain, and he was murdered by the Greeks. After his death Rhesus became an oracular spirit dwelling in caves near the the silver mines of Thrace.

Rhexenor in Greek mythology, a son of NAUSITHOUS, a king of the PHAEACIANS, who was killed by APOLLO.

Rhodas *see* **Triopas** (1).

Rhode *or* **Rhodos** in Greek mythology, a NYMPH and a daughter of POSEIDON and AMPHITRITE, who gave her name to the island of RHODES. She bore seven sons to HELIOS, the sun god, who had claimed the island for his own as it rose from the sea.

Rhodes an island in the Aegean Sea, off the southwest coast of Asia Minor, crossed by a mountain range. Rhodes was much celebrated in antiquity, being called after the NYMPH, RHODE, wife of the sun god, HELIOS, who had claimed the island for his own as it rose from the sea. It was settled by DORIANS from Greece, and the Rhodians soon became an important maritime people.

Rhodope in Greek mythology, the NYMPH of a Thracian well, the wife of HAEMUS and mother of Hebrus. She is mentioned among the playmates of PERSEPHONE.

Rhodope, Mount the ancient name of a range of mountains now situated on the border between Greece and Bulgaria. Its highest peak is Muss Allah. In Greek mythology, it is the mountain from which DIONYSUS threw LYCURGUS (1), the Edonian king, to his panthers below.

Rhone (Rhodanus), River the European river that rises in Switzerland and flows through southern France to the Mediterranean. It was possibly the river that the ARGONAUTS sailed down having sailed up the ERIDANUS, thought to be the modern Po, from the Adriatic. It is thought that they might have taken a wrong route north originally, going by the river Rhine before going by the Rhone.

river-gods in Greek mythology, a DAIMON associated with a river and considered to be the son of OCEANUS and TETHYS. There were some three thousand, the most famous of which are ACHELOUS and ASOPUS. They were represented as vigorous men with beards and a pair of horns on their brows as a symbol of strength.

Roman mythology the body of myths connected with the deities of Rome. Unlike Greek mythology, in early Roman mythology there were no picturesque legends, Roman gods and goddesses betraying fewer of the failings by which those of Greece often sink to human level. The Romans took a more practical and objective approach to religion and religious worship, striking a rural and domestic note and worshipping especially gods of nature, like FAUNUS, and those who shielded the house and family, like the LARES. Every thing and every action had its corresponding deity, even such day-to-day processes as ploughing, harrowing, etc. As Rome grew as a power, however, its mythology began to be created and state deities like JUPITER came to the fore. After Jupiter, the head of the divine world became MARS, the defender of the city, father of ROMULUS and of the Roman people, and QUIRINUS, the deified Romulus. Closer contact with Greece brought the importation and absorption of Greek mythology until the two became totally intermingled.

Rome in modern times the capital city of Italy situated on the River Tiber. In mythology, it was founded by ROMULUS and succeeded LAVINIUM and ALBA Longa as the major city of the region. Rome became a great city but, having no women, the male citizens abducted some women from the Sabine tribe who lived in the mountains. This led to war, and when it was ended the Romans and some of the Sabines joined together to form a single political unit. Power was based in Rome but shared by Romulus and Titus Tatius, the king of the Sabines. Titus was killed as the result of a quarrel, and Romulus reigned alone, although the Sabines retained some control. After the death of Romulus, NUMA POMPILIUS, who was a Sabine, ruled Rome and brought peace and law to a warlike city. The next king, TULLUS HOSTILIUS, was warlike and engaged in several wars. He also forced the people of ALBA Longa to move to Rome. Near the end of his reign, Rome was struck by a great plague. Later kings of Rome included ANCUS MARCIUS and Lucius Tarquinus Priscus, an Etruscan born of a Greek father, who named as his successor Servius Tullus, whose mother had been a Latin captive. He was a good ruler, and Rome flourished, particuarly the common people in it. His son-in-law Lucius Tarquinius Superbus had him assassinated and declared himself king. He reigned for twenty-five years by force. but he was overthrown in an uprising caused by the rape of LUCRETIA by Tarquinius's son Sextus, the rebellion being led by Lucius Junius Brutus. The Romans expelled the Etruscan Tarquins and declared Rome a republic.

Romulus and Remus in Roman mythology, the twin sons of MARS and REA SILVIA, daughter of NUMITOR, who had been appointed as a Vestal Virgin by AMULIUS, her uncle, so that she would not be able to bear children who could be heirs to the throne and prevent Amulius from ruling. When Rea Silvia was made pregnant on being seduced by Mars, Amulius was furious, and her sons were born, he threw her in prison and put the babies in a basket on the River Tiber so that they would die. However, Romulus and Remus were washed up on the shore and were suckled by a wolf until they were rescued by FAUSTULUS, who took them home to his wife Larentia for her to rear them. When they became men, Romulus and Remus were the leaders of a band of shepherds. and were held to be very brave. When their true identity was discovered, Numitor was overjoyed. Romulus and Remus killed Amulius and restored Numitor to the throne. The two brothers then decided to build a new city of their own, but each wanted to call this after himself. The brothers left this difficult decision to the gods, who were to suggest some form of contest. The details of this are unclear, but in any event Remus was killed. According to one legend, Remus was killed by Romulus or one of his men for jumping over the wall that Romulus had just laid out as the wall of his city. On the death of Remus, Romulus built the new city himself and named it Rome after himself. Rome became a great city but, having no women, the male citizens abducted some women from the Sabine tribe who lived in the mountains. This led to war, and when it was ended the Romans and some of the Sabines joined together to form a single political unit. Power was based in Rome but shared by Romulus and Titus Tatius, the king of the Sabines. Titus was killed as the result of a quarrel and Romulus reigned alone again, although the Sabines retained some control.

Rutulians *or* **Rutuli** in Roman mythology, a tribe living in LATIUM who went to war against AENEAS and his TROJAN companions.

S

Sabines *or* **Sabini** an ancient people widely spread in Middle Italy, allied to the LATINS and already an important nation prior to the foundation of ROME. Originally they were confined to the mountain districts to the northeast of Rome, and their ancient capital was Amiternum.

Salamis (1) an island of Greece, in the Gulf of Aegina, close to the shore of ATTICA. The island is said to have obtained its name from Salamis, a daughter of ASOPUS. TELAMON, son of AEACUS, fled there after the murder of his half-brother Phocus and became king of the island. His son AJAX accompanied the Greeks with twelve Salmacian ships to the TROJAN WAR.

Salamis (2) *see* **Tiryns**.

Salmacis *see* **Hermaphroditus**.

Salmoneus *see* **Neleus**.

Salus *see* **Hygieia**.

Samos a mountainous Greek island in the Aegean Sea, near the coast of Asia Minor. It was inhabited in antiquity by Ionian Greeks, and had an important position among the Greek communities as early as the seventh century BC.

Samothrace a mountainous Greek island in the north of the Aegean Sea. Homer describes POSEIDON as viewing the events of the TROJAN WAR from its highest point. It was the chief seat of the worship of the CABIRI, and DARDANUS stayed there before he went to Troy.

Sarpedon (1) in Greek mythology, a son of ZEUS and EUROPA, and a brother of MINOS and RHADAMANTHUS. After a quarrel with Minos over MILETUS, he took refuge with Cilix, whom he assisted against the Lycians, and afterwards he became king of the Lycians. ZEUS granted him the privilege of living three generations.

Sarpedon (2) a son of ZEUS and a Lycian prince and grandson of SARPEDON (1). In the TROJAN WAR he was an ally of the Trojans and distinguished himself by his valour. He was slain at Troy by PATROCLUS. APOLLO, at the command of Zeus, cleaned and anointed his body, which was carried to Lycia by Sleep and Death for an honourable burial.

Saturn in Roman mythology, an agricultural god popularly but erroneously identified with the Greek god CRONOS and by a further error sometimes identified with Time. His reign was supposed to have been the GOLDEN AGE. His emblem was a sickle, the origin of Time's scythe.

Saturnalia a festival held by the Romans in honour of SATURN, during which the citizens, with their slaves, gave themselves up to unrestrained freedom and mirth. Under the Caesars it lasted seven days, from 17th to 23rd December. While it continued, no public business could be transacted, the law courts were closed, the schools kept holiday, and slaves were freed from restraint. Masters and slaves even changed places, so that while the servants sat at table, they were waited on by their masters and their guests. In the last days of the festival presents were sent by one friend to another.

satyrs in Greek mythology, a class of woodland divinities. In later times they were inseparably connected with the worship of DIONYSUS (Bacchus) and representing the luxuriant vital powers of nature. The satyrs appear in works of art as half-man and half-goat, having horns on the head, and a hairy body with the feet and tail of a goat. They are often portrayed with a cup or a thyrsus in their hand and shown sleeping, playing musical instruments or dancing with nymphs.

Scamander *or* **Scamandrus** a river rising on Mount IDA and crossing the plain of TROY. In Greek mythology, its river-god was the father of TEUCER and Callirrhoë and grandfather of GANYMEDE.

Sceiron *or* **Sciron** (1) in Greek mythology, a robber who haunted the frontier between ATTICA and Megaris and not only robbed travellers who passed through the country but compelled them, on the Sceironian Rock, to wash his feet, during which operation he kicked them with his feet into the sea. At the foot of the rock there was a tortoise that devoured the bodies of his victims. He was slain by THESEUS in the same manner in which he had killed others.

Sceiron *or* **Sciron** (2) in Greek mythology, a son of PYLAS and grandson of Lelex. He was married to the daughter of PANDION (2) and disputed with her brother NISUS the government of MEGARA. But AEACUS, who was chosen umpire, decided that Nisus should have the government and Sceiron the command in war.

Schedius (1) in Greek mythology, a son of IPHITUS (1) and HIPPOLYTE, who commanded the Phocians in the TROJAN WAR. He was slain by HECTOR.

Schedius (2) in Greek mythology, a son of Perimedes, likewise a Phocian who was killed at TROY by HECTOR.

Scylla (1) in Greek mythology, a daughter of King NISUS of MEGARA, who, because of her love of MINOS cut off the red hair from her father's head and thereby caused his death. When Minos deplored what she had done, she drowned herself. She is often confused with SCYLLA (2).

Scylla (2) **and Charybdis** two rocks in the Strait of MESSINA between Italy and Sicily which were considered highly dangerous to navigators. In Greek mythology, one legend has it that there dwelt in the middle of the rock nearer Italy a fearful monster called Scylla, who barked like a dog, had twelve feet, six long necks and mouths, each of which contained three rows of sharp teeth. The opposite lower rock contained a hugh fig tree under which dwelt Charybdis, who three times every day swallowed the waters of the sea and threw them up again. Another legend says that Scylla was a beautiful maiden who often played with the sea nymphs and was loved by the god GLAUCUS (2). He applied to CIRCE for some means of making her return his love, but Circe was jealous of her and threw magic herbs in the well in which she bathed and so metamorphosed her in such a manner that the upper part of her body remained that of a woman while the lower part was changed into the tail of a fish or serpent surrounded by dogs. Another tradition relates that Scylla was loved by POSEIDON, and that AMPHITRITE, from jealousy, changed her into a monster. HERACLES is said to have killed her because she had stolen some of the oxen of GERYON, but PHORCYS is said to have restored her to life. Charybdis is described as a daughter of Poseidon and GE, and as a voracious woman who stole oxen from Heracles and was hurled by the thunderbolt of ZEUS into the sea where she retained her voracious nature.

Scyros *or* **Scyrus** (modern Skiros) an island in the Aegean Sea and one of the northern SPORADES. It frequently appears in Greek mythology. Here THETIS concealed ACHILLES in woman's attire among the daughters of LYCOMEDES to save him from the fate that awaited him at TROY. It was here too that Pyrrhus, the son of DEÏDAMEIA (2) by Achilles, was brought up and was fetched from thence by ODYSSEUS to the TROJAN WAR. According to another tradition, Scyros was conquered by Achilles, and this conquest was connected with the death of THESEUS. After Theseus had been driven out of ATHENS, he retired to Scyros, where he was first hospitably received by Lycomedes but was afterwards treacherously hurled into the sea from one of the rocks in the island. It was to revenge his death that PELEUS sent Achilles to conquer the island.

Seilenus *or* **Silenus** in Greek mythology, the foster-father and constant companion of DIONYSUS, and a leader of the SATYRS. He was represented as a robust old man, generally in a state of intoxication and riding on an ass, carrying a cantharus, or bottle.

Seirenes *see* **Sirens**.

Selene in Greek mythology, the goddess of the moon, daughter of HYPERION, and sister of HELIOS (the sun) and Eos (the dawn). She was also called Phoebe, and in later times was identified with Artemis. According to a popular legend, Endymion, her lover, lay sunk in eternal sleep in a cave on Mount Latmos, where he was nightly visited by Selene. In art she is often represented as a beautiful woman with large wings, a long robe, and a coronet.

Selinus *see* **Seilenus**.

Semele in Greek mythology, a daughter of Cadmus by Harmonia, and beloved by Zeus. Jealous of her husband's mistresses, Hera persuaded Semele to entreat her lover to attend her with the same majesty as he approached Hera. As he had sworn to gratify her every wish, Zeus, although horrified at this request, came to her accompanied by lightning and thunderbolts, when Semele was instantly consumed by fire. Dionysus was her son by Zeus. *See also* Agave.

Seriphos *or* **Seriphus** an islet of the Cyclades. In Greek mythology, it is the island where Danaë and Perseus were washed ashore in the chest in which they had been put by Acrisius, where Perseus was brought up, and where he afterwards turned the inhabitants to stone with the Gorgon's head.

Serpent-holder, The *see* **Ophiuchus**.

Servius Tullius the sixth king of Rome. In Roman mythology, he was the son of a slave and was favoured by the gods, especially the goddess Fortuna. During his lifetime she would visit him secretly as his spouse, and after his death his statue was placed in her temple and remained unhurt when the temple itself was once destroyed by fire. He was given as a slave by Tarquinius Priscus to Tanaquil, his wife, who recognized the future destiny of the boy and had him raised as part of the royal family. He married Tarquinius's daughter, and on the death of his father-in-law he was raised to the throne. His reign was noted for the establishment of civil rights and institutions, and he extended and beautified the city.

Seven against Thebes a group of champions under the leadership of Adrastus, king of Argos. With their troops they marched against Thebes with the aim of getting the throne of Thebes back for POLYNICES from his brother ETEOCLES. Eteocles had broken an agreement that, after the deposition of OEDIPUS, Polynices and Eteocles should have the throne of Thebes in alternate years. The force included MECISTEUS, brother of Adastrus, CAPANEUS, nephew of Adastrus, AMPHIARAUS, brother-in-law of Adastrus, Hippomedon, another relative of Adastrus, ETEOCLUS and Parthenopaeus, one of the Arcadian chieftains. These with Adrastus made up the Seven, and they were joined by Polynices himself and Tydeus, son of OENEUS, king of Calydon. When the force marched against Thebes, Adrastus assigned a champion to each of the seven gates of Thebes. As the seer Amphiaraus had foretold, the whole force from Argos was killed, except Adastrus himself. He was carried by his divine horse, ARION, from the field of battle. Capaneus was killed by a thunderbolt from ZEUS when he shouted as he scaled the walls of Thebes that not even the god himself could prevent him from burning the city. Mecisteus and Eteoclus were both killed by Theban champions, Parthenopaeus died when a huge stone crushed his skull, and Tydeus and MELANIPPUS killed each other in single combat. Amphiaraus was saved from death at a Theban's hands when Zeus split the earth with a thunderbolt and swallowed up him and his chariot. Polynices and Eteocles killed each other in single combat, thus fulfilling the curse of their father, Oedipus. With both Polynices and Eteocles dead, their uncle, CREON, became king of Thebes. Ten years later sons of the Seven avenged their fathers as the EPIGONI.

Sextus *see* **Oenoë**.

sibyl in Greek and Roman mythology, the name of certain women endowed by APOLLO with the gift of prophecy. Their number is variously stated, but is generally given as ten. Of these the most celebrated was the Cumaean sibyl (from Cumae in Campania). She was consulted by AENEAS before he descended into the underworld. She is said to have written in Greek verses the collection of prophecies known as the Sibylline books, three of which she sold to TARQUINIUS SUPERBUS.

Sichaeus *or* **Sychaeus** in Greek mythology, a wealthy Phoenician and husband of DIDO, who was treacherously murdered by her brother, who was anxious to secure his treasures.

Sicily the large triangular island at the southwestern extremity of Italy, from which it is separated by the narrow strait of MESSINA. Its highest point is the active volcano of ETNA, in the east of the island. Its earliest inhabitants were the Iberian Sicani, from Iberia (Spain), and the Siculi, from Italy, followed by the Phoenicians and Greeks, who entered the island in the eighth century BC, founded the great cities of Syracuse, Agrigentum and Messina, and spread their influence and culture over the whole island.

Sicinus *see* **Oenoë**.

Sicyon one of the most ancient cities of Greece, said to have existed under the name of AEGIALEIA or Aegiali long before the arrival of PELOPS in Greece. It was also called Mecone, under which it is celebrated as the 'dwelling place of the blessed' and as the spot where PROMETHEUS instituted the Hellenic sacrifices and deceived ZEUS. Its name Aegialeia is said to come from Aegialeius, a son of INACHUS. It was conquered by AGAMEMNON.

Side *see* **Orion**.

Sidero in Greek mythology, the stepmother of TYRO who was killed by PELIAS at the altar of HERA.

Silenus *see* **Seilenus**.

Silvanus *or* **Sylvanus** in Roman mythology, a god of the fields and forests, who is also called the protector of the boundaries of fields. He is represented as carrying the trunk of a cypress. His Greek counterpart is PAN.

Silver Age, Silver Race *see* **Races of Man**.

Sinon in Greek mythology, a young relative of ODYSSEUS whom he accompanied to TROY. There Sinon allowed himself to be taken prisoner by the Trojans and opened the WOODEN HORSE.

Sirens *or* **Seirenes** in Greek mythology, sea NYMPHS who by their singing fascinated those who sailed by their island and then destroyed them. When ODYSSEUS approached their island, on the advice of CIRCE he took the precaution of stuffing the ears of his companions with wax, while he bound himself to the mast, and so they escaped. When the ARGONAUTS passed by the Sirens, the Sirens began to sing, but in vain for ORPHEUS rivalled and surpassed them. As it had been decreed that they should live only until someone, hearing their song, should pass by unmoved, they threw themselves into the sea and became formidable rocks.

Sisyphus a mythical king of CORINTH, son of AEOLUS (2) and Enarete. He was married to MEROPE (1) and became by her the father of GLAUCUS (3) and others. He promoted navigation and commerce but was fraudulent and avaricious. For his wickedness he was severely punished in the lower world, being obliged to roll a heavy stone to the top of a hill, on reaching which it would always roll back again, thus rendering his punishment eternal.

Sithon *see* **Demophon**; **Phyllis**.

Smyrna one of the most celebrated and most flourishing cities in Asia Minor, on the Gulf of Smyrna. In mythology, it was founded by an Amazon called Smyrna or Myrrhe, who had previously conquered EPHESUS. It is one of the reputed birthplaces of HOMER.

Sois *see* **Pelasgus**.

Sol *see* **Helios**.

Somnos *or* **Somnus** in Roman mythology, the equivalent of HYPNOS.

Sophocles Greek dramatist born *c*.496 and died *c*.406 BC. He was the most popular of the three great Athenian tragedians, the others being AESCHYLUS and EURIPIDES. His characters are plausible, have recognizable human failings, and their tragic situations have a strong element of pathos. Seven of his many plays are extant, including *Oedipus Rex*, *Oedipus at Colonus* and *Antigone*.

sown men *see* **Sparti**.

Sparta in Greek mythology, a daughter of EUROTAS (1) and wife of Lacedaemon, by whom she became the mother of Amyclas and Eurydice (4). From her the the city of Sparta was believed to have derived its name.

Sparta *or* **Lacedaemon** a city of ancient Greece, the capital of Laconia and of the Spartan state, and the chief city in the Peloponnesus, in the Eurotas Valley. Sparta was a scattered city, actually a union of five villages, and was always unwalled. Unlike Athens, it was plainly built and had few notable public buildings.

Sparti (literally 'the sown men') in Greek mythology, the name given to the armed men who sprang from the dragon's teeth sown by Cadmus and who were believed to be the ancestors of the oldest families in Thebes. They were Echion (1), Udaeus, Chthonius, Hyperenor and Pelor.

Spercheius, River a river in the south of Thessaly. The Dryopians lived along the upper part of its course. In Greek mythology, its river-god became the father of Menestheus by Polydora, the daughter of Peleus, and he is also mentioned in connection with Achilles.

Sphinx in Greek mythology, a daughter of Orthus and Chimaera, or of Typhon and Echidna, or of Typhon and Chimaera, or a natural daughter of Laius. She was a monster renowned for posing an unanswerable riddle that she learnt from the Muses or that Laius taught her. She is represented as having the winged body of a lion and the breast and upper part of a woman. *See also* Jocasta; Oedipus.

Sporades the general name for a group of small islands in the Greek Archipelago, lying scattered to the east of the Cyclades. The principal islands are Scio or Chios, Samos, Cost, Rhodes, Lesbos and Patmos.

Sterope *see* **Peleus**.

Stheneboea *or* **Antaea** in Greek mythology, a daughter of Iobates and wife of Proetus. She was in love with Bellerophon, who later married her sister.

Sthenelas *see* **Tiryns**.

Sthenelus (1) in Greek mythology, a son of PERSEUS and ANDROMEDA and husband of Nicippe, by whom he became the father of Alcinoë, Medusa and EURYSTHEUS. When his brother ELECTRYON was killed by AMPHITRYON, Sthenelus seized Mycenae for himself. He was slain by Hyllus, the son of HERACLES.

Sthenelus (2) in Greek mythology, a son of CAPANEUS and Evadne. He was one of the EPIGONI who took THEBES and commanded the Argives under DIOMEDES (2) in the TROJAN WAR, being the faithful friend and companion of Diomedes. He was one of the Greeks concealed in the WOODEN HORSE, and at the distribution of the booty, he was said to have received an image of a three-eyed ZEUS which was afterwards shown at ARGOS.

Stheno *see* **Gorgons**.

Strophius (1) in Greek mythology, king of Phocis, son of Crisus and father of Astydameia and PYLADES.

Strophius (2) in Greek mythology, son of PYLADES and ELECTRA.

Stymphalus in Greek mythology, a son of ELATUS and Laodice. PELOPS, who was unable to conquer him in war, murdered him by stratagem and cut his body in pieces. For this crime Greece was visited with a famine, which however was averted by the prayer of AEACUS.

Styx in Greek and Roman mythology, the name of the principal river in the lower world, around which it flows seven times. The river is described as a branch of OCEANUS, flowing from its tenth source, and the COCYTUS is a branch of the Styx. Styx is described as a daughter of Oceanus and TETHYS, and as a nymph she dwelt at the entrance of HADES in a lofty grotto that was supported by silver columns. By PALLAS, STYX became the mother of ZELUS, NIKE, BIA and CRATOS. She was the first of the immortals to take her children to ZEUS to help him against the TITANS, and in return her children were allowed to live with Zeus for ever and Styx herself became the divinity by whom the gods took the most solemn oaths. When one of the gods was to take an oath by Styx, IRIS fetched a cup full of water from the Styx, and the god, while taking the oath, poured out the water. Zeus became by her the father of PERSEPHONE and Peiras the father of ECHIDNA.

Sybaris an ancient Greek city of lower Italy, on the Gulf of Tarentum, the first Greek colony, in mythology said to be founded by AJAX. It rapidly rose to an extraordinary degree of prosperity, and the inhabitants were proverbial for their luxury and voluptuousness.

Sychaeus *see* **Sichaeus**.

Symplegades *see* **Clashing Rocks**.

Syrinx in Greek mythology, an Arcadian NYMPH who, being pursued by PAN, fled into the River Ladon, and at her own request was changed into a reed of which Pan then made his pipes.

T

Tages in Roman mythology, a grandson of JUPITER.

Taking of Oechalia, The a lost epic poem which dealt with the capture of EURYTUS's city by HERACLES, his abduction of IOLE, and possibly his death.

Talaus in Greek mythology, a son of BIAS and PERO who sailed with the ARGONAUTS. He was king of ARGOS and father of ADRASTUS, Parthenopaeus, Pronax, Mecisteus, Aristomachus and Eriphyle.

Talthybius in Greek mythology, the chief herald of the Greek forces in the TROJAN WAR. According to legend it was his fate to perform unpleasant duties, such as telling HECUBA that her daughter Polyxena had been sacrificed by the Greeks and going with ODYSSEUS to bring IPHIGENEIA to Aulis, even though she knew that she was to be sacrificed there.

Talus (1) in Greek mythology, a giant made of brass who guarded CRETE. According to some legends he was the last survivor of the brass age (*see* RACES OF MAN).

Talus (2) in Greek mythology, a son of Perdix, the sister of DAEDALUS. He was a disciple of Daedulus and invented several mechanical instruments. Daedalus, incensed by envy, thrust him down the rock of the Acropolis at ATHENS.

Tanaquil the wife of Lucius TARQUINUS PRISCUS, the fifth king of Rome. She was an Etruscan woman who urged her husband to move to Rome to further her ambitions. She was skilled in the art of augury, the observation and interpretation of omens.

Tantalus (1) in Greek mythology, a son of ZEUS, and king of PHRYGIA, LYDIA, ARGOS or CORINTH, who was admitted to the table of the gods, but who had forfeited their favour either by betraying their secrets, by stealing ambrosia from heaven, or by presenting to them his murdered son Pelops as food. His punishment consisted in being placed in a lake whose waters receded from his lips when he attempted to drink, and of being tempted by delicious fruit overhead which withdrew when he attempted to eat. Moreover, a huge rock for ever threatened to fall and crush him.

Tantalus (2) in Greek mythology, a son of Thystes or Broteas. He was the first husband of Clytemnestra before she married Agamemnon.

Taphians the inhabitants of the Taphian Islands and Cephallenia off the coast of Arcarnania who were descended from Poseidon. They were originally called Teleboans and made their living mainly by piracy. When Athena visited Telemachus at Ithaca, she assumed the form of Mentes, the leader of the Taphians.

Taraxippus in Greek mythology, a round altar located near a very dangerous spot on the racecourse at Olympia. The altar was thought to mark a tomb of someone whose ghost haunted the racetrack. Whose ghost it was was not clear although many suggestions were made. Horses were often thrown for no reason near the altar during chariot races, and sacrifices were made at the start of races to propitiate the ghost and ensure the safety of the horses. Taraxippus means 'horse-scarer'.

Tarpeia *see* **Tarpeian Rock**.

Tarpeian Rock a precipitous rock forming part of the Captoline Hill at Rome over which people convicted of treason to the State were hurled. It was so named from Tarpeia, a Vestal Virgin (*see* Vesta) and daughter of the governor of the citadel on the Capitoline, who, coveting the golden bracelets worn by the Sabine soldiers, opened the gate to them on the promise of receiving what they wore on their left arms. Once inside the gate, they threw their shields upon her, instead of the bracelets. She was buried at the base of the Tarpeian Rock.

Tarquinius, Sextus *see* **Tarquinius Superbus**.

Tarquinius Priscus, Lucius the fifth King of Rome, supposed to have reigned from 616 to 578 BC. The family of Tarquinius was said to have been of Greek extraction, his father, Demaratus, being a Corinthian who settled in Tarquinii, one of the chief cities of Etruria. Having removed with a large following to Rome, Tarquinius became the favourite and confidant of the Roman king ANCUS MARTIUS, and at his death was unanimously elected his successor. He made war with success on the LATINS and SABINES, from whom he took numerous towns. His reign was distinguished by the construction of the Cloaca Maxima, the Forum, the wall round the city, and the Capitoline Temple. He was killed by assassins employed by the sons of Ancus Martius.

Tarquinius Superbus, Lucius the last of the legendary kings of Rome, and son of Lucius TARQUINIUS PRISCUS, who reigned from 534 to 510 BC. He abolished the privileges conferred on the plebeians by his father, banished or put to death the senators whom he suspected, never filled up the vacancies in the senate, and rarely consulted that body. He continued the great works of his father, and advanced the power of Rome abroad by wars and alliances. By the marriage of his daughter with Octavius Mamilius of Tusculum, the most powerful of the Latin chiefs, and other political measures, he caused himself to be recognized as the head of the Latin confederacy. In 510 BC, a conspiracy broke out by which Tarquinius and his family were exiled from Rome, an infamous action of his son Sextus being part of the cause of the outbreak (*see* LUCRETIA). He tried repeatedly, without success, to regain his power, and at length died at Cumae in 495 BC.

Tartarus in Greek mythology, a deep and sunless abyss as far below HADES as earth is below Heaven. According to legend an anvil would fall for nine days in order to reach it. It was closed by iron gates, and in it ZEUS imprisoned the rebel TITANS. who had warred with the gods. They were guarded by the HUNDRED-HANDED. Later writers describe Tartarus as the place in which the spirits of the wicked receive their due punishment. Sometimes the name is used as synonymous with Hades, or the lower world in general. It is also used as a personification of the region, who is said to have issued from CHAOS together with GE and EROS. He is said to have been the father by Ge of the monsters TYPHON and ECHIDNA.

Tartessus an ancient city near Gades (now Cadiz) in Spain. HERACLES returned to HELIOS his golden boat here after stealing the cattle of GERYON.

Tatius, Titus a king of the SABINES who led his troops against Rome to take vengeance on the abduction of the Sabine women by the Romans (*see* ROME). At the end of the conflict ROMULUS agreed to share power with Tatius jointly over the Romans and the Sabines.

Taurians the inhabitants of the Tauric Chersonese, the penisula on the north coast of the BLACK SEA, now known as the Crimea. They were at one time ruled by PERSEUS and later by Thoas (2). They were a barbaric people who sacrificed strangers.

Taurus (1) in Greek mythology, a Cretan noble who was the leader of MINOS's navy. He won many prizes for prowess at the Games but was defeated by THESEUS.

Taurus (2) (The Bull) one of the twelve signs of the zodiac and a constellation. Its brightest star represents the eye of the Bull and is named Aldebaran. The bull was placed among the stars to commemorate ZEUS carrying off EUROPA to Crete in the form of a bull. Close by is the group of stars called the HYADES. The constellation also contains the cluster of the PLEIADES.

Taÿgete in Greek mythology, a daughter of ATLAS and the OCEANID Pleione, the nymph of Mount Taÿgetus. ZEUS fell in love with her, and although ARTEMIS turned her into a doe to protect her, Zeus captured her and fathered a child, LACEDAEMON, by her. To thank Artemis for her help, Taÿgete inscribed the golden horns of a doe with the name of the goddess. This doe is said to have been the CERYNITIAN HIND which HERACLES captured as his third labour.

Taÿgetus, Mount a range of mountains that divided MESSENIA from LACONIA. It was named after its resident nymph, TAYŸGETE.

Tegea a city of southeast ARCADIA, the principal city of Arcadia. in early times. It was often in conflict with SPARTA in later times.

Teiresias *or* **Tiresisas** in Greek mythology, a Theban seer who was changed into a woman as a youth when he killed a female snake when it was coupling with its mate. Seven or eight years later he killed a male snake when it was coupling with its mate, and he was turned back into a male. He was called upon by HERA and ZEUS as arbitrator in their dispute as to whether a man or a woman most enjoyed sex since he had experience of being both sexes. He said that women received most satisfaction, and Hera was so annoyed that she blinded him. Zeus was pleased and granted him long life and the gift of prophecy. It was Teiresias who revealed that OEDIPUS was the killer of his father and that he had committed incest with his mother. He died after drinking from the spring of TELPHUSA.

Telamon in Greek mythology, son of AEACUS and a brother of PELEUS. He emigrated from Aegina to SALAMIS and had as his second wife PERIBOEA or Eriboea, a daughter of ALCATHOUS, by whom he became the father of AJAX. He was one of the hunters of the CALYDONIAN BOAR and a member of the ARGONAUTS' expedition. He is said to have been a great friend of HERACLES and to have joined him in his expedition against Laomedon of Troy, which city he was the first to enter. Heracles gave him Theaneira or Hesione, a daughter of LAOMEDON, by whom he became the father of TEUCER and Trambelus. On this expedition Telamon and Heracles also fought against the Meropes in Cos on account of Chalciope, the beautiful daughter of Eurypylus, the king of the Meropes, and against the giant Alcioneus, on the isthmus of Corinth. He also accompanied Heracles on his expedition against the AMAZONS and slew Melanippe.

Telchines in Greek mythology, sorcerers of RHODES. The Telchines were the sons of Thalatta (sea) and the first inhabitants of Rhodes. With the OCEANID, Capheira, they nursed the infant POSEIDON at the request of his mother to prevent his father, CRONOS, from swallowing him. The Telchines could change their shape, and they were able to bring on rain, hail and snow. They are said to have invented the art of making statues of the gods.

Teledice *see* **Niobe** (2).

Telegonus (1) in Greek mythology, the son of ODYSSEUS and CIRCE who killed his father when he was old without knowing who he was until it was too late. He later married PENELOPE.

Telegones (2) *see* **Io**.

Telemachus in Greek mythology, the son of ODYSSEUS and PENELOPE, who was an infant when his father went to TROY, and in his absence of nearly twenty years he grew up to manhood. After the gods in council had determined that Odysseus should return home from the island of Ogygia, ATHENA, assuming the appearance of Mentes, king of the TAPHIANS, went to ITHACA and advised Telemachus to eject the troublesome suitors of his mother from his house and to go to Pylos and SPARTA to gather information concerning his father. Telemachus followed the advice, but the suitors refused to go, and Athena, in the form of Mentes, accompanied Telemachus to Pylos. There they were hospitably received by NESTOR, who also sent his own son to conduct Telemachus to Sparta. MENELAUS received him kindly and communicated to him the prophecy of Proteus concerning Odysseus. From Sparta Telemachus returned home and on his arrival found his father with the swineherd Eumaeus. As Athena had metamorphosed Odysseus into a beggar, Telemachus did not recognize his father until the latter disclosed to him who he was. Father and son now agreed to punish the suitors, and when they were slain or dispersed, Telemachus accompanied his father to the aged LAERTES.

Telephassa *see* **Cadmus**.

Telephus in Greek mythology, a son of HERACLES and Auge, the daughter of King Aleus of TEGEA. He was reared by a hind and educated by King Corythus in ARCADIA. When he had grown up, he consulted the Delphic ORACLE as to who his mother was. He was ordered to go to King TEUTHRAS in MYSIA. There he found his mother and was kindly received. He married Argiope, the daughter of Teuthras, whom he succeeded on the throne of Mysia.

Telethusa *see* **Iphis** (2).

Tellus *or* **Terra** in Greek mythology, the earth and the goddess of the earth, the equivalent of the Greek GE. She is often mentioned in contrast with JUPITER, the god of heaven, and connected with DIS and the MANES.

Telphusa in Greek mythology, a spring near Haliartus in BOEOTIA and the NYMPH of the spring. The spring was the site of an ancient oracle. TEIRESIAS died when he drank Telphusa's water.

Temenus *see* **Deïphontes**.

Tempe, Vale of a valley of Northern Greece, in THESSALY, on the River Peneus, in a gorge between Mount OLYMPUS on the north and Mount OSSA on the south.

Tenedos a Greek island in the Aegean Sea, on the west coast of Asia Minor, southwest of the HELLESPONT. The Greeks are said to have waited there before returning to Troy after the Trojans had taken the WOODEN HORSE into their city.

Tereus in Greek mythology, a son of ARES and king of the Thracians in Daulis, later Phocis, or of Megaris. PANDION (1), king of ATTICA, called on the help of Tereus against an enemy and gave him his daughter PROCNE in marriage. Tereus became by her the father of Itys, and then hid Procne in the country and told her sister PHILOMELA that Procne was dead and so seduced her. When Philomela learned the truth, Tereus took out her tongue. She made the truth known by weaving a message into a peplus that she sent to Procne. Procne then killed her own son, Itys, placed his flesh in a dish before Tereus and fled with her sister. Tereus pursued them with an axe, and when the sisters were overtaken they prayed to the gods to change them into birds. Procne became a nightingale, Philomela a swallow and Tereus a hoopoe.

Termessos *see* **Parmessos**.

Terpsichore in Greek mythology, one of the nine MUSES. She was a daughter of ZEUS and MNEMOSYNE.

Terra *see* **Tellus**.

Tethys in Greek mythology, a female TITAN, a daughter of GE and URANUS. She married her brother OCEANUS and became the mother of all the river-gods and of their three thousand sisters, the OCEANIDS. During the war between the Titans and the gods she took care of her niece HERA in her house at the ends of the earth.

Teucer (1) in Greek mythology, the first king of TROY, a son of the river-god SCAMANDER and IDAEA (1), a NYMPH of Mount Ida. DARDANUS of Samothrace married his daughter BATEIA (1) and was his successor.

Teucer (2) in Greek mythology, son of TELAMON and HESIONE, and the best archer with the Greek forces in the TROJAN WAR. He would have shot HECTOR if ZEUS had not broken his bowstring. On his return from the war, Telamon refused to receive him in SALAMIS because he had not avenged the death of his brother AJAX. Because of a promise of APOLLO, Teucer sailed in search of a new home, which he found in the island of CYPRUS, which was given to him by BELUS, king of Sidon. There he founded the town of Salamis.

Teumissian vixen *see* **Cephalus**; **Laelaps**.

Teuthras in Greek mythology, king of MYSIA, who received Auge, the daughter of Aleus, and brought up her son TELEPHUS. From him the town of Teuthrania in Mysia was believed to have received its name.

Thaleia in Greek mythology, one of the nine MUSES, a daughter of ZEUS and MNEMOSYNE.

Thalia in Greek mythology, one of the GRACES.

Thallo *see* **Horae**.

Thamyris *see* **Hyacinth**.

Thanatos in Greek mythology, death and also the personification of death, the offspring of NYX. He lived with his brother HYPNOS in TARTARUS.

Thasus in Greek mythology, a son of POSEIDON or AGENOR, one of the Phoenicians in search of EUROPA.

Thasus the most northerly island in the Aegean Sea, a few miles south of the Macedonian coast. It was said to be first settled by Phoenecians led by THASUS.

Thaumus in Greek mythology, a son of PONTUS and Ge, and by the Oceanid ELECTRA (4), the father of IRIS and the HARPIES.

Thebes a city of ancient Greece, the principal city of BOEOTIA, midway between the Corinthian Gulf and the Euboean Sea. In Greek mythology, it was founded by CADMUS, was the native city of TEIRESIAS and the reputed birthplace of HERACLES and DIONYSUS. The five SPARTI were the ancestors of its noble families. When Cadmus became old, his grandson PENTHEUS became king, and after his death Cadmus went to Illyria and POLYDORUS became king. Polydorus was succeeded by his son LABDACUS, who left at his death an infant son, LAIUS. The throne was usurped by LYCUS, whose brother NYCTEUS was the father of ANTIOPE (1), who became by ZEUS the mother of twin sons, AMPHION and ZETHUS. Nycteus having died, Antiope was exposed to the persecutions of her uncle Lycus and his cruel wife, Dirce, until at length her two sons revenged her wrongs, became kings of Thebes and fortified the city. After Amphion and Zethus, Laius, father of OEDIPUS, became king of Thebes. When Oedipus was expelled, ETEOCLES and POLYNICES quarrelled for the throne, and this quarrel led to two sieges of Thebes, the SEVEN AGAINST THEBES and the War of the EPIGONI. This second siege was again led by Adastrus and consisted of the sons of the seven heroes of the first. The Epigoni gained a victory and thus became masters of Thebes, placing THERSANDER, son of Polynices on the throne.

Theia in Greek mythology, a female TITAN, a daughter of GE and URANUS. She married her brother HYPERION and was the mother of EOS, HELIOS and SELENE.

Themis in Greek mythology, a female Titan, daughter of Ge and URANUS. She was goddess of order, law and justice among the Greeks. She was the second wife and chief adviser of ZEUS.

Themiste *see* **Ilus**.

Thera (modern Santorini) a volcanic island north of CRETE. In Greek mythology it was said to have grown from a clod of Libyan earth given by TRITON to the ARGONAUT Euphemus, who threw it into the sea from the *Argo*, having been instructed to do so in a dream.

Thermius *see* **Oxylus**.

Thersander in Greek mythology, a son of POLYNICES and Argeia and one of the EPIGONI. After having been made king of THEBES, he went with AGAMEMNON to TROY and was slain in that expedition.

Thersites in Greek mythology, a Greek soldier in the TROJAN WAR noted for his ugliness and for his mocking and criticism of the Greek leaders. ACHILLES killed him and the killing led to a dispute among the Greeks. Achilles sailed to LESBOS to offer sacrifice to APOLLO.

Theseus in Greek mythology, a king of ATHENS and famous hero. He was the unacknowledged son of AEGEUS by AETHRA (1), the daughter of Pittheus of Troezen in PELOPONNESUS, although other traditions say he was the son of POSEIDON and Aethra. Brought up by his mother, when he reached maturity he set off for Athens, taking with him the sword and sandals that had been left with his mother by Aegeus. Eager to emulate HERACLES, he went by land, displaying his prowess by destroying the robbers and monsters that infested the country, including PROCRUSTES and the CROMMYONIAN SOW. At Athens Aegeus recognized Theseus because of the sword he was carrying and acknowledged him as his son and successor. Many notable deeds are told of Theseus, such as the slaying of the MINOTAUR. When the time came when the Athenians had to send to MINOS their tribute of seven youths and seven maidens for the monster, Theseus offered himself as one of the youths. When they arrived at CRETE, ARIADNE, the daughter of MINOS, fell in love with Theseus and gave him a sword, with which he slew the MINOTAUR, and a ball of thread by which he found his way out of the labyrinth. Having rescued the victims, Theseus set sail, carrying off Ariadne. Most myths speak of Theseus as losing or abandoning Ariadne on the island of Naxos. He was generally believed to have had by her two sons, Oenopion and Staphylus. As the vessel in which they sailed approached ATTICA, they neglected to hoist the white sail that was to have been the signal that the expedition had had a successful end, an omission that led to the death of Aegeus. Another adventure was his expedition against the AMAZONS. He is said to have assailed them before they had recovered from the attack of Heracles and to have carried off their queen, ANTIOPE. The Amazons in their turn invaded Attica and penetrated into Athens itself, the final battle in which Theseus overcame them being fought in the middle of the city. By Antiope Theseus was said to have had a son, HIPPOLYTUS or Demophon, and after her death to have married PHAEDRA. Theseus figures in almost all the ancient heroic undertakings. He was one of the ARGONAUTS, he joined in the hunt of the CALYDONIAN BOAR, and aided ADRASTUS in recovering the bodies of those slain at THEBES. He had a close friendship with PEIRITHOUS and helped him against the CENTAURS. Aided by Peirithous, he carried off HELEN from SPARTA while she was a girl and placed her in the care of Aethra. In return he assisted Peirithous in his attempt to carry off PERSEPHONE from the lower world. Peirithous perished in the enterprise, and Theseus was kept imprisoned until rescued by Heracles. Meanwhile, CASTOR AND POLLUX had invaded Attica and carried off Helen and Aethra. MENESTHEUS also tried to incite the people against Theseus, who on his return found himself unable to re-establish his authority and retired to Scyros, where he met a treacherous end at the hands of LYCOMEDES.

Thesprotus *see* **Atreus**.

Thessalus in Greek mythology, a son of JASON and MEDEA. who managed to escape the murder that befell his brother.

Thessaly a northeastern area of Greece, mainly consisting of a rich plain enclosed between mountains and belonging almost entirely to the basin of the River Peneus which traverses it from west to east, and falls into the Aegean through the Vale of TEMPE. Its major cities in ancient times were Larissa, Pharsalus and Pherae, which were frequently at feud with one another.

Thestius *see* **Althaea**; **Oeneus**.

Thestor *see* **Calcas**.

Thetis *or* **Thetys** in Greek mythology, a divinity, a daughter of NEREUS and Doris, and therefore one of the NEREIDS. She was brought up by HERA and when she reached maturity, ZEUS and Hera gave her, against her will, in marriage to PELEUS, by whom she became the mother of ACHILLES. POSEIDON and Zeus himself are said to have sued for her hand, but when THEMIS declared that the son of Thetis would be more illustrious than his father, both suitors desisted. Her nuptials with Peleus were celebrated on Mount PELION and were honoured by the presence of all the gods except ERIS or Discord, who was not invited and who, to avenge the slight, threw in among them the GOLDEN APPLE of discord.

Thisbe *see* **Pyramus**.

Thoas (1) in Greek mythology, a son of ANDRAEMON (1) and GORGE and king of Calydon and Pleuron in AETOLIA. He went with forty ships against Troy in the TROJAN WAR.

Thoas (2) in Greek mythology, a son of Borysthenes and king of the TAURIANS, into whose dominions IPHGENIA was carried by ARTEMIS when she was to have been sacrificed.

Thrace the south-easternmost region of Europe, separated from Asia by the Propontis, and its two narrow channels, the Bosporus and the HELLESPONT. From earliest historic times Thrace was a convenient ground for contending kings, statesmen and nations to settle their differences by the sword, and, as a highway out of the east into the west, it passed under the sway of many rulers. For the Greeks, who founded a number of maritime settlements but did not attempt to explore the hinterland, Thrace was a barren northern land and formed, with EUROPA, Libya and Asia, the whole of the known world. The designation was subsquently narrowed down to embrace only the region south of the Haemus mountain chain, and east and northeast of Macedonia.

Thyestes in Greek mythology, son of PELOPS and HIPPODAMIA, and grandson of TANTALUS (1). He seduced the wife of his brother ATREUS, who, in revenge, served up to him the body of his own son at a feast.

Thynius *see* **Idaea** (1).

thyrsus a pole which was carried by MAENADS and SATYRS while taking part in revels associated with DIONYSUS. It was tipped with a pine cone and was twined with ivy or grapevine.

Tiber, River a river of Italy, rising in the Apennines in Tuscany, and flowing into the Mediterranean. It traverses the city of Rome.

Timandra *see* **Echemus**; **Phyleus**.

Tiphys in Greek mythology, a son of Agnius or of Phorbas and Hyrmine, of Siphae or Tiphae in BOEOTIA, was the helmsman of the *Argo* on the ARGONAUTS' expedition.

Tiresias *see* **Teiresias**.

Tiryns a very ancient ruined city of Greece, in the PELOPONNESUS, in the plain of Argolis, near the sea. In Greek mythology, it derived its name from Tiryns, the son of ARGOS, and its foundation was ascribed to PROETUS. MEGAPENTHES, the son of Proetus, ceded Tiryns to PERSEUS, who transmitted it to ELECTRYON. ALCMENE, the daughter of Electryon, married AMPHITRYON, who succeeded to the crown but was expelled by Sthenelas, king of Argos. Their son HERACLES afterwards regained possession of Tiryns, where he lived for many years.

Tisiphone in Greek mythology, one of the three FURIES, the others being Alecto and Megaera.

Titans in Greek mythology, the sons and daughters of URANUS (Heaven) and GE (Earth). They were twelve in number, six sons and six daughters. They were OCEANUS, Coeus, Crius, HYPERION, IAPETUS, CRONOS, THEIA, RHEA, THEMIS, MNEMOSYNE, PHOEBE (2) and TETHYS. Uranus, the first ruler of the world, threw his sons, the HUNDRED-HANDED (BRIAREUS, Cottus, Gyes) and the

Cyclops (Arges, Steropes and Brontes), into Tartarus. Ge, indignant at this, persuaded the Titans, except Oceanus, to rise against their father. Cronos castrated Uranus and threw the part into the sea and from the drops of his blood arose the Furies. The Titans then deposed Uranus, liberated their brothers from Tartarus and raised Cronos to the throne. But he again threw the Cyclops into Tartarus and married his sister Rhea. He had been foretold by Ge and Uranus, however, that he would be dethroned by one of his own children, so after their birth he swallowed successively his children Hestia, Demeter, Hera, Pluto and Poseidon. When Rhea became pregnant with Zeus, she went to Crete, gave birth to the child in a cave in Mount Dicte and entrusted him to the Curetes and the daughters of Melisseus, the nymphs Adrasteia and Ida, to be brought up. The armed Curetes guarded the infant and struck their shields with their spears so that Cronos could not hear the voice of the child. Rhea gave Cronos a stone wrapped in cloth which he swallowed, believing it be be his newly born son. When Zeus had grown up, he called on the help of Thetis, the daughter of Oceanus, who gave Cronos a potion which caused him to bring up the stone and the children he had swallowed. United with his brothers and sisters, Zeus now waged war against Cronos and the ruling Titans. This war was carried on in Thessaly, the Titans occupying Mount Othrys and the sons of Cronos Mount Olympus, and lasted ten years. At length, Ge promised Zeus victory if he would deliver the Cyclops and the Hundred-handed from Tartarus. Zeus accordingly slew Campe, who guarded the Cyclops, and the latter provided him with thunder and lightning. Pluto gave him a helmet and Poseidon a trident. The Titans were then overcome and hurled down into a cavity below Tartarus.

Tithonus in Greek mythology, a son of Laomedon and brother of Priam. By the prayers of Eos, who loved him, he obtained from the gods immortality but not eternal youth, in consequence of which he completely shrunk together in his old age.

Triopas (1) in Greek mythology, a son of POSEIDON and Canace, a daughter of AEOLUS, or of HELIOS and Rhodos, and the father of IPHIMEDEIA and Erysichthon. He is also called the father of PELASGUS. He expelled the Pelasgians from the Dotian plain but was himself obliged to emigrate and went to CARIA, where he founded Cnidus. Erysichthon was punished by DEMETER with insatiable hunger because he had violated her sacred grove.

Triopas (2) in Greek mythology, a son of Phorbas and the father of IASUS, Agenor and Messene.

Triptolemus in Greek mythology, a prince of ELEUSIS, son of Celeus and Metaneira and brother of DEMOPHON. To make up for the loss of Demophon, DEMETER bestowed many favours on Triptolemus, including a chariot with winged dragons and seeds of wheat. He took to the skies and spread and sowed grain all over the earth. He was a great hero in the ELEUSINIAN MYSTERIES.

Triton in Greek mythology, the name of certain sea-gods. They are variously described, but their body is always a compound of the human figure above with that of a fish below. They carry a trumpet composed of a shell, which they blow at the command of POSEIDON to soothe the waves.

Troad an area of Asia Minor which took its name from its main city, TROY.

Troïlus in Greek mythology, a son of HECUBA and either PRIAM or APOLLO. He was ambushed and killed by ACHILLES during the TROJAN WAR.

Trojan horse *see* **wooden horse.**

Trojan War in Greek mythology, a war waged against the city of Troy by a league of Greek leaders. The war is said to have had its origins in the beauty contest caused by the goddess ERIS and her throwing of the golden apple. The walled city of Troy succeeded in withstanding the Greek forces for ten years, but the city fell owing to the Greek's trick with the wooden horse.

Tros in Greek mythology, the king after whom TROY was named. He was a grandson of BATEIA (1) and DARDANUS and removed his grandfather's PALLADIUM to Troy. His son GANYMEDE was carried off by ZEUS to be cup-bearer to the gods.

Troy an ancient city in the TROAD in Asia Minor, south of the HELLESPONT. It was the scene of the ten years' siege by the Greeks in the TROJAN WAR.

Tullus Hostilius the third legendary king of Rome and successor to NUMA POMPILIUS. He was a warlike monarch, in whose reign took place the combat of the HORATII and Curiatii.

Turnus in mythology, a son of DANAÜS and Venilia and king of the RUTULIANS at the time of the arrival of AENEAS in Italy. He was related to Amata, the wife of King LATINUS. ALECTO, by the command of HERA, stirred him up to fight against Aeneas after his landing in Italy. He was defeated and killed by Aeneas.

Twins, The *see* **Gemini**.

Tyche in Greek mythology, the personification of chance or luck, the equivalent of the Roman FORTUNA.

Tydeus in Greek mythology, a son of OENEUS, king of Calydon, who assisted ADASTRUS in the Argive expedition against Thebes, the SEVEN AGAINST THEBES, in the attempt to help POLYNICES get back the throne of THEBES.

Tyndareus in Greek mythology, a king of SPARTA and husband of LEDA, although legends vary as to which of her many children he fathered. He was probably the father of CLYTEMNESTRA but probably not the father of HELEN, who was probably the daughter of ZEUS. In his youth he was expelled from Sparta by HIPPOCOÖN, but was restored to the Spartan throne by HERACLES, who killed Hippocoön. He asked the advice of ODYSSEUS about selecting a suitor for Helen. Following this advice, he made each of the suitors swear to abide by his decision and to punish anyone who thereafter tried to take Helen away from her husband, a ritual that led to the TROJAN WAR. MENELAUS was selected as the husband of Helen. *See also* GOLDEN APPLE.

Typhon *or* **Typhoeus** in Greek mythology, a monster, a son of GE and TARTARUS, described sometimes as a destructive hurricane and sometimes as a fire-breathing giant a hundred heads, fearful eyes and terrible voices. He was able to speak the la guage of animals and people. He tried to overthrow the gods b was killed, after a fearful struggle, by Zeus with bolts of ligh ning. He was buried in Tartarus under Mount Etna.

Tyre one of the most celebrated cities of ancient Phoenicia, ar with the older city of Sidon, a great trading market. It was bui partly on an island and partly on the mainland. It was the hon of Dido, who fled after the murder of her husband by h brother.

Tyro in Greek mythology, the wife of Cretheus and the belove of the river-god Enipeus in Thessaly, in the form of who Poseidon appeared to her and became by her the father Pelias and Neleus. By Cretheus she was the mother of Aeso Pheres and Amythaon.

Tyrrhenian Sea the name given to that part of the Meditrranea Sea which is enclosed between the Islands of Corsica and Sa dinia on the west, the Italian Peninsula on the east, and Sici on the south.

U

Udaeus *see* **Sparti**.

Ulysses *or* **Ulixes** the Latin name of ODYSSEUS.

Underworld *see* **Hades**.

Upis *see* **Opis**.

Urania in Greek mythology, one of the nine MUSES, a daughter of ZEUS and MNEMOSYNE, said to have borne a son, Linus, by a son of POSEIDON, Amphimarus.

Uranus in Greek mythology, the sky and the god of the sky. He was the son of GE, the earth, and by her the father of the TITANS, CYCLOPS, and Hecatoncheires, the HUNDRED-HANDED. He hated his children and confined them in TARTARUS within the body of the earth, causing much distress to Ge. On the instigation of Ge, CRONOS, the youngest and wiliest of the Titans planned to overthrow and destroy his father. Ge gave him a sickle and while Uranus was lying with Ge, Cronos castrated him and flung the severed parts into the sea. APHRODITE grew from the foam that surrounded these. The FURIES, the GIANTS and the MELIAE were spawned from the blood that fell on the ground. He was overthrown by Cronos.

Ursa Major (The Great Bear); **Ursa Minor** (The Lesser Bear) constellations in the northern sky. Ursa Major is the Roman name, called Arctos in Greek. It was held in legend to be the nymph CALLISTO, who had been turned into a bear. Ursa Major is followed in the sky by Arctophylax, 'bear-keeper', who was the son of Callisto. Callisto is said to have been greatly disliked by HERA, who persuaded her foster mother, TETHYS, never to allow Ursa Major to set in the ocean.

V

Valetudo *see* **Hygieia**.

Veii an Etruscan city north of ROME. Its citizens, the Veientes, were frequently at war with Rome in the early years of its existence.

Venus in Roman mythology, the name of the goddess of love, called by the Greeks APHRODITE. She surpassed all other goddesses in beauty, and hence received the GOLDEN APPLE which was to be awarded to the most beautiful by PARIS. She was the wife of VULCAN, but also bestowed her love on the gods MARS, BACCHUS, MERCURY, and NEPTUNE, and the mortals ANCHISES and ADONIS. The myrtle, rose, poppy, apple, and other fruits were sacred to her, as were the dove, sparrow, swan, swallow, ram, hare, and tortoise. In ROME several temples were erected to her under different names. In art she was originally represented draped, in later times nude. The scene of her arising from the sea was sculpted by Phidias on the base of the statue of ZEUS at OLYMPIA, and one of the most famous pictures of Apelles represented the same subject. The Venus of Capua and the Venus of Milo represent her as Venus Victrix, with one foot on a helmet and raising a shield.

Vergil *see* **Virgil**.

Vertumnus *or* **Vortumnus** in Roman mythology, a god of fertility, particularly with regard to crops and the changing of the seasons. He is said to have been able to change his shape. He assumed the shape of an old woman who pleaded with the fruit goddess, POMONA, to accept the love of Vertumnus, Pomona being unaware that it was actually Vertumnus who was doing the pleading. Pomona accepted his love.

Vesta in Roman mythology, the goddess of the hearth, the Roman equivalent of the Greek HESTIA. She was worshipped, along with the PENATES, at every family meal, when the household assembled round the hearth, which was in the centre of the room. Her public sanctuary was in the Forum, and the sacred fire was kept constantly burning in it by the Vestal Virgins, her priestesses. The Vestal Virgins are said to have been established by NUMA. There were at first four, and afterwards six of them. They were taken in when they were from six to ten years of age and compelled to be virgins for thirty years, the term of their service, after which they were allowed to marry. They were treated with great honour and respect and had important public privileges. The punishment of a Vestal Virgin who broke her vow of chastity was burying alive. Theodosius abolished the practice of the Vestal Virgins in AD 394.

Vestal virgins *see* **Vesta**.

Virbius in Roman mythology, a minor god and companion of DIANA. He was a king of Aricia and favourite of Diana and when he died she called him to life and entrusted him to the care of the nymph EGERIA. The fact of his being a favourite of Diana seems to have led the Romans to identify him with HIPPOLYTUS who, according to some traditions, had established the worship of Diana.

Virgil *or* **Vergil** (Publius Vergilius Maro) the national poet of Rome, born 70 BC, died 19 BC. His works include his masterpiece, the *Aeneid*, an epic poem in twelve books that charts the progress of AENEAS from the fall of TROY to the founding of the Roman state.

Virgo (The Virgin) a constellation. It is not clear who the virgin in question was, although there have been many suggestions. She is variously described as being ASTRAEA or Dike (justice), Tyche (fortune), Parthenos, a daughter of APOLLO, or ERIGONE (2), daughter of CLYTEMNESTRA and AEGISTHUS.

Volscians *or* **Volsci** an ancient Italian tribe who delt in LATIUM, on both sides of the River Liris (Garigliano). Their principal city was Corili, from which Coriolanus derived his name. After having several times endangered ROME, they were conquered and disappeared from history.

Vortumnus *see* **Vertumnus.**

Vulcan in Roman mythology, the god who presided over fire and the working of metals and patronized handicraftsmen of every kind. By some writers he is said to have been born lame, but others attribute his lameness to his having been thrown from OLYMPUS. He was equated with the Greek god HEPHAESTUS. His name is remembered in the word volcano.

Wandering Rocks (Planctae) in Greek mythology, mobile rocks in the sea that destroyed ships that attempted to pass between them. The ARGONAUTS passed through them safely with the help of the NEREIDS, the sea nymphs. ODYSSEUS, however, chose to avoid them when he was about to encounter them near the island of the SIRENS and took an alternative route which involved encountering SCYLLA AND CHARYBDIS.

water-bearer, The *see* **Ganymede**.

Whale, The *see* **Cetus**.

White Island an island in the BLACK SEA said in legend to have been one of the Islands of the Blessed where some of the Greek heroes lived in eternal happiness after their adventures in the TROJAN WAR.

Women of the Sea in Greek mythology, a name given to some followers of DIONYSUS. Known as the Haliae, the women went to ARGOS to support Dionysus in a war with PERSEUS. The latter defeated them and killed most of them. Dionysus later made peace with the people of Argos.

wooden horse in Greek mythology, a cunning device thought up by the Greeks to gain entrance to TROY undetected. The plan to get the Trojans to open their gates was conceived either by ODYSSEUS or Epeius. Epeius, who was a skilled craftsman, built a large wooden model of a horse with the help of ATHENA from wood cut from trees on Mount IDA. The interior of the model horse was hollow and large enough to contain a considerable number of men. When the horse was complete, a number of the Greek leaders under the command of Odysseus climbed inside the horse. Meanwhile the rest of the Greeks packed up camp and sailed away, giving the impression to the Trojans that they had given up the struggle against them. In fact they sailed only as far as the offshore island of TENEDOS. They had left the wooden horse on the shore. When they thought that the Greeks had gone, the Trojans took the opportunity to leave their city, which had been under siege for so long. They were surprised to see the wooden horse but relieved to read the inscription on it. It read 'For their return home the Greeks dedicate this thanks offering to Athena'. There was dispute among the Trojans as to what should be done with the wooden horse. Some wished to destroy it or break into it. Others wanted to take it into their city. Because it had associations with a goddess, they thought that they should not destroy it, and some of them thought that taking care of an offering to Athena might bring them good fortune. CASSANDRA, who was noted for telling true prophecies that no one would believe, warned the Trojans that there were spears inside the horse, but they ignord her. Some of them even ignored it when LAOCOÖN, a priest of APOLLO, agreed with the warning and threw his spear at the horse. Others were more suspicious. The Greeks had anticipated these suspicions and had left behind Sinon, a young relative of Odysseus, with arms bound up and with clothes in tatters. When he was captured by shepherds and brought to PRIAM, king of Troy, he told a story about how CALCHAS, a Greek seer, plotted with Odysseus, with whom Sinon had quarrelled, to interpret an oracle to the effect that Sinon must be sacrificed to the gods to ensure a safe return home for the Greeks. Sinon had succeeded in escaping just before the Greeks left. He was extremely plausible and convincing, and the Trojans believed him and trusted him. On being asked about the meaning of the wooden horse, Sinon told them that the Greeks had angered Athena by stealing the PALLADIUM, an image sacred to Athena, from the Trojan citadel. Calchas had advised the Greeks to build a wooden horse to appease Athena and then leave for home. They had deliberately made it too large to be taken through the gates of Troy in case the Trojans received good luck from it and attacked Greek cities. The seer had also said that if the Trojans destroyed the horse Athena would be angry with them and Troy would be destroyed. The Trojans believed this story, especially because two serpents swimming in the sea snatched and ate the two young sons of Laocoön and then Laocoön himself, and the Trojans interpreted this as a punishment sent by Athena for Laocoön throwing a spear at the horse. In fact it was supposed to be a punishment sent to his priest by Apollo for some other misdemeanour. The Trojans tore down part of their city walls to admit the wooden horse. They then celebrated their supposed victory over the Greeks by eating and drinking. Sinon is said to have released the Greeks inside the horse, and the Greek fleet returned. The Greeks left the ships and entered Troy. The carousing Trojans were easily defeated.

X

Xanthe in Greek mythology, one of the daughters of OCEANUS.

Xanthippe in Greek mythology, the wife of PLEURON.

Xanthus in Greek mythology, a son of TRIOPAS (1) and Oreasis, who was a king of the Pelasgians at ARGOS and afterwards settled in the island of LESBOS.

Xanthus and Balius in Greek mythology, the immortal horses of ACHILLES. They were the offspring of the Harpy PODARGE by ZEPHYRUS. The horses were given to PELEUS as a gift to celebrate his marriage to THETIS. Xanthus was given the power of speech by HERA in order to warn Achilles of his impending death. The FURIES immediately removed the powers for fear that Xanthus might reveal some more of the god's secrets to mortals.

Xanthus an ancient city of Asia Minor, the principal city of LYCIA, on the River Xanthus.

Xuthus in Greek mythology, a son of HELLEN by the nymph Orseis, and a brother of DORUS and AEOLUS (2). He was king of PELOPONNESUS, and the husband of CREUSA (2), the daughter of ERECHTHEUS, by whom he became the father of ACHAEUS and ION. According to other legends, Xuthus, after the death of his father, was expelled from Thessaly by his brothers and went to Athens, where he married the daughter of Erechtheus. After the death of Erechtheus, Xuthus was chosen as arbitrator and decreed that the kingdom should be ruled by his eldest brother-in-law, CECROPS. As a result of this judgement Xuthus was expelled by the other sons of Erechtheus and settled at Aegialos in Peloponnesus. Xuthus is an important character in Euripides's *Ion*, a play which deals with the events surrounding the discovery that Ion is a son of Creusa by APOLLO. Xuthus remained happy in the belief that he was the young man's father.

Z

Zacynthus one of the islands lying off the western coast of PELOPONNESUS near ITHACA. In Greek mythology, it was colonized by Zacynthus, son of DARDANUS, from Psophis in ARCADIA. Its inhabitants sent forces to fight the Trojans under the leadership of ODYSSEUS.

Zagreus *see* **Iacchus**.

Zelus in Greek mythology, the personification of zeal or strife, a son of the Titan PALLAS and STYX, and constant companion of ZEUS. He was the brother of Cratos, BIA and NIKE.

Zephyrus *or* **Zephyr** in Greek mythology, the west wind and god of the west wind, a son of Eos and Astraeus. He was the father of XANTHUS AND BALIUS, the immortal horses. In some legends he caused the death of HYACINTH because he was jealous of Hyacinth's love for APOLLO.

Zetes and Calaïs in Greek mythology, the twin sons of BOREAS, the north wind and god of the north wind. They were known as the Boreades and are depicted as having wings that sprouted either from their backs or from their heads and feet. Either their wings or their hair is depicted as being purple in colour. They voyaged with the ARGONAUTS and chased the HARPIES when they were attacking PHINEUS, king of Thracia, brother-in-law of Zetes and Calaïs.

Zethus in Greek mythology, son of ZEUS and ANTIOPE and twin brother of AMPHION.

Zeus in Greek mythology, the supreme divinity; the ruler of the other gods. He is generally treated as the equivalent of the Roman JUPITER and was the son of CRONOS and RHEA, and brother of POSEIDON and HERA, the latter of whom was also his wife. Rhea, with her mother GE, tricked Cronos at the birth of Zeus by giving him a stone wrapped in swaddling clothes instead of the baby. This was because Cronos had been warned that he would be deposed by one of his children, just as he had deposed his father, URANUS. In order to get rid of his children he swallowed them. In the case of the infant Zeus it was the stone that he swallowed. For his protection the baby Zeus was hidden in a cave on Mount Dicte in CRETE. When he was an adult Zeus persuaded the Oceanid METIS to give his father, Cronos, an emetic, and he vomited up the brothers and sisters of Zeus whom he had previously swallowed. They then joined Zeus in his struggle against Cronos for control of OLYMPUS. He finally expelled his father and the dynasty of the TITANS, successfully opposed the attacks of the GIANTS and the conspiracies of the other gods, and became chief power in heaven and earth.

Zeuxippe in Greek mythology, a NAIAD, daughter of ERIDANUS and the wife of PANDION (1), king of ATHENS. He was in fact her nephew. She bore him PROCNE and PHILOMELA and twin sons, ERECHTHEUS and BUTES (2).